The China Question

For centuries, Western scholars portrayed China either as a land of superior morality, economy, and governance or as a formidable country of pagans that posed a global threat to Western values. Idealized images of China were used to shame rulers for their incompetence, while China was demonized as an external threat to cover up domestic political failures. In the twentieth century, the geopolitics of global capitalism have facilitated more nuanced perspectives, but the diversifying of knowledge about China is far from complete. In this thought-provoking study, Ho-fung Hung finds that both Western elites and China's authoritarian regime today continue to promote many Orientalist stereotypes to advance their economic interests and political projects. He shows how big-picture historical, social, and economic changes are inextricably linked to fluctuations in the realm of ideas. Only open debate can overcome extremes of fantasy and fear.

Ho-fung Hung is Henry M. and Elizabeth P. Wiesenfeld Professor in Political Economy in the Department of Sociology and Nitze School of Advanced International Studies, Johns Hopkins University.

The China Question
Eight Centuries of Fantasy and Fear

Ho-fung Hung
Johns Hopkins University

CAMBRIDGE
UNIVERSITY PRESS

Shaftesbury Road, Cambridge CB2 8EA, United Kingdom

One Liberty Plaza, 20th Floor, New York, NY 10006, USA

477 Williamstown Road, Port Melbourne, VIC 3207, Australia

314–321, 3rd Floor, Plot 3, Splendor Forum, Jasola District Centre, New Delhi – 110025, India

103 Penang Road, #05–06/07, Visioncrest Commercial, Singapore 238467

Cambridge University Press is part of Cambridge University Press & Assessment, a department of the University of Cambridge.

We share the University's mission to contribute to society through the pursuit of education, learning and research at the highest international levels of excellence.

www.cambridge.org
Information on this title: www.cambridge.org/9781009559775

DOI: 10.1017/9781009559751

© Ho-fung Hung 2026

This publication is in copyright. Subject to statutory exception and to the provisions of relevant collective licensing agreements, no reproduction of any part may take place without the written permission of Cambridge University Press & Assessment.

When citing this work, please include a reference to the
DOI 10.1017/9781009559751

First published 2026

Printed in the United Kingdom by CPI Group Ltd, Croydon CR0 4YY

Cover image: *Le voyage du prince* (France, c. 1700; source: Alamy)

A catalogue record for this publication is available from the British Library

A Cataloging-in-Publication data record for this book is available from the Library of Congress

ISBN 978-1-009-55977-5 Hardback

Cambridge University Press & Assessment has no responsibility for the persistence or accuracy of URLs for external or third-party internet websites referred to in this publication and does not guarantee that any content on such websites is, or will remain, accurate or appropriate.

For EU product safety concerns, contact us at Calle de José Abascal, 56, 1°, 28003 Madrid, Spain, or email eugpsr@cambridge.org

To Mark Selden

CONTENTS

List of Figures	*page* x
Preface	xiii
Introduction: Orientalism in the *Longue Durée*	1
Study of Orientalism since Edward Said	5
Sociology of Intellectual Change	10
Chapter Outline	15

Part I Catholic Scholarship

1 From Pax Mongolica to the Long Sixteenth Century — 23
   Medieval Fear and Fantasy of the Mongols — 25
   The Portuguese and Spaniards in East Asia — 34
   Reconciling China and the Bible — 36

2 The Seventeenth-Century Crisis and the Rise of Sinophilia — 44
   A Crisis of European Consciousness — 45
   European Views of China's Ming–Qing Transition — 48
   Jesuits' Knowledge and Fantasies about China — 54

Part II Enlightenment Philosophy

3 Early Enlightenment Sinophilia — 71
   "What Is Enlightenment?" — 72
   China as a Model for Europe — 74

4 Late Enlightenment Sinophobia — 88
   The Eurocentric Idea of Progress — 89

Sinophiles under Siege 92
Europe and the Chinese without Philosophy 97
The Political Sociology of the Rise and Fall
of Sinophilia 102

Part III Institutionalized Orientalism

5   Romantic Sinology after the French Revolution 109
The Colonial Canonization of the East 109
The Making of Academic Sinology 111
Romanticism and Orientalism 116
Sinophilic Déjà Vu 119

6   Scientific-Racist Sinology in the Age of Empire 129
Scientific-Racist Turn in Orientalism 129
Sinophobic Revival in Sinology 137

Part IV Cold War Area Studies

7   From Sinology to China Studies 149
Orientalism and Max Weber 149
Sources of *The Religion of China* 153
Modernization Theory and Cold War China Studies 158
The Unintended Openness of Area Studies 165

8   The "Asiatic Mode of Production" Myth 176
Marx's Oriental Despots and Communal Villages 176
The Bolsheviks' Asia Question 184
The Romance and Catastrophe of Maoism 187
Asian Peasants in Western Academia 195

Part V Self-Orientalism

9   Self-Orientalizing Nation Building 203
An American Political Scientist and Chinese
Monarchists 205
Orientalist Origins of Cultural Radicalism 211
Cultural Conservativism and Confucian Fascism 214

10	**Contested Confucianism**	221
	Varieties of Confucianisms in Imperial China	222
	New Confucianism after Empire	229
	Post-Cold War Asian Values	235
	Conclusion: De-Orientalizing Triumph, Re-Orientalizing Perils	243
	Eight Hundred Years of Fantasy–Fear Cycles	243
	De-Orientalization in China Studies	245
	Lasting Popular Orientalism	248
	Orientalism Strikes Back	251
	References	262
	Index	303

FIGURES

P.1 An eighteenth-century Beauvais tapestry illustrating European conceptions of China *page* [xvii]
0.1 General dynamics of intellectual rivalry and intellectual change [14]
1.1 Tartar feast: medieval depiction of Mongols' cannibalism [29]
2.1 Dutch depiction of idolatry in China [56]
2.2 Jesuit depiction of rational Confucius [60]
2.3 Rival networks and views of the Mongol/Chinese empire within the Catholic Church [66]
3.1a Voltaire's armchair, which he used in his last days in Paris, with a tilting stand on the right with China-themed painting [78]
3.1b Cup and saucer imported from China and used by Voltaire, with Chinese poem and painting [78]
4.1 Late eighteenth-century Jesuit portrait of Confucius [101]
4.2 Competing philosophical views on China during the Enlightenment [105]
6.1 Classification and geographical distribution of races, 1894 [131]
6.2 Characteristics and physiognomy of the Mongolian race [132]
6.3 Dynamics of changing Orientalism/Sinology in the nineteenth century [145]
7.1 Promoting modernization and attacking local traditions in Cold War Taiwan [161]
7.2 From Cold War China Studies to de-Orientalization of China Studies [174]

List of Figures

- 8.1 Sources and changes in Marx's view of the Asiatic mode of production [183]
- 8.2 National Emblem of the Democratic Kampuchea (1975–1979) [194]
- 9.1 Yuan Shikai and Frank Goodnow as the Walrus and the Carpenter [207]
- 10.1 Li Zhi (1527–1602), the anarchist neo-Confucianist in sixteenth-century China [225]

PREFACE

Pierre Bourdieu suggested at the very beginning of his *Homo Academicus* that his book was "a book for burning," citing the title of a late sixteenth-century Chinese book by "renegade mandarin" Li Zhi, who also happened to be one of the heroes discussed in this book (Chapter 10). If Bourdieu's book deserves burning for "divulging tribal secrets" of his own kind – the academics – this book of mine definitely meets the bar for burning, too. This book is about nonsense: nonsense in Western Sinology that, after eight centuries of accumulation and institutionalization, has been enshrined as indisputable truth. The varieties of nonsense have been so stubbornly dominant that they continue to condition politicians' and the public's views on China today despite the best efforts of many contemporary academics to undo them.

This book is the culmination of my longest project – nearly three decades in the making. In the mid-1990s, I went off the track of political economy and delved into the burgeoning literature on postcolonial and poststructuralist theories with a group of radical students and young scholars driven by the hunger for new theories. Fascinated as well as disappointed by Edward Said's critique of Orientalism and various follow-up studies on Western academic knowledge of South Asia and the Islamic world, I noticed a conspicuous absence of critical studies of Western knowledge of China, except for a few works discussing Western representations of China in literature, films, and other forms of popular culture.

With this puzzle in mind, I began my PhD studies at Binghamton in 1997. That fall, I had Immanuel Wallerstein – who was splitting his time between Paris and Binghamton and working on his Structure of Knowledge project – agreeing to guide me in an independent research project on the history of academic Sinology and its relation to the development of the capitalist world-system. This research, along with the brilliant classes that opened my eyes to world-historical social sciences with Dale Tomich, Giovanni Arrighi, and Mark Selden supported my deep dive into Western Sinological knowledge, from the Jesuits to Cold War Area Studies.

Amid the spectacular golden leaves and drifting snow of upstate New York, I managed to complete a research "paper" of over 30,000 words in early spring 1998. While the paper yielded several interesting discoveries, it also raised more questions than it answered. Then, an idea dawned on me: Why not fill these gaps, answer the remaining questions, and expand the study's time horizon to turn the project into my dissertation research?

I was excited about the prospect. However, the advice I got was nearly unanimous: It was a risky dissertation project because its time frame and geographic scope were too broad (it spanned centuries and involved Sinological works from several European countries). As an intellectual history project, it wasn't considered "solid" within sociology or even history at that time. These well-meaning warnings, along with my move to the PhD program at Johns Hopkins University, eventually led me to abandon the idea of developing the project into my dissertation. However, I continued working on it in the background, collecting more materials from historical manuscript collections at the marvelous George Peabody Library at Johns Hopkins and turning some specific findings into a journal article and a book chapter.

The notion that studying a phenomenon or process spanning centuries and multiple countries is too broad for practical research is flawed. In the natural sciences, scholars study cosmic processes measured in light years and billions of years alongside those who study subatomic processes measured in nanometers and microseconds. No one ever suggests the former is too broad to be practical. To study processes on vastly different scales, we simply need different theories and methods (e.g., general relativity versus quantum physics, radio telescope versus particle accelerator). The idea that studying processes longer than a few decades and encompassing more than a few cities is too ambitious reflects our confinement to the human scale and intuition. It shows that our knowledge production has not yet fully embraced the realm of science. Similarly, viewing the study of ideas as less "solid" than the study of income distribution, protest events, or schools is like considering the study of quarks less solid than the study of trees.

Driven by my frustration with mainstream social science's hostility toward the macro and long term, I continued to gather materials for this sidelined project over the years, confident it would one day be revived. After completing a number of projects recognized as appropriately solid and focused, I knew the time had come to finally finish this book. In retrospect, the present is a more opportune moment for completing the project. Over the past twenty-seven years, many manuscripts I once had to travel to specific rare book libraries to read have been digitized and are now much more accessible. The rise of online translation tools has allowed me to read virtually all European languages, opening up sources I could never have dreamed of accessing when the project first began.

After taking Mark Selden's course on East Asia from a world-historical perspective in the fall of 1997, I continued to benefit from my many discussions and conversations with him. Every gathering provided fresh insights into the latest works on China's history, politics, and society. I have also been inspired by his evolving views, from his years with the Committee of Concerned Asian Scholars to his recent editorship of impactful book series for multiple publishers and *The Asia-Pacific Journal: Japan Focus*, as well as his own classic works on the Chinese revolution and development. He has been a mentor, a friend, and a model of how de-Orientalized, reflexive China studies can be done. It is to him that this book is dedicated.

Naturally, this long journey has benefited from the help, support, and feedback of many. I can only mention a few whose recent generosity I wish to acknowledge here. Over the last two years, I had the opportunity to present nearly finished versions of various chapters at venues such as the School for Advanced Studies in the Social Sciences (École des Hautes Études en Sciences Sociales), the American Sociological Association Annual Meeting, Academia Sinica Institute of Sociology, and the University of Melbourne's Centre for Contemporary Chinese Studies. I greatly benefited from the audience's feedback, which included insights from Jean-Philippe Béja, Pierre Fuller, Joshua Fogel, Julian Go, Joan Judge, Ka Chih-Ming, Arnaud Orain, Anthony Spires, Tang Chih-Chieh, Wu Jiehmin, and many more. Kin Man Chan, Andy Mertha, Mark Selden, and Jeff Wasserstrom read parts of the manuscript in progress, offering invaluable guidance on sources. Johns Hopkins' Agora Institute provided a microgrant that supported my research into the works of former Hopkins president Frank Goodnow. I also thank Musée Carnavalet in Paris and *Harvest* magazine in Taiwan for granting me permission to use images of artifacts in their possession.

At the final stage of writing, I owe much to the anonymous readers of Cambridge University Press. They helped fine-tune my arguments and fill gaps in sources. As always, Lucy Rhymer has been the best editor one could hope for and entrust with the fruits of one's immense intellectual labor. I appreciate Rosa Martin's assistance at the Press, too. The final manuscript also benefited from the help of my copy editor, Sasha Milonova, and my research assistants, Rena Sasaki and Mingtang Liu. Little cat Penny, my reading, thinking, and writing companion, enabled me to have a peace of mind essential to the completion of the project. Of course, none of those acknowledged here are responsible for any mistakes in the book.

Lastly, but by no means least, I am grateful to my family – particularly Henry and Helia, who have been transitioning into adulthood as this book took shape. They unwittingly urged me not to slacken in my intellectual endeavors. They are the ultimate readers, and I hope they will appreciate this book and others.

Figure P.1 An eighteenth-century Beauvais tapestry illustrating European conceptions of China. "Le voyage du prince" (Journey of the prince) in the cover image was one of the nine tapestries that made up the *L'Histoire de l'empereur de la Chine* (The history of the emperor of China) or *Première tenture chinoise* (First Chinese tapestry) tapestry series. The tapestries were designed and woven in the Beauvais Manufactory at the turn of the eighteenth century and commissioned by members of Louis XIV's royal household, including his sons. Elements in this tapestry and others – like the prostrating subjects, the Kangxi Emperor, the pagoda, Jesuit father Schall holding a globe, and the pineapples – can be traced back to illustrations in prominent books on China at the time by diplomats or Jesuit scholars such as Johan Nieuhof and Athanasius Kircher. This tapestry set represents the height of *chinoiserie* in France and other parts of Europe, visualizing the European conception of China as the exemplar of royal absolutism during the early stage of the Enlightenment.
Source: Alamy

INTRODUCTION
Orientalism in the *Longue Durée*

In 2008, before his first earnest bid for the US Presidency, businessman Donald Trump expressed his admiration for China's economic model, where he thought businessman like him could freely pursue profits without many regulatory restraints. Trump exalted:

> In China, they fill up hundreds of acres of land, constantly dumping and dumping dirt in the ocean. I asked the builder, did you get an environmental impact study? He goes, "what?" I asked, "Did you need approval?" "No," the Chinese said. And yet, if I am the last guy to drop one pebble in the ocean here in this city [New York], I will be given the electric chair.[1]

In 2015, with the plausibility of socialist Jeremy Corbyn's Labour Party coming to power in the UK, British billionaire Lord Sugar, the host of the UK version of Donald Trump's *The Apprentice* remarked that "[i]f they ever got anywhere near electing him [Corbyn] and him being the Prime Minister, then I think we should all move to China or somewhere like that and let this place just rot."[2]

To business and political elites around the world back then, China represented a paradise of limitless capital accumulation, a welcome rising superpower, and an antidote to the "socialist

---

[1] Hohnholz 2008.
[2] Bryant 2015.

excesses" threatening capitalism and Western civilization. Bill Clinton and George W. Bush saw China as a "strategic partner" in the 1990s and early 2000s. In March 2014, the European Commission declared that the EU–China relationship was one of a "Comprehensive Strategic Partnership for mutual benefit" that needed deepening for the good of Europe.[3]

This high hope for China was shared by many intellectuals coming from the lineage of the Left. Martin Jacques, the former editor of *Marxism Today*, published the bestseller *When China Rules the World* in 2009. He claimed that China represented a more progressive and sustainable model of growth benefiting from Confucianism. This model displaced the long hegemony of the West, and this was beneficial for the world.[4] Best-selling books with a similar euphoric tone, positioning China as a sage that could enlighten the West and offer a better model of capitalism, abounded right after the global financial crisis of 2008.[5]

About a decade after the financial crisis, a new consensus emerged among the political and economic elites in the West. It became broadly agreed that China represented a diminished model of capitalism that strangled innovation and was prone to corruption and that China's expanding global influence threatened democracy and prosperity everywhere.[6] Its attempt to displace Western leadership was perceived as a threat to global stability. Its investment and assistance to other developing countries were seen as a ploy to trick them into a "debt trap."[7] The same Donald Trump, who admired the China model in 2008, became the president of a Republican administration in 2017–2021, which accelerated the all-out US–China rivalry. Democratic President of the US in 2021–2025, Joe Biden, characterized the US–China relationship as one of "extreme competition" in 2021.[8] Many European countries experienced similar shifts. In March 2019, the EU took a sharp turn in its "EU-China Strategic Outlook" report by designating China as Europe's competitor (in economic and technological issues) and rival (in values),

---

[3] European Commission 2014.
[4] Jacques 2009.
[5] E.g., Lee, Ann 2012; Ramo 2004; Newman 2011.
[6] E.g., Guardian 2020.
[7] Chellaney 2017.
[8] Associated Press 2021.

besides being a partner (in other global issues like climate change).[9] Ever since the COVID-19 pandemic and the Russian invasion of Ukraine, EU–China relations have deteriorated and become more about competition and rivalry than partnership.[10]

Michael Pillsbury, a China specialist who later became Trump's informal China adviser during his 2017–2021 presidency, published *The Hundred Years Marathon* in 2016 and spoke of China's deceptively friendly gestures and its secretive gambit since 1949 to upend US global leadership. He claimed China's strategy and tactics of global domination were drawn from Sunzi's 孫子 (Sun Tzu) *Art of War*, written more than two thousand years ago.[11] Peter Navarro, Trump's trade policy director in 2017–2021, talked of the horror of "Death by China." He warned that the "voracious … Manufacturing Dragon" exploited the global free trade system to not only destroy our jobs but also to "strangle our babies" and poison our bodies with "Chinese junk."[12]

This drastic shift was not about accidental changes in the personal views of the business, political, or intellectual elites. It was largely driven by the changing global political economy and the domestic political economy of the US and China, especially in the aftermath of the global financial crisis of 2008.[13] Western politicians' views on China might swing again in the future through a change in government or a change in the view of politicians like Trump, but the positive and negative views between the swings always carried many long-held stereotypes and assumptions that portrayed China as an undifferentiated, ahistorical, and singular entity.[14] Such stereotypes and assumptions, as well as the drastic swing between extreme euphoric and contemptuous views on China, are more common in the popular imaginations and political representation of China than in the academic study of China today. However, as I show in this book, such extreme views have emanated from eight centuries of academic knowledge production about China, from medieval Catholic institutions to eighteenth-century circles of Enlightenment

---

[9] European Commission 2019.
[10] Lizzi 2024; García-Herrero and Vasselier 2024.
[11] Pillsbury 2016: Chs. 2 & 7.
[12] Navarro and Autry 2011: 29–45; 107.
[13] Hung 2022a.
[14] Wasserstrom 2006.

philosophers to nineteenth-century universities as successive loci of knowledge production. Such privileged sites of knowledge production saw the crystallization of raw popular perceptions of China, facilitating, advancing, and legitimating them. Academic knowledge of China has manifested recurrent swings between the poles of romantic idealization and racist contempt of China until very recently.

This book shows that in the mid thirteenth century, the medieval fear of Mongol conquest led to monastic writings about the Mongols as cannibalistic, idolatrous, and evil barbarians on a quest to destroy Christianity. Ever since then, European writings have referred to Mongolia, Tartary, and China interchangeably, with the term "Mongoloid" being used to refer to all "yellow" races in the "Far East" until the mid twentieth century. However, in the late thirteenth century, Marco Polo's tales about the legendary Cathay in the Mongol Empire overshadowed the earlier, more fearful, Catholic depictions. Polo's account highlighted the fascinating achievements of the then-Mongol Emperor Kublai Khan without any mention of the negatives of the Empire. He even claimed that the Khan expressed his readiness to convert to Christianity. In the sixteenth and seventeenth centuries, Western study of China was initially dominated by the Jesuits, who asserted that the Chinese worshiped a monotheistic God and were a model of religious piety for Europeans. The Jesuits were later sidelined by their enemies in the Catholic Church, who argued that the Chinese were godless and idolatrous. This shift re-occurred with the eighteenth-century swing between the Sinophilic philosophers during the early Enlightenment, who saw China as a model for Europe in administration, economy, and morality, and the later Sinophobic thinkers, who portrayed China as the dark, decaying antithesis of Western civilization and progress. Such a swing was repeated once again in Western universities, where Romantic Sinology, which idealized China as a spiritual inspiration for Europe and was the dominant paradigm in the early to mid nineteenth century, was replaced in the late nineteenth century by racist Sinology, which viewed China as a degenerated, inferior civilization. The racist Sinology contributed to the rise of self-proclaimed universal, social scientific theories of modernization and continued to shape China Studies in the mid twentieth century until a new generation of China scholars started to de-Orientalize the field in the late twentieth century. This book depicts these recurrent shifts in Western views on China in the academic field – a privileged venue for the systematic production of authoritative knowledge in society – over the *longue durée*. It exposits the dynamics within and beyond the academic field that drive these shifts. This book also explores how academic China Studies in more recent times sought to overcome, with significant success, the polarized prejudices in old Sinology, even as the prejudices, having accumulated over centuries of academic production, continue to shape contemporary popular and political imaginations of China. The insights from the theory of Orientalism and macro-sociology of knowledge are indispensable to this endeavor to exposit the long-term change and continuity in the Western academic constructions of China.

Study of Orientalism since Edward Said

Drastic swings in the Western conception of China have been tied to the shifting Western view of Eastern civilizations in general. As Edward Said emphasized in his critique of Orientalism, Orientalism took many forms as a system of knowledge and scholarship institutionalized in nineteenth-century Europe.[15] It entailed not only racist contempt of non-Western civilizations but also romanticizing fantasies. The fundamental epistemology of Orientalist knowledge was the objectifying and othering of any non-Western civilization as timeless, undifferentiated entities ontologically different from the West. Despite his crude attempt to classify and describe different forms of Orientalist knowledge, Said has been criticized for failing to discern the dynamics that drive the changing forms of Orientalism between contempt and idealization. His conception of Orientalism was deemed oversimplified, disregarding the variations and complexities of the European colonial encounters with different peoples.[16] Said focused on how Western representation of Islamic societies and cultures has been mostly disdainful from

---

[15] Said 1978: Ch. 2.
[16] For example, see Thomas 1994.

the early modern times to the twentieth century. Parallel works on Orientalism by Anouar Abdel-Malek,[17] who critiqued Orientalists' reduction of the East to philology and religion and the use of their distant past to understand their present, and by Alain Grosrichard,[18] who analyzed French derogatory description of "Oriental despotism" in the Ottoman Empire as Europe's eternal other, also focused one-sidedly on the West's disdainful representations of the East.

The oversight of Said, Abdel-Malek, and Grosrichard, who all portrayed an invariantly disdainful Western view of the East, was related to their focus on Western learning of the Arab Islamic world. As Said pointed out, the protracted geopolitical conflict between the Islamic world and Christian Europe, as well as the former's triumph from medieval to early modern times, made Islam a lasting "trauma" to European civilization.[19] It left the Western study of the Islamic world full of contempt and hatred. Such negativity remained in the field of Arab Studies even when other fields of Area Studies – above all, China Studies – started to shed the pitfall of Orientalist epistemology in the late twentieth century.[20]

Since Said's publication of *Orientalism*, several works have deepened the discussion with respect to the Western academic learning of the Islamic world.[21] Others extended the discussion to other Asian civilizations. For example, India Studies scholars put together an edited volume, *Orientalism and the Postcolonial Predicaments*, to examine how the British Raj conditioned the Western knowledge of India.[22] These works constituted a first step in expanding the horizon of Said's original theory by identifying variations of Orientalism shaped by the different relations between Europe and the civilizations in question. However, most of these works also emphasized Europe's invariant disdain for the East instead of exploring the internal variations in the forms of Orientalism.

Scholars of Orientalism also did not differentiate academic and popular or political discourses about the East, discussing academic writings, novels, and paintings side by side and

[17] Abdel-Malek 1963.
[18] Grosrichard 1998.
[19] Said 1978: 59.
[20] Said 1985: 105.
[21] E.g., Turner 1978, 1994.
[22] Breckenridge and van der Veer 1993.

interchangeably. As academic institutions in different eras – from monasteries in medieval Europe to modern universities since the nineteenth century – enjoyed unparalleled authority and followed regularized methods to produce knowledge enshrined as the most reliable and legitimate in a given time, production of academic knowledge about the East deserves our special attention and needs to be separated from other fields of discourse production.

The Western study of Chinese civilization, a large civilization located farthest away from Europe and not having come in direct conflict or colonial encounter with Europe until the nineteenth century, has been characterized by more drastic swings and complex variations over different historical periods. The shift from admiration of China among early Enlightenment thinkers in the early eighteenth century to a more racist view at the turn of the nineteenth century was relatively well known. Many took this shift as a one-shot transformation connected to the rise of Western imperialism in Asia.[23] However, recent studies that compared nineteenth-century Western colonial discourses on different colonies discovered that colonizers' dispositions toward Chinese natives were often more complex than those of other colonial subjects and showed a mix of admiration and contempt. For example, George Steinmetz, who analyzed German colonists' nineteenth-century writings on the native peoples in German colonial possessions of Samoa, Southwest Africa, and China's Qingdao 青島, found that, unlike the racist depictions of the former two, the depiction of Chinese was a mix of racism and sympathetic condescension.[24]

Complex and interesting as it is, Europe's romanticizing knowledge of China has rarely been discussed in the context of the theory of Orientalism. This inadequacy originates from the misconception that Western admiration of non-Western civilizations is virtuous and thus does not require critical reflection. Many works even treated the Western idealization of China by the Jesuits and early Enlightenment thinkers in the eighteenth century as the antidote to later racist and contemptuous views on China. For example, historian Jürgen Osterhammel, after his meticulous examination of how late Enlightenment philosophers "unfabled" the East toward the

[23] E.g., Osterhammel 2018: 480–518.
[24] Steinmetz 2007: Chs. 6 & 7. cf. Ince 2024; Isaacs 1958.

end of the eighteenth century, expressed his nostalgia about the earlier "intercultural good taste" that was "poisoned" by the "assumption of European superiority" in around 1800, as if refabling the East can be the solution to Orientalist distortions.[25]

But as we shall see in this book, naïve idealization of a non-Western civilization was always another side of the same coin of racist contempt. Both hinged on a totalizing and reductionist assumption about the civilization in question and constituted two forms of the same Orientalism. The two forms reinforced each other and could easily transform into each other. The two forms of Orientalism could even be found in the writings of a single Orientalist scholar at different stages of their career, as some cases of Sinologists covered in the book will illustrate.

This book outlines the pattern of changing Western views on China in the *longue durée*, focusing on Western scholarly learning of China. It will explain such a pattern in terms of the macro-political, economic, and social changes of the Western and global capitalist economy. It offers a critique of both the romantic idealization and the racist contempt of China as two sides of the same Orientalist construction of China as the eternal other. This book will contribute to the theory of Orientalism, the sociology of knowledge, the history of China/Area Studies in Western academia, and the decolonization of Western social theories built upon Orientalist knowledge. It will also engage several critical intellectual movements – such as China-centered historiography, inter-Asian studies, and multiple/early modernities studies – in the search for more reflexive China/Asia Studies.[26]

There are previous works discussing Western views of China from long historical perspectives. They include Jonathan Spence's *Chan's Great Continent*,[27] Nigel Cameron's *Mandarins and Barbarians*,[28] David Mungello's *The Great Encounter of China and the West, 1500–1800*,[29] and Bradley's *The China Mirage*.[30] These

---

[25] Osterhammel 2018: 491; he also lamented that "Asia has never since been refabled or reenchanted in dominant European perceptions" (32).
[26] E.g., Cohen 2010 [1984]; Duara 2015; Eisenstadt 2002; Eisenstadt and Schluchter 1998; Chen and Chua ed. 2015.
[27] Spence 1998; see also Spence 1992b.
[28] Cameron 1989.
[29] Mungello 1999; cf. 1985.
[30] Bradley 2016.

are mostly historical accounts telling a story of long romance or misunderstanding between the two cultures. Except for Mungello, who told a meticulous story of seventeenth-century Jesuits' learning of China as the origins of Western Sinological knowledge, these accounts are mostly about popular and artistic conceptions of China or practical knowledge about China constructed by individual authors and not a systematic account of the politics and institutions of academic knowledge production.[31] The edited volume *China and Historical Capitalism: Genealogies of Sinological Knowledge* contained content that offered insightful critical analyses of Western Sinological knowledge of China in the nineteenth century, but only in one chapter among a patchwork of chapters with widely different themes.[32] The anthology *The Yellow Perils* presented an array of materials representing Western racist views on Chinese/Asians in the nineteenth and twentieth centuries.[33] Its critique focused on racist contempt of China, and Asia more broadly, in popular culture and political propaganda. It did not cover the Western romanticization of Chinese/Asian cultures, nor its latent connection to racist contempt.

Among academic books on Western learning of China, Jensen's *Manufacturing Confucianism* critically analyzed how sixteenth-century Jesuits lumped together diverse cultural traditions in China to fabricate a coherent canonical Confucianism.[34] It also delineated how twentieth-century Chinese intellectuals appropriated this idealized construction of Confucianism as the starting point of their nationalist projects.[35] Fabio Lanza's *The End of the Concern* chronicled the revolt of a group of American China Studies scholars who broke with the traditional Sinological paradigms to foster a radical revision of the academic approach to China and how some of them became attracted to an uncritical view of Maoist China as the genuine path toward communist utopia.[36] Daniel Vukovich's *China and Orientalism* focused on the Western popular or political imagination of the People's Republic of China during the post-Cold War period.[37]

---

[31] See also Zhang 1999; Carroll 2021; Brown and Deng 2022.
[32] Brook and Blue ed. 1999; Blue 1999a.
[33] Kuo and Yeats 2014.
[34] Jensen 1997: Chs. 1 and 2.
[35] Jensen 1997: Chs. 3 and 4.
[36] Lanza 2017.
[37] Vukovich 2012.

The above works are enlightening. Some of these solid analyses focused on popular culture, and others on academic production. Each focused on a particular time period. They beg for a synthetic analysis of how each particular moment of knowledge production on China was connected to the construction of China in other Western intellectual traditions in different historical periods. A systematic inquiry into the genealogy, variations, complexity, and swings in the long history of Western academic understanding of China is wanting. Analyzing large-scale, long-term intellectual changes and delineating any regularity of those changes is no easy task. The various theoretical frameworks offered by the macro-historical sociology of intellectual change and knowledge production offer pertinent tools for such tasks.[38]

Sociology of Intellectual Change

Traditional sociological theories of large-scale intellectual changes explained the changes by focusing on the dynamics and processes within the intellectual field, represented by Thomas Kuhn's *The Structure of Scientific Revolutions*, or by looking into the social changes and class politics outside the intellectual field, represented by Karl Mannheim's *Ideology and Utopia: An Introduction to the Sociology of Knowledge*.[39] To take into account both the forces within and outside intellectual fields, I integrate two recent sociological perspectives on large-scale, long-term intellectual change – the macro-world-historical perspective and the network/field perspective.

Immanuel Wallerstein, following the spirit of Mannheim, traced the rise and development of the modern structure of knowledge, as well as the dominance of certain ideas (e.g., centrist liberalism) in the structure, in the context of the expansion, consolidation, and crisis of the capitalist world-system from the eighteenth to the twentieth century.[40] More specifically, Albert Bergesen compared different dominant art forms and humanities theories in the West as examples of changing intellectual currents

---

[38] E.g., Collins 1998, Swidler and Aditi 1994; Wallerstein 1996; Mannheim 2014 [1936]; Hung 2003.
[39] Kuhn 1962; Mannheim 2014 [1936].
[40] Wallerstein 1996, 2011; Lee and Wallerstein ed. 2004.

from 1500 to the present. He discovered that successive transformations of the dominant schools of visual arts and philosophical currents constituted a cyclical movement between universalism (that emphasizes the universality of certain values and cultural forms) and particularism (that emphasizes the particularities of local cultures).[41] This cyclical movement coincided with, and can be explained by, the cycles of hegemonic stability and hegemonic rivalry within the capitalist world-system. While the height of world hegemony saw the prevalence of universalistic artistic styles and theories (such as neoclassicism, abstract expressionism, and modernization theories), times of hegemonic decline and inter-imperial rivalry favored particularistic styles and theories (such as realism and postmodernism).

Since the emergence of Orientalism was a direct result of the geographic expansion of the capitalist world-system, the formation and transformation of Orientalist knowledge should be likewise related to the changing geoeconomics and geopolitics of the system. Nevertheless, most world-systemic interpretations of intellectual change have not yet been fully worked out. If the political economy of the world-system mattered in shaping the changes in ideas, then what are the causal mechanisms and intermediate processes involved?

This question can be answered by drawing insights from Randall Collins' theory of intellectual change, which employed network analysis and symbolic interaction theory in sociology to develop Kuhn's theory and unveil the underlying logic of changes in intellectual fields.[42] An intellectual field is an arena of knowledge production constituted by chains of ritual interactions among intellectuals, who "are people who produce decontextualized ideas."[43] Individual intellectuals coalesce to form intellectual networks (or schools of thought) in an intellectual field. These networks could be based on either real relationships (such as mentor–student relations) or imagined, symbolic ones (such as inter-scholars connections established through citations of or allusions to others' ideas).[44] Through the ramification

---

[41] Bergesen 1995, 1996.
[42] Collins 1998.
[43] Collins 1998: 19.
[44] Lamont 2001: 89–90.

of intellectual networks, intellectual ideas could spread over large geographical space and transmit over a long historical time. Intellectual networks in the same field always compete for cultural capital and attention space. Since the "intellectual world lives on oppositions and by dividing up the dominant attention space ... and the opponents lived symbiotically by the attention they drew to one another,"[45] the split of an intellectual field into opposing, polarized camps was inevitable unless the field was put under the straitjacket of extraordinary external forces, such as an authoritarian regime that stamps out all but one school of thought. Collins interpreted the rise and fall of ideas as outcomes of competition among rival networks. He linked the shifts of ideas to the changes in political and economic conditions by a two-step causality. First, "political and economic changes bring ascendancy or decline of the material institutions which support intellectuals," such as monasteries and universities.[46] Then, intellectual networks form alliances and compete for space in the newly restructured intellectual field. In other words, the impacts of political and economic changes on the production of ideas are indirect.

A Bourdieuan perspective of knowledge production can enrich our understanding of how political-economic changes and ideational changes are indirectly connected. To Bourdieu, the macro-political economy and academia are two autonomous fields with independent internal rules and regulations.[47] However, politics and power dynamics could be transposed from one field to another through overlap of networks between actors within each field, and linkages between institutions within the respective fields. These dynamics of inter-field relations have been illustrated in Kay and Evans' analysis of the interaction between the trade-policy-making field and the social movement field in the case of environmental/labor movements and US trade policy.[48] It is also illustrated in Steinmetz's study of the development of French sociology during the crisis of late French imperialism.[49]

[45] Collins 1998: 625.
[46] Collins 1998: 380.
[47] Bourdieu 1988.
[48] Kay and Evans 2018.
[49] Steinmetz 2023.

The macro-world-historical approach examined intellectual changes by considering the direct influences of external political and economic forces. This approach can be synthesized with Collins' and Bourdieu's network/field perspective if we examine inter-network competition endogenous to the intellectual field not as an isolated process but as a semi-autonomous process constrained by exogenous forces. In certain political-economic contexts, some ideas would be more easily accepted or consciously promoted by the actors on whom the livelihoods of intellectuals depended. These actors included the reading public, which constituted the market for ideas and intellectual products (e.g., books), and the state and social elites, which financed intellectual activities and institutions. As such, external political and economic processes not only molded the institutional form of the field of knowledge production but also directly impacted the balance of forces between rival intellectual networks by shaping the popular sentiments and constellations/dispositions of states and social elites. The relative autonomy of the academic field vis-à-vis other fields, like politics and popular culture, varied from time to time, depending on the changing structure of financing of academic producers or institutions. In general, the academic field is never totally isolated from the influences of other fields. A general model expositing dynamics of intellectual change in institutions of academic production that integrates both the network and field approaches is summarized in Figure 0.1.

This book employs the integrated sociological perspective on intellectual change to analyze the recurrent shift between idealization and contempt of China within different loci of academic production throughout the last eight centuries, from the thirteenth-to-seventeenth-century Catholic Church, eighteenth-century Enlightenment, to the nineteenth-century universities. I will draw on representative works on China in different epochs to depict the pattern of change and division within the field. I will then explain the pattern by looking into the level of interpersonal networks of patronage, mentorship, and rivalry among intellectuals, the level of institutional politics of knowledge production, and the level of macro-political economy as nested levels with relative autonomy in each level.

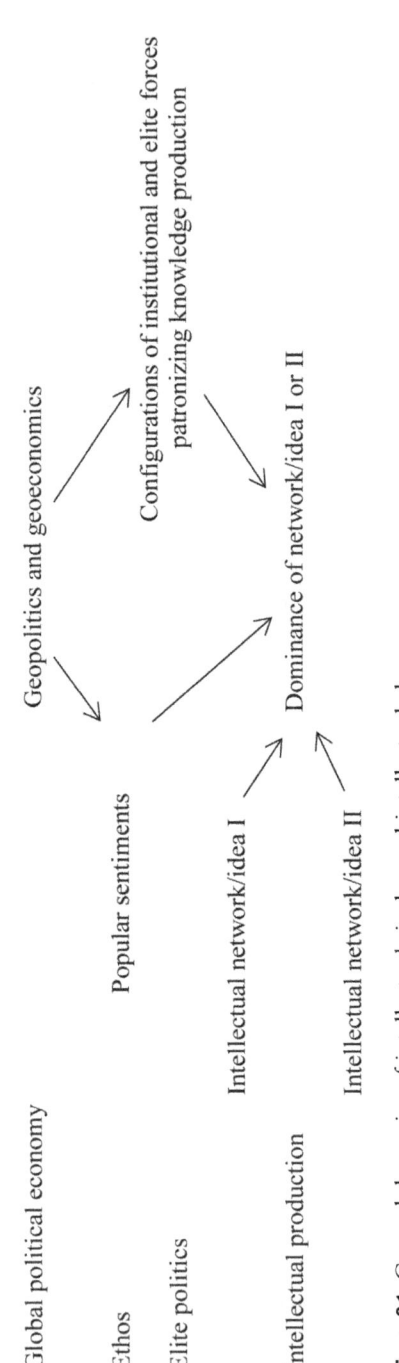

Figure 0.1 General dynamics of intellectual rivalry and intellectual change

Chapter Outline

Chapter 1 discusses how China entered Europe's consciousness through the expansion of the Mongol Empire. The travelogue of Marco Polo has been hailed as the first Western description of China. Its exhilarating portrayal of China (or the Chinese region of the Mongol Empire) and of a benign Mongol ruler ready to be baptized was the origin of the Western idealization of China. But, in fact, during medieval Europe, intellectual accounts of China were far more pluralistic than Marco Polo's account. Polo's account was the first direct and relatively accurate (but selectively positive) one on China, but Polo's notion about the readiness of the Mongol rulers to be converted to Christianity originated from earlier monastic scholarly works claiming the Mongols as descendants of the Three Magi and hence, inherently Christian.

Earlier than Marco Polo's travelogue, Matthew Paris, a Benedictine monk in England, published *Chronica Majora*, regarded as the first universal history of the world in Europe. Paris devoted a section of the book to describing the customs of the Mongols and the people living under Mongolian rule as cannibalistic and barbaric. It portrayed the imminent Mongol invasion as the greatest peril that Christianity had ever faced. Though the Mongols are not exactly Chinese, for medieval Europeans, both Mongols and the Chinese were the same alien culture from the Far Orient. Later writings on the Chinese region continued this simplification. Pseudo-scientific theories of race in the nineteenth and early twentieth century classified all human beings into the "sub-species" of "Caucasoid" (white), "Negroid" (black), and "Mongoloid" (yellow), with the last term referring to all populations in Asia. Polo's and Paris' accounts of China constituted the archetypes of the two poles of Western representation of China – simplistic idealization and disdainful fear – that continued even after Europe established direct and regular contacts with China in the long sixteenth century (c. 1450–1640).

Chapter 2 discusses the rise of Sinopilia during Europe's "seventeenth-century crisis." Amid the economic downturn and geopolitical chaos in Europe in the seventeenth century, European travelers, principally Catholic missionaries like the Jesuits, noticed the Chinese empire undergoing similar chaos during its early seventeenth-century dynastic transition. The chaos ended swiftly with the rise of the Qing 清 Empire in the latter half of the century. With political stability restored in China, the Jesuits managed to gain access to the Qing court as scientific advisers and painters of the Qing Emperor. The Jesuits also translated classic Confucianist texts into European languages. They started to publish books in Europe on Chinese history, technology, agronomy, and other aspects of life.

As the monopolistic source on China in Europe, the Jesuits presented an idealized image of China to gain the Church's and European rulers' support for their continued missionary work. They claimed classic Confucianist texts conveyed a belief in the monotheistic God and that China's uninterrupted adherence to ancient teaching, in contrast to Europe's degeneration from antiquity, made the Chinese civilization closer to pure morality and knowledge of God. Jesuits' idealizing writings on China sparked the rise of Sinophilia in all intellectual fields in Europe. The popularity of Jesuits' writings on China soon invoked attacks from other Catholic orders, who convinced the Church that the Chinese were godless and idolatrous. Jesuits' writings and their position on China did not win the argument in the Church but further aggravated the Sinophilia outside the Church.

Chapters 3 and 4 deal with the changing view of China in the early and late Enlightenment communities of philosophers, which constituted the new centers of knowledge production in the eighteenth century. Early Enlightenment thinkers, like Voltaire, were trained in Jesuit schools and served absolutist monarchs pursuing political centralization. They adopted the Jesuits' idealized image of China and Confucianism, seeing China as a model of rational deism and enlightened despotism that European princes should emulate. The Physiocrats drew from China's vast internal market, portrayed as free from bureaucratic intervention, to develop their ideas about *laissez-faire* economics. This idealized view was disputed by other Enlightenment thinkers, like Montesquieu, who represented France's aristocratic opposition to absolutism and saw China as a dark example of extreme despotism. The debate about China among mid eighteenth-century Enlightenment thinkers gave way to the consensual disdain of China during the late Enlightenment among Diderot, Kant, Hegel, and so on.

While the conflicting views on China in the early to mid eighteenth century were tied to the conflicts between absolutist monarchs and the aristocracy, the late eighteenth-century widespread disdain for China was related to Europe's newfound confidence among the ascendent bourgeoisie amid Europe's renewed economic and geopolitical expansion. Under the conception of Europe as a progressive continent, all ancient civilizations, including Christianity, were attacked as stagnant, superstitious, and detrimental to human reason and progress. Radical Enlightenment thinkers' attack on China was as fervent as their attack on the Church. While their attack on the Church paved the way to the destruction of the Church's political power in the Age of Revolution, their attack on China and other non-Western civilizations prepared the ground for Europe's imperial subjugation of the old "Orient."

Chapters 5 and 6 show that concomitant to the rise of Romanticism, which was a reaction to the perceived excesses of modernism and industrialization that allegedly threatened the integrity of humanity, was the rise of Romantic Orientalism as an academic field, institutionalized in universities and academic associations in the nineteenth century. Romantic Orientalists tasked themselves with looking to the East for the lost innocence of human minds, or pure knowledge of God, that the menace of industrial civilization had clouded. Romantic Sinologists revived many idealizing themes of the Jesuits' writings on China. They immersed themselves in Confucianist texts and folk religious practices in China to look for the uncontaminated, original human soul and God's morality.

Amid the intensifying inter-imperial rivalry at the turn of the twentieth century, Darwinism, scientific racism, and ethnonationalism replaced Romanticism as the zeitgeist of Europe's academia. As such, Romantic Orientalism gave way to scientific-racist Orientalism. The early Sinologists' Romanticist ideas about an innocent, spiritual China were replaced by the scientific-racist Sinological view that the Chinese were the principal animists and fetishists in the world trapped in an inferior culture that should be eradicated or subjugated in the inter-racial struggle for survival.

Chapters 7 and 8 examine the formative years of modern social sciences in the late nineteenth and early twentieth century. Social theorists like Marx and Weber were obsessed with explaining the rise of modernity in the West compared to the supposedly unchanging non-Western societies. The contrast between a dynamic West and stagnant civilizations outside Europe is central to their theoretical construct. These social theorists based their knowledge about non-European civilizations on the distorted views of the most prominent Orientalists of their days. They, therefore, inherited some of the most disdainful or idealizing views of the East in the Orientalist enterprise. Although those views have been rejected by a new generation of Area Studies scholars in the post-World War II era, the prejudices and fantasy in nineteenth-century Orientalist knowledge persisted covertly through the dominance of some universal, abstract social theories derived from such knowledge. These grand theories contributed to the many variants of the modernization theory, dependency theory, or the theory of Oriental Despotism in Cold War Western academia, which generated serious intellectual, policy, and political consequences, such as the marginalization of local cultures and the catastrophe of top-down agrarian collectivization.

The idealized and disdainful views on China, generated by centuries of scholarly knowledge production, continued in Western popular imaginations throughout the twentieth century. At the same time, Sinology, when morphing into postwar China Studies, was among the first Area Studies fields that de-Orientalized by ridding itself of centuries of reductionist and essentializing epistemology. Such a de-Orientalizing process started at the fringe of Sinology in the mid twentieth century and benefited from novel social science perspectives and methods. It culminated in the turbulent 1960s, when many postwar assumptions and ideologies were challenged, and China's geopolitical relations with the West underwent a drastic reversal following the Sino–Soviet split.

Chapters 9 and 10 explore how Chinese intellectuals and state builders appropriated the Western Orientalizing views of China in their modern nation-making projects. Both the cultural radicals, who advocated total eradication of traditional Chinese culture because they viewed it as the biggest impediment to modernization, and the cultural conservatives, who defended traditional Chinese values against the pressure of Westernization, based their understanding of Chinese traditions on the Western Orientalist construction of Chinese cultures. The chapters will also explore the quixotic attempts by some twentieth-century New Confucianism scholars who strove to rescue Confucianism by recovering the full complexity of the Confucianist traditions. At the turn of the twenty-first century, those scholarly attempts have been increasingly overshadowed by the Chinese state's ambition to revive the idealizing fantasy about a communalistic and filial Confucianist culture to legitimize its persistent authoritarian rule. Such self-Orientalizing efforts of the Chinese state constituted one source of the persistence of Orientalist views on China in Western popular and political discourses, despite the progress of de-Orientalization in Western China Studies.

The internal dynamism of the field of China Studies, after all, is constrained by popular and political ideologies shaped by the forces of geopolitics and geoeconomics. In the Conclusion, I take stock of the de-Orientalizing achievements of the China Studies field in the last four decades. I discuss how the revival of Orientalist views of China in the Western popular imagination, as well as the self-Orientalism of China's authoritarian state in the context of intensifying US–China rivalry, jeopardizes the de-Orientalizing achievements of academic China Studies.

Part I
CATHOLIC SCHOLARSHIP

1 FROM PAX MONGOLICA TO THE LONG SIXTEENTH CENTURY

Up until the mid twentieth century, the term "Mongolian race" or "Mongoloids" had been often used to refer to all peoples in East Asia, including Chinese, Mongols proper, Koreans, and Japanese (see Chapter 6). In early modern times, Mongolia, Tartary, China, and Cathay were often used interchangeably in European writings on the East. Medieval Europe's fantasy and fear of the Mongols constituted the templates of Europeans' fantasy and fear of China in the centuries to come.

In 1882, young Theodore Roosevelt supported the Chinese Exclusion Act of the US by saying: "No greater calamity could now befall the United States than to have the Pacific slope filled up with a Mongolian population."[1] In 1901, a Chinese Exclusion Convention was held in California. Participants included "Supervisors, City Councils, trade, commercial and civic organizations to the number of three thousand" from the state. The Convention issued a memorandum to the US president and Congress to urge for a continuation of the Exclusion Act. The memorandum repeatedly referred to the Chinese as Mongolians, emphasizing, "[t]he Caucasian will not tolerate the Mongolian ... the white population of this country will not without resistance suffer itself to be destroyed." It invoked the fear of the yellow peril by emphasizing the history of the waves of Asiatic and Mongolian invasion of Europe, noting that "[c]ivilization in Europe has been frequently attacked and imperiled by the barbaric hordes of Asia."[2]

---

[1] Cited in Dyer 1980: 140; see also Bradley 2015: 44.
[2] San Francisco Call 1901.

During World War II, US General George S. Patton Jr., who commanded the US invasion of Germany after the Normandy landing, openly spoke against the US alliance with the Soviet Union toward the end of the war and referred to the communist Russians as the new Mongol invaders of Europe:

> The Russians are Mongols ... From Genghis Kahn to Stalin, they have not changed. They never will and we will never learn, at least, not until it is too late. Poland is under Russian domination, so is Hungary, so is Czechoslovakia, and so is Yugoslavia ... We have destroyed what could have been a good race of people and we are about to replace them with Mongolian savages and all of Europe with communism.[3]

The memory of the Mongol invasion continued after World War II. At the inception of the Cold War, the shock of China turning communist in 1949 and the rise of a Soviet–China alliance brought back the fear of an autocratic Eurasian landmass resembling the thirteenth-century Mongol Empire that threatened to invade Europe and Japan. As George Kennan, the architect of the US Cold War strategy of containing the Soviet Bloc, famously remarked in 1951:

> [I]t was essential to us ... that no single Continental land power should come to dominate the entire Eurasian land mass. Our interest has lain rather in the maintenance of some sort of stable balance among the powers of the interior, in order that none of them should ... conquer the seafaring fringes of the land mass ... [W]e have had a stake in the prosperity and independence of the peripheral powers of Europe and Asia: those countries whose gazes were oriented outward, across the seas, rather than inward to the conquest of power on land.[4]

Such medieval fear of the Mongol invasion and the US Cold War priority of "preventing a hostile power (or coalition) from controlling the Eurasian land mass" was behind Nixon–Kissinger's rapprochement to China as a move to split that autocratic Eurasian power bloc.[5]

---

[3] Patton 1944; see also Patton 2002: 269.
[4] Kennan 1951: 4–5.
[5] Burr 2010.

The memory of the Mongol invasion was also strong in the Soviet Union and played a part in the Soviets turning against China in the 1960s. In 1964, when Sino-Soviet relations deteriorated, Moscow accused Beijing of glorifying Genghis Khan. Soviet communist theoretical journal *Kommunist* attacked the Chinese Communist Party for "wiping the blood" off Genghis Khan's hands and preaching "yellow supremacy" by claiming Mongol invaders brought "higher culture" to the conquered peoples, including the Russians.[6]

Medieval Fear and Fantasy of the Mongols

The memory of the Mongol invasion is deep and has shaped Western conceptions of China for centuries. The conflation of the Mongols and Chinese in the West originated in the thirteenth century when Latin Christianity started seriously learning about the East beyond the Muslim world when confronted with the westward expansion of the Mongol Empire.

In Janet Abu-Lughod's "thirteenth-century world-system," different parts of the Eurasian continent were connected through overlapping regional trade circuits under the Mongol Empire's hegemony in most of the Eurasian continent.[7] However, regular, direct trade links and contacts between the two ends of Eurasia did not yet exist. Up to the medieval times, Europe's scholarly understanding of the East in the Church, the locus of authoritative knowledge production at the time, did not stretch beyond the Muslim world, which had been in direct contact with Europe through trade, diplomacy, and wars. Writings about the land farther east often portrayed the area as the home of strange men and monsters. From clerical encyclopedias to Church architecture, we find illustrations of dog-headed men, men with one foot as large as an umbrella, men with faces on the chest, and the like, as the inhabitants of the East. There were also writings arguing that the East was the seat of Paradise or the Garden of Eden.[8]

---

[6] New York Times, 1964.
[7] Abu-Lughod 1989. See also Zarakol 2022: 47–88.
[8] Gordon 1986: 46–7.

Into the twelfth century, at the height of European conflict with the Arab world through successive crusades, the Catholic Church saw the rise of the legend about Prester John. Many European monarchs, priests, and scholars started to believe that Prester John, a mythical and mighty Christian warrior king, a descendant of the Magi who had built a prospering, expanding Christian kingdom in the Far East, would one day join the Crusaders in the West to crush the Muslims from the other side. A forged letter from Prester John addressing European authorities circulated at the time, with more exaggerations and embellishments added with every version. The legend of Prester John was fueled by the various travelers' accounts of Nestorian Christian communities in Central Asia and India.[9] Nestorianism was a theological doctrine in the early Church that inspired the formation of Christian sects that spread eastward after it was banned as a heresy in Rome.

In the early thirteenth century, when the news about the rise of the Mongol Empire that invaded Muslim lands in the Near East reached Europe, the Church and monarchs were initially jubilant. Learning of the tales about repressed Christian communities under Muslim rule liberated by the Mongols, many Europeans started to refer to the Mongol Emperor Genghis Khan as King David, believed to be a son or grandson of the long-awaited Prester John.[10]

The Fear of Mongol Invasion

When the Mongol army invaded Poland and Hungary in 1241–1242, all fantasy about the Mongols as Christian liberators vanished into thin air. The brutality of the Mongol army that razed Christian towns and cities to the ground, the massacre of Christians, and the enslavement of women and artisans brought panic around Europe. After Poland and Hungary, the Mongol army reached Austria and was about to invade Vienna in the spring of 1242. Foreseeing the destruction of Christendom by the Mongol army, the Pope and aristocrats throughout Europe started to prepare for a crusade against the Mongols and to defend Europe. Suddenly, the Mongol army turned away and disappeared without attacking

---

[9] Jackson 2018: 22–4.
[10] Jackson 2018: 49–52.

Vienna. To this day, historians debate why the Mongols suddenly turned back. Hypotheses include the arrival of the news of the death of the Great Khan, the lack of grassland in Europe that deprived the horse-dependent Mongol war machine of its fuel, and the wet weather in spring 1242 that turned the pathways of invasion into swamps unpassable by horses.[11]

After the retreat of the immediate threat, Europeans learned that the Mongol army was still rampaging the Muslim world in the Near East. Pope Innocent IV sent Franciscan and Dominican friars to the Mongol land in the mid 1240s to establish contact with the Great Khan and probe his intentions regarding Europe. They were also to explore the possibility of a diplomatic relationship and even an alliance against the Muslims. The Pope's envoys traveled extensively in the Mongol Empire and reached its capital, Karakorum. The diplomatic mission failed, as the Mongol lords presented the Pope's envoys with an ultimatum from Guyuk Khan, the grandson of Genghis Khan, requesting that the Pope attended the Mongol court in person to pledge subjugation of the Christian world to the Khan. The envoys also reported serious military preparation for a fresh invasion of Europe.[12]

After traveling extensively in the Mongol Empire, the Pope's envoys produced several manuscripts of ethnographic and historical accounts of the lands occupied by the Mongols. These accounts were the first of their kind in Europe. Two of the better-known examples include C. de Bridia's *Historia Tartarorum* (History of the Tartars) (c. 1247), believed to be based on the travel records of the Franciscan envoy Giovanni da Pian del Carpini, and a book of the same name by Simon of Saint Quentin, a member of the Dominican envoys, also published in 1247. Based on collections of documentary materials, first-hand observations, and legendary accounts the authors gathered, these books were filled with hatred and wild imagery of the Mongols. For example, Bridia's book talked of strange countries of people who lived solely on sniffing steam and not eating anything, people with human heads, dog faces, and ox feet who mixed human languages with barking,

---

[11] Jackson 2018: 65–81; Büntgen and Di Cosmo 2016.
[12] Jackson 2018: 92–116.

and people with only one foot and one arm, in different parts of the Mongol Empire.[13]

Quentin's *Historia Tartarorum* did not mention half-human beings and monsters. But it portrayed the Mongols as cannibalistic and extremely cruel, devilish beings:

> They are so cruel that they neither respect the elderly, nor do they have any mercy on children. The spilling of blood is considered among them like the spilling of water, and human bodies strewn about are reckoned as a pile of shit; they rage for the annihilation of not just one nation, but also Christians and every other group of people ... They devour the flesh of men like lions, either roasted with fire or boiled, sometimes out of necessity, sometimes for the pleasure of it, and other times in order to incite fear and horror in people who will hear about it.[14]

These accounts also referred to the legend of Prester John. But instead of seeing the Mongol overlord as a descendant of the mystical Christian king, these writings saw the Mongols as the subjects of King David, son of John. Under the leadership of Genghis Khan, they murdered King David and slaughtered his whole family to found the Mongol Empire.

The rise of the Tartars and their invasion of Europe was recorded in the English Benedictine monastery by the scholar Matthew Paris in *Chronica Majora* (Major Chronicle) (1259), regarded as the first universal history of the known world. By incorporating extensive written sources at the time, Paris depicted the Mongols as inhuman and demonic in the 1241 entry of the chronicle, with gruesome illustrations of their cannibalism (see Figure 1.1):

> For the [Tartar] men are inhuman and bestial. They should be called monsters rather than human beings, thirsting after and drinking blood, tearing apart and devouring the corpses of dogs and humans. They are clothed in the skins of bulls, are armed with iron lances, short in stature, stocky and compact in body, vigorously strong, invincible in war,

---

[13] Bridia 1996 [1247]: 74.
[14] Simon of Saint-Quentin 2019 [c. 1253]: xxx, 77.

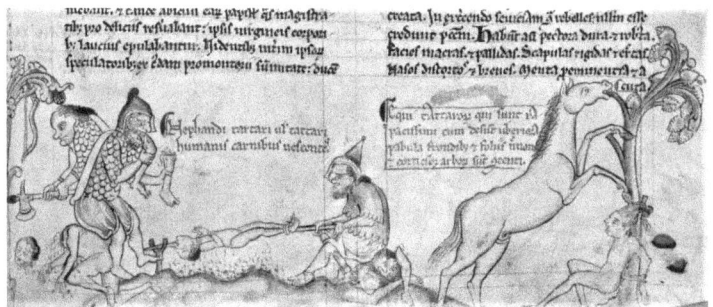

Figure 1.1 Tartar feast: medieval depiction of Mongols' cannibalism
Source: Paris 1259: MS 16, folio 167r

untiring in labor ... Devoid of human laws, they have no knowledge of clemency; they are more ferocious than lions and bears. ... The leaders, along with their dinner guests and other lotus eaters, fed on their [Christians] corpses as though they were bread, leaving nothing for the vultures except bones. ... The old and deformed women they gave to the cannibals ... as food, as if it were a daily ration. They did not eat the beautiful women immediately. Rather they suffocated them under a mass of rapists as they cried out and wailed. They raped virgins until they died, and then their breasts were cut off, which they kept for their leaders as delicacies, and they feasted on their virginal bodies in a more splendid manner.[15]

Paris also reiterated a common conspiracy theory that the Mongols were descendants of the "lost tribes of Israel," asserting the Mongols were Jewish in origin. He alleged that "[t]hese Tartars ... are believed to have been from the ten tribes who followed after golden calves, having abandoned the Law of Moses." Later, they were locked up in a mountain by Alexander the Great. Because of millennia of isolation from civilized humans, they "followed after alien gods and unknown rites, ... their way of life is transformed into feral and senseless cruelty."[16] Paris accused the Jews in Europe,

---

[15] Paris 1259, translated in Andrea 2020: 337–9.
[16] Paris 1259, translated in Andrea 2020: 338.

who allegedly resented Christian rule and saw the Mongol Khan as the Messiah, of devising a treacherous plot to bring down their Christian leaders, supplying arms to the invading Mongols, and intending to open their city gates to welcome the invaders.[17]

Fantasizing about Mongols' Conversion to Christianity

Into the late thirteenth century, the new Mongol invasion of Europe never materialized, while the Mongols continued their campaign against the Muslim Near East. Christians' fear of the Mongols abated, and European rulers started to consider a Christian–Mongol alliance against the Muslims again. They even fantasized about converting the Khan to Christianity and making the Mongol Empire a mighty Christian force.

The fantasy about converting Mongol rulers to Christianity was reflected in Riccoldo da Monte di Croce's *Libellus ad nationes orientales* (A Little Book to the Eastern Nations), written in 1300.[18] It was one of the first attempts at comprehensive ethnographies of all the nations in the East. The book was intended to be a manual for Catholic priests to convert different peoples they encountered when they traveled to the East. To Riccoldo, all peoples or nations in the East could be categorized into Nestorian Christians, Jews, Muslims, and Tartars. According to Riccoldo's hierarchical schema, the Tartars were more readily convertible to Christianity than the Muslims, and the Muslims more readily than the Jews. Noting that the "great emperor of the Tartars gladly keeps the [Christian] brothers in his court and treats them with honor," Riccoldo was hopeful that "the Tartars can be brought back [to Christianity] by way of verbal and rational communication and by miracles. And we must begin with the kings and their elders."[19]

Besides emissaries from Rome who wanted to establish diplomatic and alliance relations with the Great Khan and to convert the Mongols, merchants from Europe and other parts of Eurasia started to travel freely across the Mongol Empire. They mingled and exchanged notes with one another. Under a unitary Mongol

---

[17] Menache 1996.
[18] Jensen 1998.
[19] Riccoldo da Monte di Croce 2009 [1300]: section 5.

Empire's protection, trade routes across Eurasia via land and sea became much safer. The abolition of tariffs for goods transported from one locality to a faraway one across the continent made long-distance trade more profitable. In many instances, merchants in cities under Mongol attack would undermine their rulers to facilitate the invading Mongols, as they expected that Mongol rule could open their cities to free trade across the empire.[20]

Marco Polo traveled to Karakorum and Mongol-ruled China with his father and uncle in the late thirteenth century in the midst of blooming diplomatic, religious, and trading activities across Eurasia. The Polos were not pure traders, as Marco's father and uncle also played the role of messenger between the Great Khan and the Pope. The Kublai Kahn employed Marco Polo as an administrator in his Empire. Some even hypothesized that Marco Polo devised his book about travel not for traders and travelers but as an instrument to bid for a diplomatic career himself.[21]

Marco Polo's account of Mongol China was filled with his fascination with big ships and magnificent bridges, roads, granaries, warehouses, and advanced production that Europeans had not seen since ancient Roman times. The Mongol rulers, in Polo's eyes, were no longer devilish and cannibalistic. The Mongol rule in China, according to Polo, was far from repressive and extractive, nor was it plagued by racial discrimination, administrative malfunction, or monetary chaos, as depicted in Chinese sources.[22] On the contrary, Polo described Kublai rule as an exemplar of benevolent rule that European rulers should emulate:

> Now let me tell you something of the bounties that the Great Khan confers upon his subjects. For all his thoughts are directed towards helping the people who are subject to him, so that they may live and labor and increase their wealth. You may take it for a fact that he sends emissaries and inspectors throughout all his dominions and kingdoms and provinces to learn whether any of his people have suffered a failure of their crops either through weather or through locusts or other pests. And if he finds that any have

[20] Jackson 2018: 255–82.
[21] Spence 1998: 1–18; Jackson 2018: 279–82; 338–51.
[22] Waterson 2013; Atwood 2021; Rossabi 1994: 473–82.

lost their harvest, he exempts them for that year from their tribute and even gives them some of his own grain to sow and to eat – a magnificent act of royal bounty ... Let me now tell you how the Great Khan bestows charity on the poor people of Khan-balik [Beijing]. When he learns that some family of honest and respectable people have been impoverished by some misfortune or disabled from working by illness, so that they have no means of earning their daily bread, he sees to it that such families ... are given enough to cover their expenses for the whole year.[23]

Such a social security system in Mongol China has not been documented anywhere else. These descriptions could be based on hearsay from earlier times. By the time Polo served in the Mongol court in the late thirteenth century, the Mongol state was in decline after the failed invasion of Japan.[24] Polo also portrayed the Kublai Khan as having great respect for Christianity. Not only did the Khan offer generous liberty to Christians in his realm, but he was also ready to be converted to Christianity, according to Macro Polo:

[O]n the Great Khan's own showing he regards as truest and best the faith of the Christians, because he declares that it commands nothing that is not full of all goodness and holiness. ... [Kublai to Polo:] "You go to your Pope and ask him on my behalf to send me a hundred men learned in your religion, who in the face of these idolaters [among Mongol aristocracy] will have the knowledge to condemn their performances and tell them that they too could do such things [magics] but will not, because they are done by diabolic art and evil spirits, and will show their mastery by making the idolaters powerless to perform those marvels in their presence. On the day when we see this, I too will condemn them and their religion. Then I will be baptized, and all my barons and magnates will do likewise, and their subjects in turn will undergo baptism. So there will be more Christians here than there are in your part of the world."
And if ... men had really been sent by the Pope with the

---

[23] Polo 1958 [c. 1300]: 155–7.
[24] Atwood 2023: 122–3, 132–8; Rossabi 1994: 473–88.

ability to preach our faith to the Great Khan, then assuredly he would have become a Christian. For it is known for a fact that he was most desirous to be converted.[25]

Besides praising the Mongol rulers, Polo also showed admiration for the propriety, chastity, and humility of the Chinese subjects of the Great Khan, as the "young ladies of the province of Cathay excel in modesty and the strict observance of decorum ... the same applies to young lads of good family."[26]

There have been disputes about whether Marco Polo visited all the places he claimed to visit in person. There were obvious omissions of mentions of the Great Wall, foot-binding, and food, besides many of the unlikely "facts" not corroborated by other sources, as seen in these examples.[27] Nonetheless, the most important point of Polo's writings was its lasting influence on Europe's stereotypes of China. Just as the mid thirteenth-century monastery depictions of the Mongols became the prototype of negative views on China in the centuries to come, Polo's flattering accounts of the Mongol Empire set the tone of the idealizing fantasy about China. Polo's assertion that the Mongol rulers were ready to be baptized and that the Empire could become Christian was nothing new. The significance of Polo's writings is that he incorporated ideas that had been developed in scholarly monastic knowledge (such as the idea that Mongol rulers were descendants of the Three Magi or Prester John, inherently Christian, and that their rule was an exemplar of benevolence and generosity) and popularized them through his book, which was widely read through the subsequent centuries.

The monastery production of knowledge about the Mongols did rely on systematic methods to collect evidence, credible or not, through citing other written sources in the Christian or Islamic world (e.g., Mathew Paris) or through reference to direct ethnographic observation (e.g., C. de Bridia). The driving force behind the assembling of evidence into coherent views about the Mongols was the geopolitical intent of the authorities (the Pope and the monarchs) and popular sentiments about the Mongol Empire.

---

[25] Polo 1958 [c. 1300]: 119–20.
[26] Polo 1958 [c. 1300]: 196–7.
[27] Wood 1997; Spence 1998: 1–18.

As such, the religious institutions of learning did not enjoy much autonomy in constructing and verifying their knowledge. They were more or less subservient to feudal power and created ideologicalized knowledge serving such power and fed the imagination of the reading classes. The two competing notions about the Mongols/Chinese, one portraying them as "same as us" and inherently Christian, and the other projecting them as "radically different from us" and a demonic threat, continued to be the foci around which scholarly knowledge about China revolved around in the centuries to come.

The Portuguese and Spaniards in East Asia

With the Black Death and nationalist revolts against Mongol rule across Eurasia that ended Pax Mongolica in the fourteenth century, Europe turned inward amid the disintegration of trading circuits across Eurasia. When Europe recovered from the Black Death and its economy entered the expansionary "long sixteenth century" (c. 1450–1640), the blocking of the trade route to the East by the rising Ottoman Empire after the fall of Constantinople in 1453 urged Portugal and Spain, the new dominant powers in Europe, to explore new sea routes. It resulted in the unexpected conquest of America in 1492 and the Portuguese arrival in Calcutta after the journey around the Cape of Good Hope in 1498. Following the Portuguese conquest of Goa and Malacca in 1510 and 1511 and the Spanish conquest of America, the two Iberian empires continued to try to reach China, the legendary, prosperous Cathay described by Marco Polo.

The Portuguese galleon arrived at Guangzhou 廣州 (Canton) in South China in 1517 and requested a trade. Being declined, the Portuguese moved to the mouth of the Pearl River and stationed on today's Lantau Island in the Hong Kong region. This triggered the Sino-Portuguese war in 1522–1523, in which the Portuguese fleet was defeated and expelled. Afterward, when the state of the Ming 明 Empire – founded in 1368 by Han Chinese rebels who expelled the Mongols – became less hostile to maritime trade, the ban on sea trade that originated in the 1430s began eroding. In 1553, the Portuguese landed on Macao and offered to submit an annual tribute to the Ming government. A Portuguese–Ming agreement ensued. The Ming government tolerated the Portuguese occupation of Macao in exchange for Portuguese arquebus as part of the Portuguese tribute. These Portuguese weapons were useful to the Ming efforts in its frontier war in the northeast of the empire.[28] The Portuguese also established themselves in the Japanese port of Nagasaki. They built a trade network spanning from Lisbon to Guangzhou and Nagasaki via Macao, Malacca, and Goa. These became the trade routes for European mercantile and missionary travelers.

The Portuguese maritime empire was grounded on the Portuguese holding of a few coastal cities. It was politically and militarily vulnerable, especially at the eastern end.[29] Their presence in East Asia was only possible through the toleration of local rulers, such as the Ming state in China. They counted on a symbiotic relationship with the Chinese merchants to stay profitable.[30] Chinese traders brought goods from Guangzhou to Macao, while the Portuguese purchased and brought them to the Malacca markets.[31]

In 1493, the Vatican divided the world into the Eastern and Western hemispheres, granting the Portuguese dominance in the former and the Spaniards in the latter. The Spaniards, absorbed in consolidating their territorial empire in the Americas, did not come to the other side of the Pacific Ocean until the mid sixteenth century. Stimulated by the Portuguese settling in Macao, the Spanish court sought to establish a direct trade route with China in the 1550s. In 1565, a Spanish fleet landed on the Philippines Islands and built a colony centered on Manila, which served as a springboard for the China trade.

Upon establishing themselves in Manila, the Spaniards were attacked by an armed Chinese merchant fleet in 1574. After repelling the attack, the Spaniards sent their first mission to the southeastern coastal province of Fujian 福建 to ask for permission for trade and missionary work there in 1575. The mission was led by two Augustinian friars, Martin de Rada and Jeronimo Marin, plus two military observers. Their proposal was opposed fiercely by the Portuguese, who did not want to see Spanish competition in the thriving China–Nagasaki trade. Chinese local officials who allied

---

[28] He 1996: 34–6.
[29] Boxer 1969: 50, 56–7; He 1996: 42–3; Chaudhuri 1981: 232.
[30] Bryan Souza 1986: 130–1; Hui 1995: 45, 62.
[31] Hui 1995.

with the Portuguese and their Chinese merchant collaborators were against the Spanish presence, too.[32] A Spanish Franciscan mission visited Guangzhou in 1578 to ask for trade there. The mission faced the same resistance.

Rejected by Chinese officials, the Spanish governor of the Philippines proposed a military expedition to invade China. They believed the Chinese to be militarily incompetent and that they could conquer China with as little effort as they did the Americas. Though the king of Spain, Philip II, rejected the proposed attack of China in 1576, the voice for aggression did not abate among the Spaniards in Mexico and the Philippines.[33]

The Spanish hostility toward China increased with the intensifying competition from Chinese merchants in the Manila market. Spanish merchants in the Philippines could not break their Chinese counterpart's monopoly of the silk trade in Manila. The textile manufacturers in Spain also lost their American market to Chinese products.[34] This hostility resulted in recurrent ethnocide of the Chinese inhabitants in Manila by the Spanish authorities in 1603, 1639, 1662, and 1686.[35]

Reconciling China and the Bible
Early Missionary Writings on China

The Eurocentric, theological worldview that Europe was at the center of the world and the unique recipient of God's grace still held after Europe's discovery of the world. The Asians, with their exotic customs, were seen as savages to be converted to Christianity.[36] To recover from its loss of influence in Europe during the Reformation, Rome initiated the Counter-Reformation program in the fifteenth and sixteenth centuries. It involved an attempt to convert the newly encountered peoples to Catholicism to make up for the loss to Protestantism. The Vatican founded the Society of Jesus in 1540 to train missionaries, who then traveled to different

---

[32] Lach 1965: 746; He 1996: 61.
[33] Lach 1965: 746, 786–7.
[34] Quan 1971: 363–4; Bryan Souza 1986: 70.
[35] Hui 1995: 71.
[36] Gordon 1986: 46–51.

1 From Pax Mongolica to the Long Sixteenth Century

corners of the world to spread the gospel. As well as the Jesuits, other orders in the Church – the Franciscan, Dominican, and Augustinian – also attempted to extend their influences in Asia and the Americas by traveling on either Portuguese or Spanish ships. Under the patronage of the Iberian colonizers, the Catholic priests became the major writers about Asia.

The first book systematically describing China was written in 1569 by a Portuguese Dominican, Gaspar da Gruz, titled *Tractado em que se cõtam muito por estēso as cousas da China* (Treatise in which the matters of China are recounted in great detail) (Evora, 1569). Other well-known reports on China included one by Galeote Pereira, a Portuguese nobleman, published in 1565, a report by Martín de Rada, the Spanish Augustinian leading the 1575 missions to China, and the reports of his companions. Portuguese and Spanish Jesuits frequently mentioned China in their letters and reports published as compilations.[37]

These early writings relied on the authors' first-hand experiences and Portuguese or Spanish informants working in the coastal cities in south and southeast China. They also cited each other as secondary sources. Most of the works show the authors' fascination with the fertility of Chinese agricultural land, the productivity of the porcelain and silk industries, the nonexistence of beggars in the cities, effective administration, and the large population of the Chinese empire.[38]

Concerning the religions of the Chinese, the writers split into laudatory and critical camps. The division between the two coincided more or less with the authors' nationalities. Rada, the Spanish Augustinian, emphasized the idolatry of the Chinese. He found that "each house has its own idols besides the multitude which they have in temples," and "there is hardly a large rock which does not have idols carved thereon." He regarded the rites and ceremonies of the Chinese as "very ridiculous."[39] Rada was among the most earnest advocates for a military crusade against China. He asserted that China was militarily weak despite its wealth. He argued that China could only be converted through force.[40]

---

[37] Lach 1965: 742–3.
[38] Lach 1965: 751–86.
[39] quoted in Lach 1965: 785.
[40] Lach 1965: 749, 785–6.

The belief in the necessity of using force to bring China to submission was shared by many Spanish Jesuits.[41]

On the other side, Cruz and Pereria, the two Portuguese writers, advocated the peaceful conversion of the Chinese. Though they noticed the idolatry of the Chinese civilians, they insisted the Chinese were not very serious about their gods. They also tried to find some parallels between Chinese religious ideas and Christianity. They believed the Chinese lacked the true knowledge of God, and they could easily be converted after the introduction of such knowledge by Europeans.[42] The divergence between the Portuguese and Spanish views on China was related to the Portuguese alliance with the Chinese court and merchants, in contrast to the Spanish hostility toward them.

Despite the divergent views between the Portuguese and Spaniards, the general opinion of Europe was more sympathetic to China. The most authoritative and widely read book in sixteenth-century Europe on China was *Historia de las cosas mas notables, ritos y costumbres del gran Reyno de la China* (History of the Most Notable Things, Rites, and Customs of the Great Kingdom of China) (Rome, 1585) by Juan González de Mendoza, an Augustinian who wrote the book under the command of Pope Gregory XIII to produce a compendium on the history and general description of the Chinese empire.[43] The book synthesized preceding works by Portuguese and Spanish authors, including Cruz, Radar, and Pereria. After its publication in Rome, it was swiftly translated into different vernacular languages across Europe. By the end of the sixteenth century, the book was reprinted forty-six times in seven European languages. It appeared as a key source of information in almost all major succeeding works on China. It was still regarded as a classic in the nineteenth century.

Though the book drew from both laudatory and critical sources on China, it was generally on the side of the former.[44] Mendoza tried to show the similarities between Christianity and popular Chinese religious beliefs. He interpreted the Chinese belief

[41] Lach 1965: 798.
[42] Lach 1965: 784–5.
[43] Lach 1965: 742–3.
[44] Lach 1965: 749–50.

in immortality and transmigration as a belief in heaven and that good people would become angels after death. He thought the Chinese would not hesitate to become Christian once they came in contact with the knowledge of God.[45] Mendoza irritated the Spanish militants. Soon after the publication of the Spanish edition in 1585, Juan Fernández de Velasco, Constable of Castile and a former high army officer, issued a letter to Rome to attack it as full of "clear and manifest" errors. The letter called for a ban on its second printing unless it was revised.

Jesuits Accommodation Policy toward China

As the Portuguese and Spanish missionaries competed to establish the first missionary station in China, and the debate about a military crusade against China continued in Spain and in Rome, Alessandro Valignano, an Italian Jesuit, proposed an approach of cultural accommodation based on his successful experience in Japan, where he converted the "king of Bungo," a lord of five kingdoms in the pre-unified Japan, by assimilating concepts of Buddhism in Catholicism.[46] Valignano, together with the Jesuit leaders in Rome, deplored Spanish militarism. He tried to prevent the further demarcation of the Society of Jesus along nationality lines by recruiting Jesuits from outside Portugal and Spain and letting them work under the patronage of the Portuguese.[47]

Valignano visited Canton with some Portuguese merchants in 1580. The Chinese officials warmly welcomed them. In 1583, the Chinese government permitted the permanent residence of the Jesuits. In September of that year, the first Jesuit station in China was established by Matteo Ricci and Michele Ruggieri, who were later joined by many others.[48] In 1585, Pope Gregory XIII issued a decree prohibiting other religious orders from entering China. The decree was to avoid disagreements and to let the Jesuits try their method of accommodation. The Chinese state allowed the Jesuits to travel freely in China. With such privileged access, Jesuit writings

---

[45] Lach 1965: 785.
[46] Sebes 1988: 23; Spence 1992a: 41; Lach 1965: 799.
[47] Lach 1965: 800.
[48] Lach 1965: 800–1.

became the authoritative sources of knowledge on China and shaped the European conception of China for more than a century. The approach of preaching Christianity through native languages and native cultural concepts, as well as converting the natives through collaborative efforts with the local ruling elite, underlined Ricci's missionary work in China. Before entering China, Ricci only knew of Buddhism and other idolatrous popular religions among common Chinese. When he first arrived, he was dressed as a Buddhist bonze or monk.[49] When Ricci and other Jesuits realized that Confucianism was the state ideology and the literati despised Buddhism, they shifted their attention from Buddhism and all other layman religions to Confucianism.[50]

The accommodation policy urged the Jesuits to study Confucian texts to identify elements reconcilable with Biblical teachings. Ricci found many. He discovered that in the classic Confucianist texts, *Shangdi* 上帝 (*Shang-Ti*) and *Tian* 天 (*Tin*) were frequently mentioned with praise and respect. Under the prominent interpretation among the Confucianists contemporary to Ricci, *Shangdi* was the Supreme Order of Nature, while *Tian* meant the physical sky. This interpretation was under the increasingly influential neo-Confucianist school formulated by Zhu Xi 朱熹 in the twelfth century. This school of Confucianism brought forth a materialist interpretation of the classics and grounded the Confucianist doctrines on an understanding of the "natural order" (see more discussion in Chapter 10). Ricci tried to argue against this atheist interpretation of Confucianism. He contended that *Shangdi* was exactly God and *Tian* was the same as Heaven.[51]

Ricci further stated that ancient Chinese worshipped a monotheistic God, which was the same as the God in Catholicism.[52] The Jesuits portrayed the ancient Chinese as a group of humans who received direct revelation from God. They also asserted that the belief in a monotheist God faded after the massive book burning in the Qin 秦 dynasty (c. 213 BCE). Despite the loss of its theological core, the remaining Chinese moral philosophy inherited from the

[49] Sebes 1988: 40.
[50] Dirlik 1996; Rule 1986; Jensen 1997.
[51] Mungello 1985: 61–2, 93.
[52] Mungello 1985: 63.

ancient Chinese was still compatible with Christianity. Confucius claimed he did not invent new morality but only recorded the morality in ancient China. As such, the Jesuits believed the Confucianist classics were key to revealing the ancient Chinese monotheism. The Jesuit program in China was to reformulate Confucianism by reinstating the "lost" theological core in it. It led to a systematic and thorough study of China's classic texts. This first organized study of Chinese culture by the West was the origin of Western Sinology.[53]

Ricci was an admirer of the Chinese language. He and many Jesuits praised the Chinese language's antiquity, beauty, and simplicity over European languages. Once Ricci started learning Chinese, he mentioned that Chinese was much easier to learn than Greek and German, and "the greatest advantage of this is all the countries [provinces] that use these letters can understand each other's correspondence and books, even though the languages [dialects] are different. That is not so with our letters."[54]

With regard to Chinese society, Ricci reproduced Marco Polo's image of a prosperous and militarily strong China. But he also mentioned the cunning merchants, the corruption in the imperial court, the tyranny of local officials over ordinary people, as well as the existence of slavery.[55] Ricci remarked that the Chinese had "no conception of the rules of logic," and the "science of ethics with them was a series of confused maxims and deductions at which they have arrived under guidance of the light of reason."[56] Ricci also detested Chinese arts and claimed they were particularly "primitive" in portraiture.[57]

The Jesuits described Confucian morality as originating from the same Biblical teachings as Western Catholicism. However, they also asserted that the Chinese had lost the knowledge of God and God's grace. To the Jesuits, it was the Europeans' responsibility to recover Chinese culture from its sin of atheism. The Jesuits distinguished philosophical sins from theological sins. The latter usually involved idolatry and was an offense against God, while the

---

[53] Mungello 1985; Zürcher 1995.
[54] quoted in Spence 1992a: 45.
[55] Spence 1984: 210–12; 219.
[56] Ricci 1953: 30.
[57] Ricci 1953: 22.

former was only caused by ignorance of God. Philosophical sin did not deserve eternal damnation and could easily be rectified by revelation by the missionaries.[58] Before the eighteenth century, Rome considered the Chinese sin of not recognizing the existence of God as a philosophical one.[59]

The Discourse of Universal History

The aforementioned European views on China were not unique. Sixteenth-century Europe treated other newly encountered peoples and societies more or less similarly. These views were well reflected in several sixteenth-century attempts to expand European historiography to deal with the non-Christian world in the writing of "Universal History."[60]

The global economic expansion of sixteenth-century Europe fomented sentiments of optimism and arrogance. The European conquest of Asia and the New World were praised as glorious achievements of Christendom. The idea of progress and the word "civilization" to describe a stage of society after successive evolution appeared for the first time in the century.[61] André Thevet, a Franciscan monk, traveler, and royal cosmographer in France, wrote in his popular *Les singularites de la France antarcitque* (The Singularities of France Antarctique) (Paris, 1558) that, although the high civilizations of India, Japan, and China were respectable, they were still all savages or barbarians, for their non-Christian religions were idolatrous. However, he also believed that there existed some similarities between the religious practices of these people and Christianity, such as the resemblance between the Indian custom of washing in the Ganges and Christian baptism. He then proposed a theory of "lost Christianity" – that all those high civilizations were Christians in the distant past. He felt confident in their eventual Christianization. Thevet applied this theory not only to Asian civilizations but also to the Brazilian "barbarians." He asserted that the indigenous Brazilians, like the East Asians, were superior to

---

[58] Guy 1963a: 42.
[59] Lach 1965: 802–5.
[60] Lach 1977: 323.
[61] Lach 1977: 316; Huppert 1971.

the European Protestants.⁶² Thevet's worldview was essentially the same as reflected in the Jesuits' accommodation policy.

Other authors of Universal History in France, such as François de Belleforest, Jean Bodin, and Louis Le Roy, varied in their appreciation of non-European cultures and their belief in European superiority. However, they shared some basic conceptions about the newly discovered peoples in Asia.⁶³ First, they regarded highly their accomplishments in government, architecture, and craftsmanship as superior to the European ones, as in the case of printing. The theory of diffusion of printing technology from China to Europe, and that printing originated in China, was formulated in the mid sixteenth century when the Europeans became aware that the Chinese began printing much earlier than Europe.⁶⁴ Second, these authors still believed in Europe's ultimate superiority. God had singularly favored Europe and let it possess the true way to Christianity. The Asians and Americans might possess knowledge about God in a half-conscious way that was passed down from their distant ancestors, but they did not know the true way of worship. Christianizing missions, therefore, were necessary to convert those pagans. The authors believed that the different peoples in the world shared some universal instincts, such as the instinct for government, agriculture, waging war, and, most importantly, the instinct to worship God. As a result, these writers were all optimistic about the success of the Vatican's global conversion campaign.

Ricci's and other Jesuits' views on China were part and parcel of this general discourse on the world outside Europe in the sixteenth century. In this discourse, the Eurocentric and theological worldview was not shaken but modified to incorporate knowledge about the newly discovered cultures. These Eurocentric sentiments, however, started to weaken amidst the chaos of the seventeenth-century crisis.⁶⁵

---

⁶² Gordon 1986: 54–8; Lach 1977: 303–5.
⁶³ Gordon 1986; Lach 1977: 301–13.
⁶⁴ Lach 1977: 319.
⁶⁵ Lach 1977: 560.

2 THE SEVENTEENTH-CENTURY CRISIS AND THE RISE OF SINOPHILIA

The circulation of Ricci and other early Jesuit writings on China was limited before the seventeenth century. The only Ricci materials circulated in sixteenth-century Europe were a few letters appearing in various Jesuit letter collections.[1] The reason for this limited dissemination was both religious and political. The Rome authorities and Portuguese government greatly restricted the publication and circulation of materials related to Asia. As early as 1558, Pope Paul IV issued the *Index Librorum Prohibitorum* (Index of Book Censorship), prohibiting the publication of works by certain authors and topics. The Church had been aware of the potential challenge that foreign religions and civilizations posed to the Catholic orthodoxy. Many works related to the newly discovered societies were on the prohibition list. In 1606, Ricci complained to Rome that he could not obtain the Church's permission to publish his books.[2] The Portuguese government adopted and extended Rome's *Index* to formulate its own in 1561. According to the Iberian state, publications related to the East disclosed valuable information about the Asian trade. Such disclosure could threaten its control over the trade routes.[3]

The situation changed in the mid seventeenth century when the patronage of Jesuit missionary work shifted from the Portuguese to the French court. The shift brought about fewer restrictions on

---

[1] Lach 1965: 802.
[2] Lach 1977: 41.
[3] O'Neill 1986: 283.

publishing Jesuit materials about China. By the early seventeenth century, Portugal (and Spain) was declining and could no longer fulfill its duty of appointing and providing financial support to bishops in regions outside Europe. As a result, many bishoprics remained vacant for years. Rome began recentralizing the administration of the global missions. In 1622, the Sacred Congregation for Propagation of the Faith was created in Rome, and the activities of the Jesuits were freed from Portuguese restrictions.[4] France, a latecomer to the Asian trade, joined the struggle for control over the missionaries. To follow in the footsteps of Portugal and Spain and to catch up with England and Holland in long-distance trade, the French court saw the Jesuits, who had already established themselves among China's ruling elite, as useful in developing its relationship with Chinese officials to enhance its business there. The establishment of the Société des Missions Etrangères in Paris in 1663 marked the final success of the French state in patronizing the Society of Jesus.

Beginning in the late seventeenth century, the Jesuits traveled between China and Europe on the ships of the *Compagnie des Indes Orientales*, the French chartered East Indian Company monopolizing France–Asia trade. They received funding from the French government and published their books in Paris. The Jesuits found a more favorable environment for propagating their ideas there, and Paris became the center of the study of China.[5] The wider dissemination of knowledge about China was also facilitated by two events that aroused popular enthusiasm in China: the Manchu Conquest of China and the Rites Controversy, which I will discuss later in this chapter. The two events unfolded in the context of expanding trade with China and Europe's century-long economic, political, and identity crises.

A Crisis of European Consciousness

After the expansion in the long sixteenth century (c. 1450–1640), the European economy entered a long contraction between *circa* 1600 and 1750. The downturn was known as the general

---

[4] Neill 1964: 178–9.
[5] Neill 1964: 180–2; Mungello 1985: 25.

crisis of the seventeenth century. Symptoms of the crisis included widespread economic and demographic contraction, famines and plagues, the Thirty Years War, upheavals in England, Ireland, Scotland, France, Sweden, Catalonia, Portugal, Naples, Holland and Spain, and the intensification of conflicts between the emerging sovereign states.[6] The 1630s and the 1640s were the most turbulent and rebellious years. The only exception was the Netherlands, which ascended to become Europe's hegemonic power and enjoyed increasing economic fortunes amid the chaos. The economic and political turmoil in the seventeenth century ended the optimism and the incipient notion of progress, while the tales of great civilizations outside Europe generated wide interest. The resulting crisis of confidence in Christian civilization fomented what is deemed a crisis of European consciousness, or *La Crise de la conscience européenne*, toward the end of the seventeenth century.[7]

The Christian–Latin identity of Europe and its theological worldview in the Middle Ages started to dissolve amid the crisis of feudalism in the fourteenth and fifteenth centuries. With the long contraction of the European economy, the medieval states, seigniors, and monasteries encountered a deepening financial crisis.[8] The increasing involvement of the financially stringent Church in secular affairs contradicted its spiritual ideals and undermined its intellectual and moral authority. It created the conditions for the early modern intellectuals, whose means of livelihood became increasingly independent of the Church under aristocratic and royal patronage, to begin thinking outside the framework of religious orthodoxy.[9]

The crisis of feudalism fostered an intellectual climate of pessimism, under which the present age was conceived of as an age of corruption and degeneration from the Golden Age of Greek and Roman antiquity. The yearning for the restoration of the Golden Age paved the way for the fifteenth to sixteenth-century Renaissance, followed by the sixteenth-century Reformation. The latter constituted a serious blow to the Christian–Latin identity of Europe. The

---

[6] Stone 1981: 166–7; Trevor-Roper 1967: 46–7; Wallerstein 1980: 24–6; Parker and Smith ed. 1997; Braudel 1992.
[7] Hazard 1935; Weitzman 1967: 1851.
[8] Wallerstein 1974: 14–65.
[9] Gilchrist 1969: 83, 95.

shaken Catholic worldview managed to reconsolidate itself, though not totally, through the Church's Counter-Reformation program, which was to reform the Church and fight back against Protestant powers militantly. At the same time, Europe's Christian worldview and identity were retained in Protestantism with variations. Europe regained its self-confidence and optimism with the renewed economic expansion, European colonization of the Americas, and its entrance into Asia in the long sixteenth century. But the renewed economic contraction and social and political chaos during the seventeenth-century crisis shook Europe's optimism and confidence again. Though the seventeenth-century crisis was less severe than the fourteenth and fifteenth-century crisis of feudalism economically and politically, it was much more unsettling ideologically. This crisis gave a final blow to the Christian–Latin worldview of the Middle Ages. The wave of new scientific discoveries and technological innovations during the seventeenth-century Scientific Revolution fueled the Enlightenment that started toward the end of the century. The vast increase in the knowledge about the East, particularly the Chinese civilization that appeared to be superior to Europe and "had prospered for over a thousand years without benefit of Christian teachings," exacerbated the crisis to an unprecedented extent.[10]

While the fourteenth-century crisis of feudalism fomented a breakdown of Europe's economic system at the end of the period, the seventeenth-century crisis led to a breakdown of Europe's Christian–Latin worldview. It was coincidental with the rise of new political boundaries defined by the Westphalian system of sovereign nation-states after the Treaty of Westphalia in 1648. The final demise of the Christian–Latin worldview opened new ground for formulating new worldviews and identities that culminated amid Europe's renewed economic and geographical expansion in the latter half of the eighteenth century.

The intellectual crisis during the crisis of feudalism brought forth a temporal comparison of Europe with Occidental antiquity. It led to the Renaissance, which strived to restore a lost Gold Age of Greco-Roman antiquity. Thus, the solution to the crisis was found in Europe's own past. On the other hand, the intellectual crisis

[10] Weitzman 1967: 1851.

during the seventeenth century invoked a spatial-temporal comparison of Europe with Oriental antiquity. The solution to the crisis was found outside Europe, that is, through emulating an idealized Oriental, especially Chinese antiquity. Whether it was Occidental or Oriental antiquity, the authority of the ancients over the moderns was common in both intellectual crises. The authority of antiquity continued until it was finally discarded and replaced by the idea of progress in the later phase of the Enlightenment in the late eighteenth century, as we will see in Chapter 4.

European Views of China's Ming-Qing Transition

Asia in general and China in particular was also impacted by the seventeenth-century crisis, which was a global crisis.[11] Parallel to Europe, the 1630s and the 1640s were the most turbulent years of the Ming Empire, which saw its final breakdown in 1644 when the Manchus invaded and established the Qing Empire. The collapse of Ming China was related to the silver connection between its economy and the European economy. In the sixteenth century, the Chinese economy underwent silverization, when imported silver replaced the out-of-control paper currency as the standard currency of taxation and government salary payments. Silver also became the principal means of bulk market transaction in the commercializing economy. China was short of silver supply and relied mainly on American silver brought by European traders, particularly after Japan stopped its silver export under the Tokugawa Seclusion policy starting in c. 1635.[12]

The economic downturn in Europe, triggered by the fall in agricultural output worldwide amid the "Little Ice Age" and the imperial decline of Spain and Portugal, led to contractions of all global trade routes on which China depended for silver. A silver dearth in the 1630s and 1640s precipitated deflation, a drastic drop in state revenue, peasant anti-tax rebellions, corruption of government officials and the army, and class antagonism in the Ming Empire.[13] The Manchus invaded the crumbling Ming from the northeast,

---

[11] E.g., Wakeman 1986; Atwell 1977, 1982; Brook 2023.
[12] Quan 1969; Flynn and Giraldez 1995; Atwell 1977; Wakeman 1986.
[13] Atwell 1982; Brook 2023.

establishing the Qing dynasty in 1644. Though it was not until 1683 when the regional war between the Chinese merchant-prince Zheng Chenggong 鄭成功 (or Koxinga) and his family (known to Europeans as Koxinga, who established an armed trading maritime empire in Taiwan to resist the nascent Qing Empire in the 1660s) and the Manchu state was settled, the Qing Empire already resumed stability in most areas in mainland China by 1650. The Manchus rebuilt an effective bureaucracy. The recovery of imperial China was so great that a Qing historian concluded, "The Chinese polity and the society it governed were able to recover from the seventeenth-century crisis sooner than any major power in the world."[14]

Against this backdrop, the popular interest in China and Sinophilia grew in Europe in the latter half of the seventeenth century. The Catholic Church was concerned about the future of its missions in China, while European traders worried about their fortunes under China's new rulers. The Jesuits became the single most important source of news about the dynastic transition. In 1654, Martino Martini, who had been sent back to Rome from China in 1653, published his *De bello tartarico historica* (The History of the Tartar War) (Antwerp, 1654). The book became the most detailed and authoritative description of the Manchu Conquest. The Latin edition of the text was republished seven times and translated into nine vernacular European languages. By the end of the century, at least twenty-five editions and translations of the book had appeared in Europe.[15]

Martini's account was in favor of the Manchus. In his eyes, the fall of the Ming resulted from God's punishment of the Wanli Emperor's persecution of the Jesuits in 1618, as well as the corruption of the Ming administration. According to Martini, the Manchus were originally barbarians. However, in the course of conquering China, they became increasingly civilized. He praised the new rulers for their ability to establish an intelligent and humane government and their generous treatment of the Jesuit missionaries remaining in China.[16]

Later Jesuit literature on the Manchu Conquest mostly followed the interpretation and description of Martini, supplemented

---

[14] Wakeman 1986: 17.
[15] Van Kley 1973: 561–7.
[16] Van Kley 1973: 566–7.

with new eyewitness accounts emphasizing the reconstruction after the Conquest. Most of these works manifested a favorable view of the Manchus. Another major account of the dynastic transition was authored by Juan de Palafox y Mendoza, a bishop in Spanish Mexico, and published in Paris in 1670. He saw the Manchu Conquest as another dynastic transition and regarded the Qing regime as a legitimate successor of the Ming. He even argued that Qing rulers were better rulers than Ming monarchs as the former was less hostile to foreigners and missionaries. He compared the Qing Empire to the ancient Roman Empire and saw the Manchu Conquest as a parallel to the Roman conquest of Carthage. The Chinese civilization was advanced, not destroyed, by the Conquest.[17]

One reason for the Jesuits' favorable attitudes toward the Manchus was their eagerness to continue their missions and accommodation policy under China's new non-Han rulers. Their views were shared even by their opponents in the Church, who had called for an end to the Jesuits' activities in China. Domingo Fernández Navarrete, a Dominican missionary, wrote in 1676 to refute Martini's account of the Conquest. However, his criticism was mostly "personal and trivial." Though he emphasized the cruelty of the Conquest, he could not avoid agreeing with Martini that the Qing Empire was a continuation of the Ming and that the Chinese civilization was restored under Qing rule.[18]

After the mid seventeenth century, the Manchu Conquest of China and the recovery of the Chinese empire became a symbol of the strength of the Chinese civilization in Europe. The dramatic suicide of the last Ming emperor and his killing of his daughter had appeared again and again as the motif of exotic novels and dramas in Europe for one hundred years after the Conquest. These novels and dramas were mostly tragedies, with tragic endings infused with admiration for the civilizing of the Manchus by Chinese culture and the restoration of prosperity in China. One of the most famous ones was Voltaire's *L'Orphelin de la Chine* (The Orphan of China), written in 1755. The play was regarded as one of Voltaire's early representative Sinophilic works. The civilizing influence of the Chinese virtues upon the Manchus was praised in the script and poems in

[17] Van Kley 1973: 570–4.
[18] Van Kley 1973: 575–7.

the drama, and Voltaire deliberately used the play to promote his admiring views of the Chinese culture and political system.[19] We will turn back to Voltaire's embellishing views on the Chinese civilization in Chapter 3.

Comparison between Europe and the East had been central to all European writings about Asia since the sixteenth century.[20] The seventeenth-century laudatory literature on the Manchu Conquest and the rapid restoration of prosperity to Chinese civilization hinged on the comparison with the long-lasting turmoil in Europe over the same period. The prolonged crisis in Europe, in contrast with the rapid recovery of China, helped precipitate the rise of Sinophilia in the latter half of the seventeenth century, when the Chinese empire was becoming the model for Europe in the mind of the educated elite.

The relation between Sinophilia and the different paces of recovery of China and Europe amid the seventeenth-century crisis is illustrated by the deviant interpretation of the Manchu Conquest in the Netherlands, the nation that prospered amid the crisis, as compared to the interpretations in other European states in turmoil. Although the Dutch relied on similar Jesuit sources to describe the dynastic transition, they expressed little sympathy, let alone praise, for Qing China. Interestingly enough, Martini's *De bello tartarico historica*, with the full title of *De bello Tartarico historia in qua, quo pacto Tartari hac nostra ætate Sinicum imperium inuaserint, ac fere totum occuparint narratur; eorumque mores breuiter describitur cum figuris* (The History of the Tartar War, which narrates how the Tartars in our age invaded and almost entirely occupied the Chinese Empire; and their customs briefly described with illustrations), appeared in a 1660 Dutch edition with a more colorful title *Het verwoest Sina, door den wreeden Tartar : Vervaatende de schrickelycke Landt-verdervende Oorlogh, By de Tartars In't Ryck van Sina aangevangen* (China Devastated by the Barbarous Tartar: Including the Dreadful Ruinous War Begun by the Tartars in the Empire of China) (Amsterdam, 1660). A poem entitled "The Devastation of China by the Tartars" was added on the back of the title page to emphasize the bloody and destructive aspects of the Conquest.[21]

---

[19] Guy 1963a: 218–31.
[20] Lach 1977: 319.
[21] Van Kley 1973: 567–8; see also Dijkstra 2021: 70.

The Dutch attitudes toward the Conquest were expressed more directly in a report of the first Dutch embassy to the Manchu court in 1655–1657. The embassy's secretary, Johan Nieuhof, authored and published the report in 1665. The report relied on both the author's first-hand experiences in China and Martini's and other Jesuit writings. The report rejected the view that the Manchu Conquest was comparable to the Roman conquest of Carthage. Instead, it shared other Dutch writers' comparison of the Conquest to the "barbarian invasion" of Rome.[22] Speaking of a South China city, which he visited in the aftermath of the Manchu invasion, Nieuhof lamented:

> The ancient Greeks and proud Romans, who once traveled so much of the world, never subjected their conquered and subdued peoples to as much suffering and unbearable misery as these rough and merciless Tartars (by whom, during the last invasion, these regions were so miserably mistreated, and nearly all cities, towns, and villages were destroyed to the ground and turned into heaps of rubble and nests for birds and wild animals) have done. ... In this last war, the Tartars, that rough people, miserably destroyed this small town, ravaged it, and brought it almost to ruins.[23]

The Conquest was seen as a death knell of Chinese civilization.

The Dutch translations of Martini's work and Nieuhof's report were the rule rather than the exceptions of the Dutch view of the Manchu Conquest. The "end of Chinese civilization" thesis appeared in many Dutch exotic novels and plays. For example, the Dutch poet Joost van Vondels' *Zungchin, of ondergang der Sineesche heerschappye* (Chongzhen, or the Downfall of the Chinese Empire) (Amsterdam, 1667) again compared the Manchu Conquest to the barbarian invasions of Rome. Further, he tried to convey that no earthly power was permanent, and even such impressive empires as Roman and Ming China were eventually brought down. In the 1680s, when the recovery of China was so evident, a Dutch scholar still claimed that the Conquest had spelled the end

---

[22] Van Kley 1973: 569–70, 579.
[23] Nieuhof 1693 [1665]: 58–9, ChatGPT and Google translation.

of Chinese civilization. The Dutch attack was not confined to the Manchus; it was extended to the Han Chinese. In the literature, the remaining Ming loyalist forces in Taiwan, led by merchant-prince Zheng Chenggong and his family from the 1650s to the 1680s, were portrayed as inhumanely cruel.[24]

Other than the economic ascendancy and the triumphalist sentiments of the Dutch Republic in Europe, the Dutch contemptuous view of China was also attributable to their intense competition with the Chinese in Asian waters. In the 1640s, they conquered Malacca and struggled with competition from the Chinese overseas traders in Dutch Batavia, where they massacred all Chinese residents in 1740. Farther East, they successfully established a colony in Taiwan in the 1620s and fought the Ming loyalist forces of Zheng Chenggong, who strived to establish themselves on the island. Zheng eventually expelled the Dutch from Taiwan in 1662, turning Taiwan into a base of resistance against Manchu rule before it fell to the Manchus in 1683. In the meantime, the Dutch robbed and sank every Chinese ship they encountered on the Manila trade route. The Dutch allied with the Japanese government and tried to oust the Chinese from the Nagasaki trade route, as well.[25] Believing in the Calvinist doctrine of predestination, the Dutch never had any religious interests in converting the Chinese and grounded their view of them solely on commercial grounds. Unsurprisingly, they viewed their most formidable competitors in Asia with contempt.

Though the Dutch understanding of China was marginal compared to the general admiration for it in seventeenth-century Europe, the Dutch view was a rehearsal of the racist Sinophobia that prevailed after the mid eighteenth century, when prosperity came back to most of Europe and European colonization of Asia accelerated. In any event, the literature on the Manchu Conquest had brought vast knowledge about China to the general readers in Europe. It produced the picture of a prosperous and stable China that became an object of fantasy among many Europeans (with the Dutch exception), who were eagerly searching for an escape from the wars and upheavals in their homeland.

[24] Van Kley 1973: 578–9, 581; see also Lach and Van Kley 1993: Chapter XXI.
[25] Hung 2000; Hung 2017: 175–7; Andrade 2008, 2013.

Jesuits' Knowledge and Fantasies about China

The Rites Controversy was another event in the seventeenth century that contributed to the rising popular zeal over China and Sinophilia. At first, it was just a debate within the Catholic Church, in which the enemies of the Jesuits condemned China and argued for an end to the accommodation policy. Paradoxically, when the Jesuits were losing ground in the debate, and the Church was shifting to a more contemptuous stand toward China, Jesuit works in defense of their position (of idealizing China) were diffusing to the public at a much greater rate, leading to a surge of Sinophilia outside the Church. Moreover, the known antiquity of the Chinese language according to the Chinese chronology suggests that the Chinese ancestors predated the Tower of Babel according to the orthodox Biblical chronology. This was already noticed by a limited number of European writers in the sixteenth century and was made known to the public during the debate. This gave rise to the belief that the Chinese civilization and language were superior to the European ones in that they had greater proximity to God.

Jesuits' Enemies and the Rites Controversy

The monopoly of the Society of Jesus over Chinese affairs invited envy among other Catholic orders, which were also eager to establish themselves in China. The demand was so strong that in November 1586, Pope Sixtus V rescinded the decree on the Jesuits' monopoly and granted the Franciscans permission to work in China. The rescission was confirmed by Pope Clement VIII (1600), Pope Paul V (1611), and at last Pope Urban VIII (1638).[26]

The Franciscans and the Dominicans entered China in the 1630s. Trying to distinguish themselves from the Jesuits and delegitimize the Jesuit method of conversion, they started giving a different picture of China, a more negative one, and attacking the accommodation policy. They observed that the Chinese, literati, and ordinary people alike performed rites to worship their deceased family members, their ancestors, and also Confucius by burning incense in front

---

[26] Sebes 1988: 51.

2 Seventeenth-Century Sinophilia

of the tablets inscribed with their names. The Mendicants regarded these rites as a manifestation of idolatry and accused the Jesuits of concealing this fact from the Church. This began the dispute over the meaning of these Chinese rites, known as the Rites Controversy, within the Church.[27]

The Controversy was further inflamed by the French Jansenists, who were critical of the Jesuits' proximity to the throne in France and their control of the Société Des Missions Etrangères in Paris.[28] Louis XIV's confessor was Fr. Michel Le Tellier, a Jesuit. In the last years of Louis XIV's rule, Le Tellier was accused of exerting a sinister influence on the court.[29] Blaise Pascal (1623–1662) was one of the leaders of the Jansenists and accused the Jesuits of casuistry and of forfeiting their principles to win converts and to retain the goodwill of the prominent and powerful.[30] In seventeenth- and eighteenth-century France, Jansenists commanded a significant following among the aristocrats opposing the centralizing monarch.[31] Different from the Jesuits, who believed that all men on earth had equal opportunities to receive God's grace and earn salvation, the Jansenists believed that God's grace was bestowed more over some men (Europeans) than others (Chinese). They denied the possibility of salvation for all mankind and were theologically close to Protestant Calvinism. They were highly critical of the Jesuits' tolerant attitudes toward the Chinese. The Jansenists' view received much sympathy from the theologians in Sorbonne, which was then a prestigious theological center in France. During the debate, the Jesuits' idealizing views and the anti-Jesuits' condemning descriptions of China became increasingly polarized. The Church was divided into the Jesuit Sinophiles on the one side and the Sinophobes on the other.

The Sinophobes' contrarian image of China as a land of idolatry was well reflected in the report by Johan Nieuhof, the Dutch ambassador to the Manchu court in the 1650s, as we see in the previous sections. The Dutch Republic, a rising power and

---

[27] Sebes 1988.
[28] Mungello 1985: 292, 298.
[29] Mungello 1985: 332.
[30] Davis 1983: 533.
[31] Van Kley 1975: 6–61.

Figure 2.1 Dutch depiction of idolatry in China
Source: Nieuhof 1693[1665]: Chapter 8, p. 87

a confident, prosperous nation in Europe amid the seventeenth-century crisis, was least touched by Sinophilia relative to other European powers at the time. We have already seen how Nieuhof depicted the Manchu Conquest as a barbaric end to Chinese civilization. Regarding religions in China, the Jesuit notion about the hidden monotheistic Confucius orthodoxy did not gain much traction in the Dutch Republic, which was dominated by Protestant Calvinists believing in predestination and that idol worshippers outside Europe were destined for hell. The Republic also harbored a lot of Jansenist sympathizers from France who shared the Calvinist belief in predestination and detested the Jesuits. As such, it is not surprising that Nieuhof depicted China as full of idolatry, animism, and fetishism sunken in decadence (Figure 2.1):

> Of all the heathen customs that have come to the knowledge of Europeans, none have been found to be less misguided than the Chinese customs in the earliest centuries or at the beginning of the world... they [the Chinese] also revered various spirits of mountains, rivers, as well as those who govern the four parts of the world...[T]he Chinese have performed many good deeds for the service of their

country and the common good... But since corrupt nature, without the help and grace of God, always deteriorates, so, over time, this light of reason darkens to such an extent that, if there are still some who abstain from the worship of idolatrous images, there are few who do not fall deeper into paganism.[32]

The Jesuits defended themselves by arguing that the Confucianist rites were not religious but social. The rites were occasions for the elders to teach the youth to respect their parents, ancestors, and Confucian morality.[33] The debate between the two camps in the Church encouraged the publication of many writings on China supporting the feuding sides. Through the debate, missionaries' writings on China began to be disseminated among the reading public. When defending the accommodation policy and rallying public support for the continuation of their mission in China, the Jesuits further idealized China. They tried to construct a more rationalized image of Confucianism to counter the accusation of its idolatrous nature.

Out of the works of Jesuits defending their position, *Confucius sinarum philosophus, sive, Scientia sinensis latine exposita* (Confucius, Philosopher of the Chinese, or, Chinese Knowledge Explained in Latin) (Paris, 1687) by Philippe Couplet et al, Louis Le Comte's *Nouveaux mémoires sur l'état présent de la China, qui contiennent une description exacte de cette vaste empire, de la politique, du gouvernement, du commerce, des moeurs et de la religion des habitans; ainsi que des connoissances très étendues dans les sciences & dans les arts, & des remarques intéressantes sur les voyages & sur la cour de Pékin* (New Memoirs on the Present State of China, which contain an exact description of this vast empire, of the politics, government, commerce, customs, and religion of the inhabitants; as well as very extensive knowledge in the sciences and arts, and interesting remarks on travels and on the court of Peking) (Paris, 1696), and Jean-Baptiste Du Halde's *Description géographique, historique, chronologique, politique et physique*

---

[32] Nieuhof 1693 [1665]: Part 2, p. 67; ChatGPT and Google translation; see also Dijkstra 2021: 47–92, 225–64.
[33] Mungello 1985: 88.

de l'Empire de la Chine et de la Tartarie chinoise (Geographical, Historical, Chronological, Political, and Physical Description of the Empire of China and Chinese Tartary) (Paris, 1735) were the most representative and influential ones. These works became widely available in Europe and were the foundations of Europe's knowledge about China in the early eighteenth century.

Three Jesuits' Classics on China

Confucius Sinarum philosophus (Paris, 1687) was the first effort to translate the Confucian classics in Europe. The translation was a group effort undertaken by seventeen known Jesuits and several Chinese co-writers. Jesuit commentaries were added to the texts, and a *Proemialis Declaratio* was written preceding the text. It can be regarded as the official Jesuit interpretation of Confucianism. It served as a text for the Jesuit missionaries and as a key to understanding the Confucian philosophy for the Enlightenment thinkers in the seventeenth and eighteenth centuries. Once published in Latin, it was quickly translated into several vernacular languages in Europe.[34]

In the *Proemialis Declaratio*, the authors declared that the aim of the translation was to wash out the superstitious contamination of Buddhism over the original corpus of Confucianism, to open Christians' eyes to the "pure simplicity of the golden age" in China. It denounced the Chinese intellectual currents during the closing decades of the Ming dynasty that advocated that the teachings of Confucianism, Taoism, and Buddhism were essentially the same and should be synthesized into one unified doctrine. The *Proemialis Declaratio* also emphasized the Jesuits' positions that rites were social rather than religious and that ancient Chinese believed in a monotheistic God.

By comparing the translation of the same paragraph of Confucius' *Da Xue* 大學 (Grand Knowledge) in *Sapientia Sinica*, which was published in 1662 and contained a partial translation of several of Confucius' works by Inacio da Costa, a Portuguese Jesuit having been in China since 1634, and the translation in *Confucius Sinarum philosophus*, David Mungello found that a phrase

---

[34] Davis 1983: 538.

translated as "illuminating spiritual power [of men] by means of virtue" in the former was translated into "refining or improving the rational nature [of men]." He concluded that, "If the *Sapientia Sinica* translation was overspiritualized, then the *Confucius Sinarum philosophus* rendering was overrationalized, perhaps in order to allow it to meld more fully with the Jesuits' interpretation of the Chinese Classics in terms of natural religion."[35]

The book also showed an illustration of Confucius, who was portrayed as a fair-skinned, gentle-looking scholar in front of a vast book collection (Figure 2.2). Such rational representation became the template image of Confucius in the century to come.

Le Comte's *Nouveaux mémoires sur l'état présent de la Chine* (Paris, 1696), which was published nearly ten years after *Confucius Sinarum philosophus*, was aimed at popularizing the Jesuits' understanding of Chinese morality among ordinary readers. The book put forward a more idealized and rationalized image of Confucian philosophy. It induced the most aggressive reactions from the anti-Jesuit forces.

Le Comte repeated other Jesuits' claims that Chinese culture originated in about 2952 BCE and was continuous until their times. In the sixteenth century, there were two Biblical chronologies. One asserted that the Noachian flood occurred in 2349 BCE, and the other believed it occurred in 2957 BCE. The Chinese chronology was calculated by considering both legends and written records of Chinese history. The Chinese chronology was regarded as evidence proving the second Biblical chronology and disproving the first one, which had been the dominant one. Le Comte stated further that the ancestor of China was a son or grandson of Noah, who went to the Yellow River Basin and settled there soon after the flood. He stated that the ancient Chinese received Biblical morality directly from God and that the morality was preserved perfectly over the years and manifested in the everyday practice of the Chinese of their time:

> [the Chinese had] the knowledge of the true God and practiced the purest maxims of morality, while Europe and almost all the rest of the world lived in error and corruption...[the Chinese] people had preserved for over 2,000

[35] Mungello 1985: 258.

Figure 2.2 Jesuit depiction of rational Confucius
Source: Couplet 1687 cxvi

years the knowledge of the true God, and had honoured Him in a manner which can serve as an example and as instruction even to Christians.[36]

[36] Le Comte 1696: 141, 146–7; translated in Mungello 1985: 338.

2 Seventeenth-Century Sinophilia

In other words, the Chinese had known about God long before the Europeans, according to the Jesuits. Notably, most Jesuits since Ricci had emphasized the antiquity and continuity of the Chinese civilization in defending their positive views on the empire. They believed the ancient Chinese received the Biblical teachings directly from God.

The idealized and rationalized image of China culminated in Du Halde's *Description géographique, historique, chronologique, politique et physique de l'Empire de la Chine et de la Tartarie chinoise* (Paris, 1735). Du Halde's book targeted secular readers.[37] It was an encyclopedia of the Chinese empire consisting of information about the empire's geography, history, political system, economy, customs, scientific development, and Confucian philosophy. Du Halde restated all the Jesuit praise and admiration of China and concentrated them into one book. It also glorified the achievements of the Society of Jesus. Du Halde's book further rationalized Confucius's image and screened out other religious images of China.

Du Halde praised China's political system and regarded the Chinese empire as a land of great peace and happiness, governed by a benevolent ruler who "possessed, in the highest degree, the Art of Reigning, and united in his Person all the Qualities that serve to form the Great Prince and the Fine Gentleman."[38] Du Halde emphasized that he and other missionaries were merely confirming and expanding on Marco Polo's account of China as a magnificent civilization that Europe should emulate:

> China has for a long time past excited the curiosity of Europeans, also the first accounts they had of it gained very little credit among them. The narrative published by the Venetian who travelled over some provinces of that Empire, in the retinue of the Tartars, passed for a Romance. All he recounts concerning the antiquity of this monarchy, the wisdom of its laws and government, the fertility of its lands, and richness of its trade, as well as the prodigious multitude of its inhabitants, the politeness of their manners,

---

[37] Rowbotham 1942: 256.
[38] Du Halde 1738 [1735] vol. 3: 35.

their industry to promote arts and husbandry, their taste and zeal for the sciences; all this, I say, was looked on as mere fiction, which had not so much as the air of probability... But by degrees these prejudices diminished, and that author's veracity began to be acknowledged, especially when it appeared that what he had advanced agreed with the accounts of the first missionaries, who towards the end of the 15th century found admittance into China... It appearing from these evidences, that the fundamental principles of the government have been always maintained in China by a constant observance of them, it is no wonder at all that a state of such vast extent has subsisted for so many ages, and still subsists in all its splendor.[39]

Du Halde's description of the Kangxi 康熙 Emperor of his time resonated with Marco Polo's description of the Kublai Khan as a benevolent and effective ruler abiding by the law:

China enjoyed a profound peace, which was owing to the wisdom and superior abilities of the Emperor. The indefatigable application of this Prince to all the affairs of state; his equity and penetration in the choice of proper persons to fill the principal places of trust; his frugality and aversion to luxury with respect to his own person, joined to his profuseness and magnificence with reference to the public; his tenderness for his people, and forwardness to relieve them; his steadiness in maintaining the laws in their full vigour; his continual watchfulness over the conduct of his vice-roys and governors; and the absolute dominion which he had over himself; all these put together kept up a perfect subordination among the members of this vast Empire, without which there commonly is nothing but trouble and confusion.[40]

Du Halde's representation of the Chinese political system shaped many early Enlightenment thinkers' political philosophy, which we will turn to in Chapter 3.[41]

---

[39] Du Halde 1738 [1735] Vol. 1: i, v.
[40] Du Halde 1738 [1735] Vol. 1: 232.
[41] Rowbotham 1942: 264.

Growth of Jesuits' Popularity outside the Church

The Jesuits' suggestion that Europeans should learn from China, not only politically and economically but also morally and religiously, antagonized the Jansenists and other religious orders hostile to the Jesuits. The three Jesuit books on China inflamed the struggle between the Sinophilic and Sinophobic factions in the Church.

The first two books received widespread attention in the early 1700s. Concerning the *Confucius Sinarum philosophus*, Jesuits' enemies published books and articles accusing the Jesuit translators of distorting the Confucian text by deliberately mistranslating words suggesting spirituality and hiding all superstitious legends mentioned in it. There were also accusations claiming that the translated text had screened out two-thirds of Confucius' texts unfavorable to the Jesuits' interpretation.[42]

In April 1700, the director of the Société des Missions-Étrangères, which had come under the control of factions sympathetic to the Jesuits' enemies, drafted a letter to the Pope to protest against Le Comte and urged that his book be censored. Jesuits' enemies called for an official examination of the Jesuits' books on China. The Jesuits attempted in vain to prevent the examination and in August, a commission of 160 faculty was formed in Sorbonne to examine the books. After two months of examination, an overwhelming majority of the commission voted to censor the books. The books were condemned as "false, rash, scandalous, erroneous, injurious to the holy Christian religion."[43]

After the examination, Pope Clement XI decreed in 1704 to formally denounce the Jesuits' accommodation policy and dictated that missionaries must not participate in Chinese rites. This position of the Vatican remained unchanged until the issue was reexamined in the twentieth century. The Pope's decision offended the Kangxi Emperor, who insisted that the Jesuits in China must continue their accommodation policy and participate in the rites. Jesuit missionaries in China evaded both the Pope's decision and Kangxi's order as long as they could. However, when both sides reiterated their positions and stood firm, the Jesuit missionary works in China

---

[42] Mungello 1985: 292–7.
[43] Mungello 1985: 329–53.

became increasingly impossible, and more and more of the Jesuits left China. Kangxi's son, Yongzheng 雍正 Emperor, whose reign started in 1722, eventually banished all missionaries in 1724 and only kept those necessary for astronomy in China.[44] It was the first battle lost by the Jesuits. Since then, Jesuit influence in the Catholic Church had declined. Their missionary work in China ceased. When Du Halde's book was published, the Jesuits had already been defeated in the Church, and its audience was primarily the educated elite outside the Church who grew increasingly indifferent, if not hostile, to the Church amid the Enlightenment.

While the Church decided to see China as a land of idolatrous and ungodly superstitions, the educated elite outside the Church were more willing to accept the view that China was superior to Christian Europe. When the Jesuits were crushed in the Church, their reputation in the secular public improved. In the context of growing discontent against the Catholic Church in Europe and an increasing hunger among Europe's educated elite for a model for society and polity independent of religion, the Jesuits' defeat in the Church made them more popular outside. Their defeat was seen as a vindication of the Church's corruption and dogmatism. The three main texts of the Jesuits on China turned out to be the classics for the early Enlightenment thinkers, with Voltaire as a representative. The chronological question and Confucianism's non-religious political and moral philosophy, as depicted by the Jesuits, were used as a weapon against the Catholic establishment. While the Church censured Jesuits' Sinophilia, their admiration of China as a rational model of economy, society, and governance fueled the rise of Enlightenment philosophy in the eighteenth century. It even triggered a *chinoiseries* in European arts that imitated the style and motif in Chinese paintings, architecture, and home decorations, helping fuel the rise of the Rococo artistic movement that celebrated asymmetry and curves and revolted against the neat geometry and straight lines of Classicism.[45] The intellectual landscape of Enlightenment Europe was shrouded in an obsession with China.[46]

---

[44] Perkins 2004: 199; Swen 2021: Ch. 9.
[45] Johns 2016.
[46] The cover image of this book that comes from the "L'Histoire de l'empereur chinois" tapestry series is a good illustration of this cultural atmosphere of the time (see Eidelberg 2021; Standen 1976).

The Jesuits' and their nemesis' writings about Chinese religions, economy, technology, administration, and society were not all factually wrong. In retrospect, many of their descriptions were accurate and elaborate, even by today's standards. The problem with their portrayals, as in the problem of other Orientalist scholarship in the succeeding centuries, is the reductionism and essentialism under which each author was compelled to generalize a very particular aspect of the vast and complex Chinese civilization, valid in one time and place, to the whole civilization as an undifferentiated, unchanging whole. There were no systematic, consistent, or rational rules for generalization. The generalizations were always premised on some a priori, even mythical, belief of the author. For example, the Jesuits, believing in universal salvation and universal ancient Christianity, selected bits of evidence from ancient Chinese texts and contemporaneous practices to project the Chinese civilization as essentially monotheistic and rational. In contrast, the Jansenists and Calvinists, believing in predestination and the impossibility of salvation for the Chinese, picked up on other evidence to verify their conviction that the Chinese civilization was invariably idolatrous and irrational. Their study and presentation of the particular evidence might be rigorous and precise, but it was their ideologically driven production of generalized knowledge from such evidence that was problematic. At times, their eagerness to attain a certain picture of China urged them to fabricate and exaggerate facts, with many of their assertions about evidence of Chinese worship of the Biblical God as a case in point.

When Enlightenment thinkers debated about China based on texts on China written by the Jesuits or their enemies, they were not only influenced by the concrete information carried in those religious writings. They also inherited the central question and the fantasy or fear of many of those religious interpretations of China: Did China share the same morality with Europe, and was it a superior model, or was China totally alien to European morality and, thus, a threat? The polarity of the two views does not mean that only these two views exist. But those two opposite views became dominant, overshadowed the ideas in between, and served as foci around which rival networks of intellectuals galvanized. While earlier Jesuits' learning of Chinese culture, like those by Ricci in the sixteenth century, tended to be more nuanced and combined both

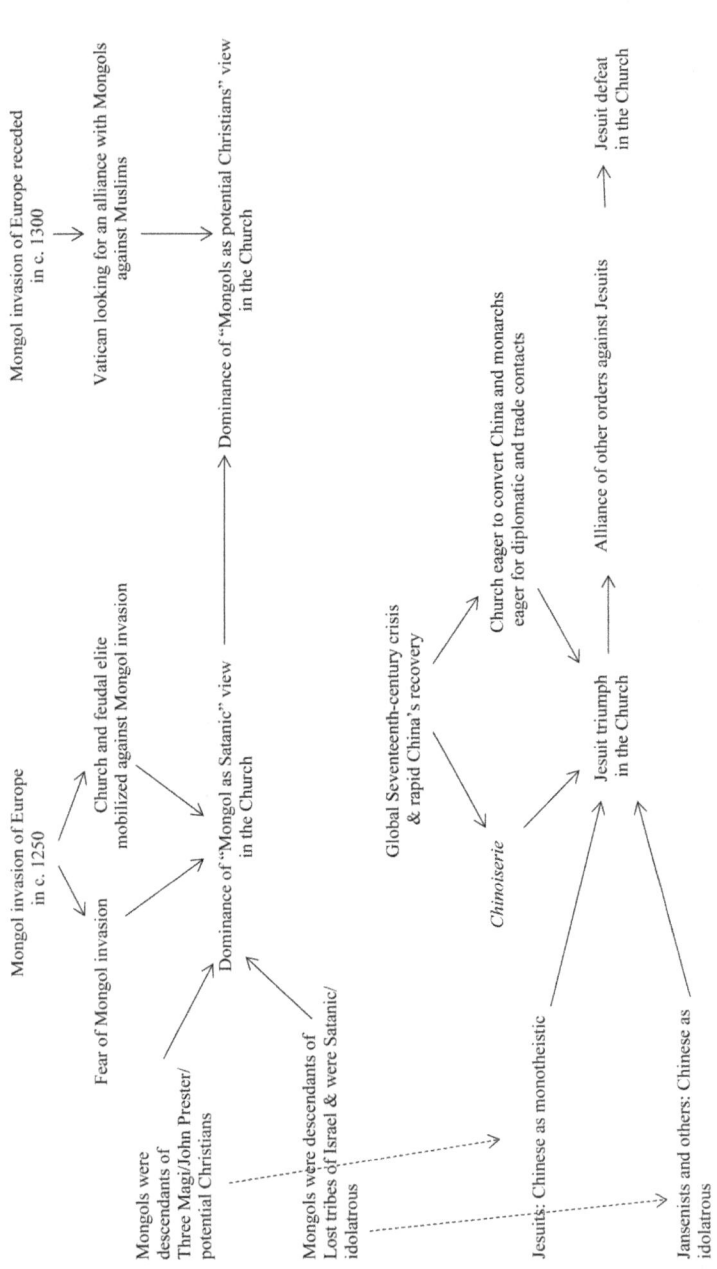

Figure 2.3 Rival networks and views of the Mongol/Chinese empire within the Catholic Church

admiration and criticism, the Jesuits' view became increasingly one-sided in its praise of China in response to their opponents.[47] For another example, seventeenth-century English scholar John Selden introduced a technically advanced Chinese maritime map to Oxford University's Bodleian Library. The map, believed to have been made by a Chinese or Arab cartographer based in Southeast Asia for a Chinese private sea merchant, showed a highly accurate and detailed depiction of Asia centered at the South China Sea. Serious study of this map would have yielded extensive, sophisticated knowledge about navigation, commerce, and geography of China. But after some initial effort to decode and annotate the map by an early English Sinologist and a Jesuit scholar in the 1680s, interest in the map died down altogether by the turn of the eighteenth century when Europe's center of scholarly attention to China was on religion and was engulfed in the polarizing debate about whether the Chinese were monotheistic or idolatrous. The map was forgotten and was never mentioned again for centuries until a US historian rediscovered it in 2008.[48] This dynamics of polarization and simplification through the rivalry between competing intellectual networks that suppresses more sophisticated and thorough knowledge is all too common in different intellectual fields.

The rival, polarized views on China were not new in the seventeenth century. As we saw in Chapter 1, the medieval Church also vacillated between the fantastical and fearful views of the Mongols (or Tartars and Chinese). The Mongols were seen either as descendants of the Three Magi and Prestor John, ready to be Christianized and superior in governance and morality, or as Satanic, cannibalistic, and a threat to the Christian world. Which view prevailed at a specific time depended on the geopolitical reality shaping Europe's relationship, or potential relationship, with the Mongol Empire at the time. In the seventeenth century, which of the two polarized views on China prevailed was shaped by Europe's perception of its own economic standing and governance effectiveness relative to China. The dynamics shaping Europe's Catholic knowledge about China from the medieval times to the seventeenth century are summarized in Figure 2.3.

---

[47] For Ricci's interpretation of China, see Chapter 1.
[48] For a magnificent account of the "Selden Map," see Brook 2013.

Part II
ENLIGHTENMENT PHILOSOPHY

3 EARLY ENLIGHTENMENT SINOPHILIA

The production and circulation of knowledge about the East, as in other fields, were under the monopoly of the Church in medieval times and Europe's Age of Great Discovery. Tales by travelers like Marco Polo were an exception rather than the rule. Even the popularity of Marco Polo's narrative was tied to the Church's agenda of finding a way to convert the Mongol rulers to Christianity.

The crisis of feudalism in the fourteenth and fifteenth centuries resulted in the weakening of feudal states and seigniors, as well as a financial crisis of the Church, which had lived on their taxes, rents, and other financial contributions.[1] The Church's financial crisis and the subsequent Reformation brought the demise of the monastic monopoly of knowledge. Monastic libraries started to sell books to pay off their debts. Catholic institutions lacked the economic means to compete with private collectors as patrons of the increasing number of books after Johannes Gutenberg invented the printing press.[2] Over the sixteenth century, the center of knowledge production, accumulation, and circulation shifted from the Church to non-religious institutions. They included printing presses, private libraries, royal academies, museums, communities of encyclopedists, and, later, de-theologizing universities.

This shift shaped the content of the knowledge being produced. The expanding knowledge from Europe's geographical

[1] Wallerstein 1992: 606–8.
[2] O'Neill 1986: 278–81.

encounter with the rest of the world was created, distributed, and consumed within the rising secular institutions and among secular readers. It was within these non-religious spheres that Jesuit writings on China were disseminated. It was also where the seventeenth-century Scientific Revolution met Jesuits' Sinophilia, giving rise to many Enlightenment ideas in the eighteenth century.

"What Is Enlightenment?"

Many see the Enlightenment as an eighteenth-century intellectual movement that was grounded on the idea of progress and advocated the freeing of human morality and reason from religious bondage. In 1784, Kant wrote in an authoritative essay, "What Is Enlightenment?," that Enlightenment was a constant critique of the old and the creation of the new with the use of reason. Kant repudiated the perpetuity of traditional authority and rules that the Church and monarchs upheld. He contended that "to agree to a perpetual religious constitution which is not publicly questioned by anyone would be, as it were, to annihilate a period of time in the progress of man's improvement. This must be absolutely forbidden."[3]

If *reason* is one keyword of Enlightenment, *progress* has to be another. Enlightenment thinkers believed in the abolition of all restraints on natural human progress and the constant replacement of the old by the new. This time consciousness departed from the established time consciousness that privileged antiquity and saw human civilization as a struggle against the corruption that eroded the legacies of a past golden age. All achievements in the Renaissance, for example, were conceived as a revival of the Greco-Roman Golden Age. The conception of Enlightenment as a new time consciousness that privileged the present over the past, the modern over the ancient, has been repeated in many later works, including Foucault's essay, also titled "What Is Enlightenment?"[4]

Though this conception of Enlightenment could capture the ethos of Enlightenment thinkers like Kant himself in the late eighteenth century, it was at odds with the ideas of many philosophers in the early phase of Enlightenment. Early Enlightenment thinkers

[3] Kant 1996 [1784].
[4] Foucault 1984.

did share a hostility toward the Church and faith in human reason. However, they were not necessarily supporters of the idea of progress or the inevitable evolution of human societies as we understand it today. As this chapter will show, Voltaire was a prominent example of early Enlightenment thinkers who did not see that moderns were always superior to the ancients.[5] Enlightenment should be alternatively and more broadly conceptualized as a movement against the Church and advocacy of the use of reason.

The early Enlightenment movement was, on the one hand, a continuation of the Scientific Revolution in the seventeenth century and, on the other, a continuation of the Jesuits' Sinophilia of the seventeenth century. The Scientific Revolution provided a convincing demonstration for the exercise of reason in attaining knowledge without relying on the authority of the Church and biblical orthodoxy. The Jesuit Sinophilic literature, which caused a sensation among the educated elite during the seventeenth-century *chinoiserie*, as described in Chapter 2, aggravated the discontent of European intellectuals against the Church. The Jesuits praised China as a country of great antiquity, with its people worshipping God much earlier than the Europeans. They also painted China as an ancient empire that had been prosperous, populous, strong, and moral for thousands of years without gripping religious institutions comparable to the Catholic Church. This image of China laid the foundation for Enlightenment philosophers to imagine an alternative and superior intellectual order without organized religious authorities. The existence of the Jesuits, Buddhists, and other religious sects in China was seen as a demonstration of religious tolerance. It contrasted with the censorship and cruelty against heresies and rival sects in Protestant and Catholic nations of Europe at the time. China became a model that sparked the onset of Enlightenment. A German intellectual historian went as far as entitling Confucius as "the patron-saint of Enlightenment."[6]

It is not an accident that China stood out as a unique civilization to be idealized and admired by many early Enlightenment thinkers. By the eighteenth century, the Qing Empire was the only Asian state still welcoming Europeans, predominantly the Jesuits

[5] Suckling 1967.
[6] Reichwein 1925: 77.

working in the Qing court. In the sixteenth century, European enthusiasm for the East laid equally on the cultures of India, Japan, and China. However, after the Muslim Mughal empire builders defeated the Portuguese and expelled their missionaries in the early seventeenth century, Indians were widely portrayed in European writings as "stubborn, wrong-headed, and immoral."[7] Similarly, the positive disposition toward Japan faded in the early seventeenth century, when the Tokugawa government banned Christianity, massacred Christian Japanese, and ousted or executed European merchants and missionaries as it moved toward a centuries-long seclusion policy. Buddhism, which was seen as a form of ancient God-worshipping Christianity by the early Jesuit advocates of the accommodation policy in Japan, no longer enjoyed its prestige in the eyes of Europeans.

China as a Model for Europe

In the late seventeenth and early eighteenth century, leading intellectuals in philology, moral philosophy, political philosophy, political economy, and natural sciences all wrote a lot about China. Many of them were influenced by Jesuits' Sinophilic reports on China. Some even argued that the birth of the Enlightenment and the growth of secular knowledge at the expense of theological knowledge were so much indebted to the influences of China, or the perception of China, that the movement should be characterized as an "Oriental Enlightenment."[8]

Although significant in the first phase of the Enlightenment, China's influence died down toward the end of the eighteenth century. As the European disposition toward China changed from idealization to contempt, China's central role in shaping the array of fields of inquiry in the early stage of the Enlightenment was largely forgotten.

Philology: In Search of the Primitive or Universal Language

The seventeenth-century search for the Primitive Language originated from religious concerns. It was also closely associated

---

[7] Lach 1977: 561.
[8] Clarke 1997.

with the early linguistic scientists' attempt to construct a Universal Language that would facilitate transparent communication of mankind. Since the Middle Ages, Biblical scholars believed that God had given Adam a pure, transcendent, and simple language, which all mankind spoke before it was lost in the Tower of Babel. For years, philologists saw the search for this *Lingua Adamica*, or human's primitive language spoken by Adam, as essential to a better understanding of God's teaching. Different theories were formulated to argue that the Primitive Language was Chaldean, Gothic, Phoenician, or ancient Hebrew.[9]

In the seventeenth century, the Jesuits claimed to discover that the Chinese language had been used continuously without fundamental change for thousands of years. At the time, literal and orthodox interpretations of the Biblical chronology concluded that the earth and the universe were no older than six thousand years. Consequently, an increasing number of philologists believed that the Chinese language was the Primitive Language lost in Babel. The most influential work supporting this position was John Webb's *An Historical Essay Endeavouring a Probability that the Language of the Empire of China is the Primitive Language* (London, 1669). Webb claimed that the Chinese language fit most of his proposed features of the Primitive Language: "antiquity, simplicity, generality, modesty of expression, utility, and brevity."[10] He also asserted that not all people in the Far East went to the faraway Babel. Those who stayed at home preserved the Primitive Language and became the ancestors of the Chinese.[11]

In contrast to those who searched for a Primitive Language, the proponents for a Universal Language either denied the existence of such a Primitive Language or argued that the Primitive Language had been lost forever and there was no hope of reconstructing it. The seekers of the Universal Language were stimulated by more secular and pragmatic concerns, such as the facilitation of international trade. The anti-Roman Catholic, and therefore anti-Latin, sentiments were also a significant stimulus to the search, especially in England. Different from the traditional philological

---

[9] Lach 1977: 501–8.
[10] Webb 1669: ii.
[11] Webb 1669: 24.

methods adopted in the search for the Primitive Language, the construction of a Universal Language was grounded on mathematical logic and experimental methods, which were becoming dominant approaches of intellectual inquiry in the rising scientific societies. For example, Descartes, in 1629, proposed a mathematical basis for reducing and clarifying languages into an incisive tool that could be quickly mastered. It is known as the Cartesian model of Universal Language.[12]

Other advocates of a Universal Language were influenced by the theory that Chinese was the Primitive Language. These advocates included both biblical and non-biblical scholars, including Francis Bacon, a major figure of the Scientific Revolution and a member of the London Royal Society of Science. The other representative figures in the search included Athanasius Kircher, a German Jesuit scholar teaching at the Roman College, and Gottfried W. Leibniz, a German leader of the Scientific Revolution (whom I will turn to later). Many supporters of the Universal Language, like Francis Bacon, noticed that the Chinese written language had effectively connected people of different tongues (dialects) in a vast geographic area as the means of written communication over thousands of years. They claimed that Chinese had a grammatical structure much simpler than European languages and that the Chinese language was based on a one-on-one relationship between words and meanings. They asserted that Chinese was a very easy language to master and should be the foundation for constructing a Universal Language. This is known as the Baconian model of Universal Language.[13]

Moral Philosophy: Deism and Natural Religion

Tired of the Church's dogma, many European thinkers started advocating the principles of natural religion, or deism. They contended that God had let the world run independently once he set up the natural laws regulating nature's operation. Hence, one does not need to receive the revelations of God

---

[12] Mungello 1985: 183–97.
[13] Mungello 1985: 189; see also Lux 2015.

3 Early Enlightenment Sinophilia

through the priests to know how to act morally. One only needs to rely on reason to discern the moral laws implanted into human minds by God.

Based on the Jesuits' description of China, the deists found China to be a great example that supported their theory. In their eyes, the Chinese were a people who had acted morally without any explicit knowledge of God and rested their morality purely on the strength of their humanistic ethic system. Many deists regarded Confucianism as an exemplary natural religion and asserted that Chinese morality was derived from exercising natural reasoning. The Confucian idea of *li* 理 (principles) was compared with the deist idea of natural laws.[14]

Voltaire was a leading advocate of deism. Trained in a Jesuit school, Voltaire's understanding of China originated nearly exclusively from Jesuit writings.[15] Volatire's household belongings, as displayed in the Musée Carnavalet in Paris today, show that he was shrouded in the *chinoiserie* of the time, as many items manifest a Chinese theme or were imported from China (see Figure 3.1a & b).

The publication of Voltaire's *Essai sur les moeurs et l'esprit des nations; et sur les principaux faits de l'histoire, depuis Charlemagne jusqu'à Louis XIII* (Essay on the Manners and Spirit of Nations, and on the Principal Facts of History from Charlemagne to Louis XIII) (Paris, 1756) marked the zenith of the admiration of China in Europe.[16] The book, supposed to be a Universal History of humankind, started with a chapter on China. It opened with the assertion that, "The empire of China, even in those days, was larger than that of Charlemaign, especially if we include Corea and Tonquin, provinces at that time tributary to the Chinese.... This state has subsisted in splendour above 4000 years, without having undergone any material alteration in its laws, manners, language, or even in the mode and fashion of dress."[17]

Talking about "the religion of China," he mentioned that Confucius was a man who

---

[14] Davis 1983: 525.
[15] Reichwein 1925: 88.
[16] Reichwein 1925: 79.
[17] Voltaire 1759a [1756]: 10.

Figure 3.1a Voltaire's armchair, which he used in his last days in Paris, with a tilting stand on the right with China-themed painting (photo taken by author on May 2, 2024 at Musée Carnavalet, Paris, with permission of Musée Carnavalet)

Figure 3.1b Cup and saucer imported from China and used by Voltaire, with Chinese poem and painting (photo taken by author on May 2, 2024 at Musée Carnavalet, Paris, with permission of Musée Carnavalet)

has no divine honours paid him, these being due to the Deity alone; but he has such as a man deserves, who has given the purest ideas that human nature unassisted by

3 Early Enlightenment Sinophilia

revelation can form of the supreme Being: for which reason father le Comte and the other missionaries have remarked that the Chinese acknowledged the true God, when other nations were idolaters, and that they sacrificed to him in the most ancient temple in the universe.[18]

Provided with the antiquity of Chinese morality, Voltaire celebrated it in many of his other writings as the purest form of ethics directly received from the children of Noah. So he declared, "If, as a philosopher, one wishes to instruct oneself about what has taken place on the globe, one must first of all turn one's eyes towards the East, the cradle of all arts, to which the West owes everything...What should our European princes do when they hear of such examples? Admire and blush, but above all imitate."[19]

For Voltaire, a golden age existed in Chinese history under the legendary reign of Fu Xi 伏羲 (Fu Hsu), who was supposed to have lived some three thousand years before Christ. The Golden Age was supposedly the time when natural morality was closely followed. The Classics of Confucius preserved the moral code practiced in that period. By following the teachings of Confucius, generations of Chinese emperors reenacted this ancient religion. Observing present-day Chinese conduct and studying the Classics were equally useful in deciphering the Golden Age's morality that Europe should follow.[20]

Voltaire's image of Confucianist philosophy was borrowed from the Jesuits. Both Voltaire and the Jesuits attributed the Chinese superiority in morality to its antiquity. For them, antiquity implied purity, naturalness, and proximity to God. It was echoed by the admiration of China by Abbe Baudeau, a Physiocrats of the time, who exclaimed that, "The Chinese are the only known people, whose philosophers were, from the earliest ages, penetrated by that supreme truth, which they call simply Order, or the voice of Heaven. They base all measures on this one law: Be guided by the Will of Heaven."[21]

---

[18] Voltaire 1759a [1756]: 23.
[19] quoted in Reichwein 1925: 90.
[20] Guy 1963a: 253, 265.
[21] quoted in Reichwein 1925: 109.

Political Philosophy: Enlightened Despotism

The reasoning that China's superiority lay in its antiquity was also applied to Chinese politics and economy. Early Enlightenment thinkers argued for leveling noble powers and proposed enlightened despotism as an ideal political system. According to many political philosophers of the early Enlightenment, the Chinese political system, which allegedly operated successfully and uninterruptedly for centuries, reflected natural laws. It was conceived as a system ruled by "philosopher kings" who were checked by the laws and advised by mandarins trained in Confucian ethics and recruited in meritocratic examinations. It was proposed as a model for the West.[22]

The admiration of China's political system appeared in Voltaire's passages everywhere. As we shall see, such admiration was based on many erroneous conceptions and wild fantasies about China's political system at the time. For example, he asserted that:

> The Chinese empire was much happier at the beginning of the seventeenth century, than India, Persia, or Turkey. Mankind cannot possibly frame a better government than where every thing is decided by great tribunals, subordinate to each other, the members of which are not admitted till after severe examination... In such a government, it is impossible the emperor should exercise any arbitrary power. The general laws flow from him: But, according to the constitution, he can do nothing without taking previous advice of persons educated in the study of the laws, who are elected by votes. ...Now, if ever there was a government where the life, honour, and estate of the subject are secured, it is that of China. The more numerous the depositaries of the law, the less arbitrary is the administration; and if the sovereign sometimes abused his power against the few who venture to come near him, he cannot abuse it against the multitude, who know him not, and who live under the protection of the laws.[23]

To Voltaire, the Manchu Conquest disrupted the happiness and ideal function of the Chinese state. But soon, "the Tartars have

---

[22] Leites 1978: 143–51.
[23] Voltaire 1759b [1756]: 296–8.

adopted the laws, customs, and religion of the Chinese," and by the late seventeenth century, the Chinese empire was under the Manchu Kangxi Emperor "as a model of perfect prince" and was "equally respected both by the Tartars and the Chinese." As such, "the empire was happy under this prince."[24]

Likewise, Pierre Poivre, a naturalist and French Indian Company officer, wrote in the *Voyages d'un Philosophe, ou Observations sur les moeurs et les arts des peuples de l'Afrique, de l'Asie et de l'Amérique* (Travels of a Philosopher, or Observations on the Manners and Arts of the Peoples of Africa, Asia, and America) (Paris, 1769), which is a popular book describing the horticulture and botany of the Orient, that, "China offers an enchanting picture of what the whole world might become, if the laws of that empire were to become the laws of all nations. Go to Peking! Gaze upon the mightiest of mortals; she is the true and perfect image of Heaven."[25]

The praise for China's bureaucratic system and its centralized and meritocratic examination system for selecting state officials was a recurrent theme in both the Jesuits' and the Enlightenment's literature.[26] Eighteenth-century authors even translated Chinese governance manuals referencing the idealized rulership of ancient emperors, such as the seventh-century Emperor Taizong during the most prosperous times of the Tang dynasty (CE 618–907), into different European languages. They used the manuals to illustrate the universal good governance model and advise their monarchs on administrative reform.[27]

Political Economy: The Idea of *Laissez-Faire*

Similarly, the Chinese economic system was conceived of as a manifestation of natural law because of its success and antiquity. The doctrine of *laissez-faire* can be traced back to Adam Smith and the Physiocrats to China.[28] François Quesnay, a founder of the

---

[24] Voltaire 1759b [1756]: 303–4.
[25] quoted in Reichwein 1925: 92.
[26] Guy 1963b.
[27] De Weerdt 2022.
[28] Davis 1983: 546.

Physiocratic school, attributed much of his economic theory to the political and economic theories of ancient China.[29] Quesnay outlined most of the important doctrines of the Physiocrats in his *Le Despotisme de la Chine* (The Despotism of China) (Paris, 1767). Quesnay's use of "despotism" to describe China's political system did not carry the usual negative connotation that many of his contemporaries meant. For Quesnay, "despots" simply meant "sovereigns who exercise an absolute power regulated by laws."[30] In particular, Quesnay asserted that China's "constitution is founded on wise and irrevocable laws, which the Emperor observes, and which he himself observes exactly."[31]

For Quesnay, China was an empire whose form of government and economy had maintained the "peace and happiness" of its inhabitants for centuries.[32] He suggested that the Chinese economic system was characterized by its simplicity of taxation on land, the primary importance of agriculture, and the government's non-intervention in commerce. Goods could be bought and sold across the vast Chinese empires without tariffs when crossing provincial borders. It was equivalent to a hypothetical tariff-free trade within all of Europe. Quesnay regarded these characteristics of the Chinese economy as the basics of a natural economy and as the key to China's long-lasting prosperity. Based on this conception of the Chinese economy, Quesnay proposed reform to European agricultural production by implementing a single tax on land and abolishing tariff barriers across countries. According to Quesnay, a "natural," *laissez-faire* market economy would be the result. He believed the Chinese example showed that a vibrant market economy required management by an efficient state that abided by natural law. Therefore, Quesnay's praise of China as the economic model for Europe in the book's conclusion paralleled Voltaire's praise of the Chinese state:

> In this immense empire, all the errors and malfeasances of the chiefs are continually disclosed by public writings authorized by the government, to secure, in all the

---

[29] Reichwein 1925: 107.
[30] Quesnay 2011 [1767]: 6, trans. by MS words.
[31] Quesnay 2011 [1767]: 6, trans. by MS words.
[32] quoted in Reichwein 1925: 107.

> provinces of so great a kingdom, the observance of the laws against the abuses of authority, always enlightened by a free complaint, which is one of the essential conditions of a secure and unalterable government. ...Are not duration, extent, and permanent prosperity secured in the empire of China by the observance of natural laws? Does not this nation, so numerous, rightly regard other peoples, governed by human wills and subject to social obedience by arms, as barbarous nations? Does not this vast empire, subject to the natural order, present an example of a stable, permanent, and invariable government, which proves that the inconstancy of transient governments has no other basis, nor any other rule, than the very inconstancy of men?[33]

Though Quesnay's thought was also indebted to other sources, the influence of the image of (or fantasy about) China was of primary importance. His pupils honored him as a continuator of the work of Confucius and gave him the title of "the Confucius of Europe."[34] The relation between his economic thought and the Confucian philosophy was more explicitly stated in the funeral oration on him by one of his disciples:

> The whole teaching of Confucius aimed at restoring to human nature that first radiance, that first beauty, that it had received from Heaven, and which had become obscured by ignorance and passion. He, therefore, exhorted his countrymen to obey the Lord of Heaven, to honour and fear him, to love their neighbours as themselves, to overcome their inclinations, never to make passion the measure of action, but rather to subject it to reason, and not to do, or think, or say, anything contrary to reason. It would be impossible to add anything to this splendid diadem of religious morality; but the most essential part still remained to be done – to bind it upon the brows of earth; and this was the work of our master [Quesnay], whose keen ear caught

---

[33] Quesnay 2011 [1767]: 120–1, trans. by MS words.
[34] Reichwein 1925: 104.

from the lips of our common mother Nature the secret of the "net product."[35]

Quesnay rated Chinese philosophy above all others. Speaking of the Confucian Classics, he says, "They [Confucian Classics] all deal with good government, virtue, and good works; this collection is full of principles and moral sentences, which surpass those of the Seven Sages of Greece."[36]

The influence of the image of the Chinese economy was not restricted to Quesnay. Anne Robert Jacques Turgot, another founder of the Physiocratic school and Controller-General of Finances in the French government in 1774–1776, had met Aloys Ko (Gao Lei'en 高類恩) and Étienne Yang (Yang Dewang 楊德望), the two Chinese Catholic priests brought by the Jesuit missionaries to Paris, just as they were about to return to China in 1766, after about a decade of training in science, technology, and arts in France. Turgot asked them to research China's economy, society, and institutions and provided fifty-two questions to guide the research.[37] The questions ranged from methods of taxation on land to daily wages for workers in China.[38] The questions, together with their explanations and commentaries, were published as *Réflexions sur la formation et la distribution des richesses* (Reflections on the Formation and Distribution of Wealth) (Paris, 1769–1770).[39] It has become a classic text of economic theory of the eighteenth century and is regarded as a precursor of and inspiration for Adam Smith's *Wealth of Nations*.[40] The two Chinese scholars did send the information back to the Jesuits in Paris via the missionaries in Beijing, though little of that information made it to the 16 volumes of *Mémoires concernant l'histoire, les sciences, les arts, les moeurs, les usages, etc. des Chinois* (Memoirs Concerning the History, Sciences, Arts, Manners, and Customs, etc., of the Chinese) (Paris, 1776–1814), the last major collection of information about China published by the Jesuits in China in the late eighteenth century.[41]

---

[35] quoted in Reichwein 1925: 104.
[36] quoted in Reichwein 1925: 105.
[37] Rowbotham 1942: 286; Will 2023: 528–9; Finlay 2019: 93–7.
[38] Davis 1983: 539–40.
[39] Nguyen & Malbranque 2014.
[40] Rowbotham 1942: 286.
[41] Will 2023: 529.

Mathematics and Natural Sciences: In Search of the Key to All Sciences

The Jesuits' missionary enterprise and the academies of science in Europe – which were the institutions of the Scientific Revolution, with Accademia dei Lincei of Rome (of which Galileo was a member) as the forerunner – were closely related in the seventeenth century. The Jesuits used mathematical and scientific knowledge as gifts to win the support of the Qing Emperors, and many Jesuits were trained in the latest discoveries of the Scientific Revolution. Jesuit schools became academic institutions that cultivated scholars who contributed to the Revolution.[42]

Jesuit missionaries and representatives in the Revolution shared many ideas and admiration for the Chinese civilization. The coincidence between Bacon-Leibniz's attempt to construct a Universal Language based on the Chinese language and the Jesuits' identification of Chinese as the Primitive Language, as discussed previously, was just one of the many examples. Many scientists and mathematicians were connected personally with the Jesuits. The royally chartered academies of science and Jesuit missions were often institutionally linked to each other. For example, Louis XIV inducted four Jesuits from the Chinese mission into the French Academy of Sciences in Paris and offered the Jesuits financial support to learn astronomy.[43]

The collaborative efforts between Joachim Bouvet, a Jesuit missionary working in China, and Gottfried Wilhelm Leibniz, a major figure of both the German Enlightenment and the Scientific Revolution, to search for a fundamental principle of natural sciences in the ancient Chinese text of *Yi Jing* 易經 (*I Ching*, or the *Book of Changes*), best illustrated the Sinophilia in the field of mathematics and science. Bouvet and Leibniz met each other around 1695 through another Jesuit in Paris. From then on, the two extensively discussed *Yi Jing* in their uninterrupted correspondence. Leibniz's study of *Yi Jing* was key in his theory about cultural exchange and mutual learning between different civilizations. To Leibniz, each of the civilizations developed a partial, relative understanding of

---

[42] Wallace 1991.
[43] Mungello 1985: 32.

God's absolute, universal truth, and exchange between these civilizations was key to achieving a more complete understanding of God's truth.[44]

Yi Jing is an ancient pre-Confucius oracle text in China used for divination. It was claimed to have been written by the mythical Emperor Fu Xi, with no known date of completion. Bouvet believed that it was not only the oldest text of China but also the world's oldest text.[45] As the text was so archaic, cryptic, and full of strange symbols, nobody could be sure what it meant. Combined with the belief that the ancient Chinese possessed a perfect knowledge of the world directly obtained from God, Bouvet contended that *Yi Jing* was the true key to all knowledge of nature. He tried decoding the mysterious hexagrams in the text using Leibniz's binary mathematics. He asserted that a mathematical system was concealed in the hexagrams and constituted the fundamental principle for all scientific and mathematical knowledge.[46]

Bouvet kept Leibniz informed of any progress made in his study. Leibniz was very much impressed by the project and began propagating Bouvet's idea in Europe. He founded the *Akademie der Wissenschaften* in Berlin in 1700, with the "opening up of China and interchange of civilizations between China and Europe" as one of the primary objectives.[47] He directed much of the Academy's efforts to facilitate Bouvet's decoding of the hexagrams in *Yi Jing*. In one of his memorandums to the king of Prussia, Federick II, summarizing the services rendered by the Society since its foundation, Leibniz reported that: "[C]ertain very ancient symbols of the Chinese have been elucidated, which for two thousand years past they have themselves been unable to understand, and which nevertheless contain a new mathematical key."[48]

The admiration of China by early Enlightenment thinkers and their views of China as a model for Europe is very well known. What receives little attention is that this Sinophilic view of China

---

[44] See Perkins 2004.
[45] More recent scholarship dated the origin of the book at around third century BCE. See Weinberger 2016: sixth para.
[46] Mungello 1985: 312–28.
[47] Reichwein 1925: 81.
[48] Quoted in Reichwein 1925: 82.

is premised on an assumption about a monolithic, historically unchanging China that was superior because of its antiquity and, hence, proximity to God. Even China's ancient divination manual of obscure origins was fantasized as an embodiment of all secrets of the universe. Such reifying construction of China, in fact, prepared the ground for the rise of Sinophobia in the later phase of Enlightenment in the late eighteenth century.

4 LATE ENLIGHTENMENT SINOPHOBIA

The expansion of the European capitalist economy, the Industrial Revolution, and formal or informal colonization of the world in c. 1750–1850 ushered in a revolution in Europe's consciousness.[1] The idea of progress re-emerged. The moderns were seen as superior to the ancients in all political, economic, and moral senses. Europe was supposed to inevitably and incessantly progress toward a higher civilization.

As seen in Chapter 1, the proto-idea of progress was already established in the sixteenth-century literature on Universal History. The idea continued into the seventeenth-century crisis, though it subsided in dominance among the intellectuals of the time. This proto-idea of progress differed from the idea of progress that prevailed during the late Enlightenment. For example, late seventeenth-century millenarian philosophers in England argued that history was a gradual unfolding or progression of God's plan for salvation, and a kingdom of God and the second coming of Christ at the end of the millennium was the final stage of such a teleological process.[2] To other early Enlightenment thinkers, progress only meant improvement through human efforts rather than a guaranteed, unidirectional, and inevitable natural evolution.[3]

To the Sinophilic Enlightenment philosophers like Voltaire, antiquity or Oriental antiquity still enjoyed authority over the

---

[1] Wallerstein 1989, 1996, 1991.
[2] Spieckermann 1983: 328–9.
[3] Suckling 1967: 1461–6.

present. Despite its celebration of reason, the early Enlightenment in the early and mid eighteenth century had not shed the time-consciousness of the Catholic Church and the Renaissance. The ancients were still superior to the moderns in all possible senses.

The Eurocentric Idea of Progress

After decades of debate between the ancients and the moderns, the idea that progress was a secular, inevitable, unidirectional improvement of humanity over time became prevalent in the late eighteenth century. The belief that human society (or European society) was evolving and perfecting owing to some natural forces independent of human efforts became the philosophy of the day. The authority of antiquity over the present was reversed. Any argument referring to the Golden Age (either Occidental or Oriental antiquity) was attacked as nostalgic and contrary to the natural law of evolution.[4] This belief in progress and the natural force of history manifested most clearly in the worship of nature in the languages of the French Revolution, such as the renaming of months and days after natural weather and logic in the Revolution's calendar.[5] For some, the French Revolution constituted a cultural revolution enabling the people to finally become cognizant of the changes in Europe's capitalist economy since the long sixteenth century.[6] To others, it was the pinnacle of a cultural revolution that started in the middle of the eighteenth century.[7]

The Scientific Revolution and the early Enlightenment were insufficient in bringing the idea of progress to the center stage of Europe's intellectual world. It was not until the renewed prosperity and expansion of European powers brought a revival of popular optimism that the philosophers began to feel proud of Europe's achievements of the century. Martin Bernal discerned a sudden mid eighteenth-century change in European attitude toward ancient Egypt, from seeing it as the cradle of Greco–Roman civilization to

---

[4] Suckling 1967: 1466–80.
[5] Sewell 1985: 78.
[6] Wallerstein 1989: Ch. 2.
[7] Chartier 1991.

seeing it as an inferior culture. He pointed to the rising dominance of the idea of progress as a driver of such a shift:

> The concept of "progress" had existed in Europe since the 16th century, when people began to realize that they now possessed products and inventions that the Ancients had lacked – sugar, paper, printing, windmills, the compass, gunpowder, etc. – all of them introductions from Asia. But during the devastating Wars of Religion from 1560 to 1660, it was difficult for such a view to spread or even to take firm root. The century from 1670 to 1770, however, was one of great economic expansion, scientific and technical development, and increased concentration of political power. The popular writer Perrault and the "Moderns" in France were not merely fawning when they compared the age of Louis XIV to that of Augustus, and considered both the splendour and morals of their own times greater than those of the Ancients.[8]

By the seventeenth century, the medieval worldview that non-Europeans were idolatrous, cannibalistic, and even non-human had been threatened by the Great Discovery, the Reformation, and the Scientific Revolution. The Church was under attack. The vernacular languages replaced Latin. Europe became fragmented. This European identity crisis fueled the Sinophilic Enlightenment, which belittled Europe and called for Europe's emulation of China. With the renewed expansion of Europe beginning in the mid eighteenth century, European arrogance came back in a non-religious form. Radical philosophers during the late Enlightenment started to conceptualize Europe as a progressive continent, whereas other civilizations were said to be trapped in stagnation and retardation.

The shifting distinctions between ancients versus moderns and East versus West are well illustrated in the evolution of the writing of *historia philosophica* from the late seventeenth to the late eighteenth century. Such writing was a key part of European intellectuals' search for a new identity for Europe.[9] The writings first focused on different vernacular and national philosophies rather

---

[8] Bernal 1987: 177; see also Nisbet 1980: 171–8; Lach 1977: 565–6.
[9] Piaia 1996.

than a unified European philosophy. By emphasizing German, English, French, and other philosophical traditions, early historians of philosophy in the seventeenth century had not yet downplayed the superiority of Greek philosophy and Chinese philosophies. Sinophilia was integral to the writings, and China was seen as the birthplace of philosophy, with Confucius portrayed as the greatest philosopher in the world. As already mentioned in Chapter 3, Indian and Japanese reputations in Europe have been tarnished since the early seventeenth century after their expulsion of European missionaries. Meanwhile, the Islamic Ottoman had never been seen as a rival of Christian Europe. As such, China and ancient Egypt became the major models in the cult of the Orient in the seventeenth century, though Egypt was seen as a lost civilization while China was regarded as a living one.[10]

When the idea of progress and the authority of the moderns over the ancients took root in the latter half of the eighteenth century, the sentiments expressed in the *historia philosophica* shifted. The idea of a "European concert" that regarded Europe as a container of nationally differentiated philosophies emerged. The commonality of European philosophies was constructed on the one hand by distinguishing the modern philosophies from the Classical ones (i.e., Greek philosophy) and emphasizing the former's superiority.[11] It was also constructed by characterizing Eastern thought as no more than random "wisdom," in contrast to the systematic, rational "natural philosophy" of the West.[12]

The association between this new philosophical identity of Europe and the sense of European superiority was shown explicitly in Johann Jacob Brucker's authoritative *Historia critica philosophiae a mundi incunabulis ad nostram usque aetatem deducta* (Critical History of Philosophy from the Beginnings of the World to Our Own Times) (Leipzig, 1742). The book argued that genuine philosophy was born after the ancient schools of philosophy dissipated. Brucker also rejected the thesis, upheld by many historians of the fifteenth through the seventeenth centuries, about the Eastern origin of philosophy. In the book, he discussed

---

[10] Bernal 1987: 172.
[11] Piaia 1996: 595–6.
[12] Bernal 1987: 198; Piaia 1996: 601.

non-European philosophies of the Chinese, Indochinese, Japanese, and Canadian Indians in an appendix. He regarded those traditions as merely a mixture of philosophical teachings and religious beliefs. European philosophy was defined as *philosophia eclectica* and the highest form of human consciousness, in contrast to *philosophia sectaria* (the fragmented national traditions of philosophy) and *philosophia exotica* (philosophies outside Europe).[13] This Eurocentric writing of the history of consciousness of humankind was a precursor to Hegel's all-out attack on Chinese and Oriental philosophies in his grand History of Philosophy project at the turn of the nineteenth century, which we shall turn to later.

This new European identity grounded on the self-consciousness of a superior, modern, eclectic philosophy culminated during the French Revolution and the Napoleonic Wars when philosophers from different nations called for building a "higher and more lasting unity" of Europe based on reason to replace the archaic unity given by the Church.[14] To rid European philosophy of the strong Sinophilia that defined the early Enlightenment, late Enlightenment philosophers devoted much of their efforts to attacking China. Such an attack was as central to the construction of a new European identity as attacking the Christian religion.

Sinophiles under Siege

While the sense of European supremacy and the dominance of the idea of progress grew with Europe's economic and geographical expansion over the eighteenth century, Sinophobic sentiments increasingly took hold of Enlightenment philosophers. To the rising group of Sinophobic philosophers, Europe's superiority over the Orient was as natural as Europe's progress. Philosophers of these views emerged in the early eighteenth century as challengers to the dominant Sinophilia in philosophy.

For example, François Fénelon, archbishop of Cambrai and tutor to the royal children in the French court, was an early eighteenth-century expert of Greek philosophy and an early advocate of universal human rights. He plotted a debate between

[13] Piaia 1996: 602–5.
[14] Thompson 1994.

Socrates and Confucius as one of the dialogues in his *Dialogues des Morts* (Dialogues of the Dead) (Paris, 1712), with the chapter title of "Confucius et Socrate: Sur la prééminence tant vantée des ChinoisSur la prééminence tant vantée des Chinois" (Confucius and Socrate: On the Much Vaunted Preeminence of the Chinese). The book was part of his teaching materials to the hires of the French king. In the dialogue, Socrates staged a severe critique of all aspects of Chinese culture, putting Confucius in a defensive position. The Chinese were accused of inventing gunpowder to bring destruction to humankind. Their architecture was criticized as insensible to proportion, and their paintings had no composition, and so on.[15]

Fénelon tried to reveal the fundamental difference between Confucius and Socrates, and hence, between the East and West they represented. Unable to argue against Socrates' accusation, Confucius turned humble and asked whether their great antiquity was not a ground for praise. He said he had to first take counsel with Yao 堯, one of the oldest mythical emperors of China. Socrates replied that for knowledge of Greece, he needed not to rely upon Cecrops, nor on the Homeric heroes or any ancients, but on himself. In Fénelon's defense of Greco-Roman culture, reliance on antiquity was condemned. Such reliance was seen as a betrayal of human reason. This attitude toward antiquity radically differed from the dominant Sinophiles of the day, who saw antiquity as proof of naturalness and reason.[16]

In 1721, Montesquieu, another pioneer in resisting Sinophilia in philosophy, wrote in the *Lettres persanes* (Persian Letters) (Cologne, 1721) that Europe was a "scientific" and "progressive" continent, and he attributed this primacy to Europe's beneficent and temperate climate. He asserted that Asia's geography and climate gave rise to despotism.[17] Montesquieu was also Voltaire's empathetic rival and showed a great distaste for China. He was a deist philosopher who graduated from the Oratorian College in France in 1705. At the time, the Oratorians were allies of the Jansenists, the archenemy of the Jesuits.[18] Montesquieu was among the first to

---

[15] Fénelon 1917 [1712]: 164–79.
[16] Fénelon 1917 [1712]: 164–79; see also Reichwein 1925: 97–8.
[17] Bernal 1987: 204.
[18] Van Kley 1975: 36.

systematically make a case against China. In the *Lettres persanes*, he accused Louis XIV of exercising arbitrary power and imitating the despots of the Orient.[19] In 1748, he published *De l'esprit des lois* (The Spirit of the Laws) (Genève, 1748), advocating the protection of traditional feudal rights and protesting against the centralizing monarchs in Europe. The concept of Oriental despotism was coined, and the Chinese state was depicted as an exemplar of a corrupt tyrant. To Montesquieu, Oriental societies had no civil society and were constituted by atomized slaves terrorized by the despots:

> [U]nderlying the unanimity of Asiatic despotism, that is, every government where power is not checked, there is always a more serious type of division. The tiller of the land, the soldier, the merchant, the magistrate, the noble are related only in the sense that some of them oppress the others without meeting any resistance. If this be union, it can be so not in the sense that citizens are joined to one another, but rather that sense in which corpses are united when buried in a mass grave.[20]

Nonetheless, in the early eighteenth century, Sinophilia was still dominant. Voltaire overshadowed Montesquieu and attacked *De l'esprit des lois* as a reactionary defense of aristocratic privileges. The book was taken out of circulation in France after the Church placed it on the Index of Censorship.[21]

Sinophobia, though not yet mainstream, grew in different fields of inquiry as a resistance to the dominant Sinophilia. The Chinese language was regarded as a "dead language" by the pioneers of scientific linguistics.[22] Giambattista Vico, who characterized the Chinese as people "having no dealings with other nations for centuries," claimed that Confucian philosophy was "rude and clumsy" and entirely devoted to "a vulgar moral code." The Chinese language was a "vulgar language [that] has no more than three hundred articulated words [sic]" in his *New Science* in 1744.[23]

---

[19] O'Leary 1989: 61-2.
[20] Montesquieu 1990 [1734]: 101.
[21] O'Leary 1989: 62-3; Anderson 1974: 108; Collins 1998: 604-5; Blue 1999a: 70.
[22] Rowbotham 1942: 288.
[23] Vico 1948 [1744]: 30, 139; see also Zhang 1988: 116.

4 Late Enlightenment Sinophobia

Sinophobia grew in influence over the eighteenth century and replaced Sinophilia as the dominant intellectual disposition toward China after the 1750s. This shift of attitudes had nothing to do with any new sources of information about China or any drastic social transformation of the Chinese empire. This was no more than a reflection of the rupture in the intellectual climate in Europe, marked by the new dominance of the idea of progress. When the discourse of antiquity gave way to the discourse of progress, Chinese civilization's great antiquity, which had attracted wide admiration and the call for emulation, suddenly became a liability that invoked contempt and attack.

This distaste of antiquity was intense among the atheists and naturalists gathering around the *Encyclopédie* (1751–1780), a key platform for the radical Enlightenment in France. Denis Diderot, the compiler of the *Encyclopédie*, had written relentlessly against the Sinophiles since the 1750s. He condemned the Chinese as sinners against the law of progress, accusing that their culture, raised to such a high standard many centuries earlier, had in more recent times been static and unproductive. He also denounced all chronologies, both the Biblical and Chinese, and declared he had no interest in the proof of antiquity of Europe or China.[24]

Diderot was trained in Sorbonne, known for its sympathy to the Jansenists and its censuring of the Jesuits in the Sorbonne examination of 1700 (see Chapter 2). Diderot was hostile to Sinophilia at the outset. He was also much influenced by Jacob Brucker's *Historia critica philosophiae* and believed in the superiority of European philosophy.[25] Diderot was regarded as the representative of the radical Enlightenment, which embraced popular sovereignty, rejected religion and despotism, and directly inspired the French Revolution. He was regarded as a "genuine dissenter" of Sinophilia.[26] In 1780, he wrote the article "État de la Chine, selon ses détracteurs" (The State of China according to its detractors) to stage an all-round attack of Sinophilia. In the text, Diderot listed 20 common Sinophile arguments and systematically attacked them one

---

[24] Rowbotham 1942: 282; Cohen 1986: 223.
[25] Cohen 1986: 222.
[26] Cohen 1986: 230.

by one, with an appeal to reason and the general law of nature.[27] Near the end of his attack, Diderot exclaimed:

> And one dares, after what has just been heard, to stubbornly call the Chinese nation a people of sages! ... A people of sages, where children are exposed and smothered; where the vilest debauchery is common; where men are mutilated; where there is neither prevention nor punishment for crimes caused by famine; where the merchant deceives both the foreigner and the citizen; where knowledge of the language is the ultimate goal of science; where for centuries they have kept a language and writing barely sufficient for the commerce of life; where inspectors of morals are without honor and integrity; where justice is venal beyond example, even among the most depraved peoples; where the legislator, in whose name people bow their heads, would not deserve to be read if the poverty of his writings were not excused by the ignorance of the time in which he lived; where, from the emperor to the lowest of his subjects, it is but a long chain of rapacious beings who devour one another, and where the sovereign only lets some of these intermediaries grow fat in order to suck them dry in turn and to obtain, with the spoils of the corrupt official, the title of avenger of the people.[28]

Likewise, Jean-Jacques Rousseau, a fierce late eighteenth-century critic of Voltaire, asserted that the Chinese were hypocritical. Rousseau followed Montesquieu's Eurocentric geographical determinism and stated that people's virtue and political capacity depended on climate and topography and that Asian geography created despots.[29] He picked up the issue of the Manchu Conquest in the 1640s again. He repeated the seventeenth-century Dutch argument that the Conquest was, in nature, a conquest of civilization by barbarianism. The Conquest was proof of the weakness and failure of the Chinese civilization.[30] Rousseau regarded the Chinese

[27] Cohen 1986: 228.
[28] Diderot 1780: 245–6, translation by ChatGPT and Google.
[29] Bernal 1987: 204.
[30] Bien 1986: 364; Guy 1963a: 227–31.

government as mere tyranny, ruled by sticks and terror. He criticized Voltaire's conception of a golden age in Chinese history as contradictory to the idea of human progress.[31]

Europe and the Chinese without Philosophy

Kant, who celebrated the Enlightenment as a constant replacement of the old by the new and a rejection of all authority of antiquity, wrote that "philosophy is not to be found in the whole Orient ... concept of virtue and morality never entered the head of the Chinese."[32] On the eve of the French Revolution, China was commonly perceived as a land of stagnation, resisting human progress. In 1773, Friedrich Melchior, Baron von Grimm, a leading German-born French literary and cultural theorist, compared China to an old man: cold, harsh, and dominated by prudence, mistrust, stubbornness, and weakness.[33] The notion of human evolution was more systematically articulated by Marquis de Condorcet, a major theorist of the French Revolution, in his *Esquisse d'un tableau historique des progrès de l'esprit humain* (Sketch for a Historical Picture of the Progress of the Human Mind) (Paris, 1795). China was classified as a society at a low stage of evolution, retarded by the superstition of an ignorant priesthood and trapped in the state of "shameful immobility" and "eternal mediocrity."[34]

All these late eighteenth-century currents of Sinophobia converged later into Hegel's monumental lectures on the *Philosophy of History* and *History of Philosophy* as a manifestation of the zeitgeist of the time. Hegel renounced Confucius's writing as "highly tasteless prescriptions for cult and manners,"[35] with "a circumlocution, a reflex character, and circuitousness in the thought, which prevents it from rising above mediocrity."[36] He denigrated European enthusiasm for Chinese philosophy since the Jesuits as a

---

[31] Guy 1956.
[32] quoted in Ching 1978: 169.
[33] Rowbotham 1942: 288.
[34] Condorcet 1796 [1795]: 59–61; see also Rowbotham 1942: 288; Blue 1999a: 91.
[35] quoted in Kim 1978: 174.
[36] Hegel 2001 [1822]: 154.

disservice to the European mind, for Chinese philosophy was nothing more than practical wisdom:

> [T]hey [the Chinese] cannot find their place with us, that we could not allow of their giving us satisfaction.... We have conversations between Confucius and his followers in which there is nothing definite further than a commonplace moral put in the form of good, sound doctrine, which may be found as well expressed and better, in every place and amongst every people. Cicero gives us *De Officiis*, a book of moral teaching more comprehensive and better than all the books of Confucius. He is hence only a man who has a certain amount of practical and worldly wisdom – one with whom there is no speculative philosophy. We may conclude from his original works that for their reputation it would have been better had they never been translated. The treatise which the Jesuits produced is, however, more a paraphrase than a translation.[37]

Besides Confucius's works, according to Hegel, the Chinese were inferior to Europe in all other aspects of knowledge in the fields of mathematics, physics, and astronomy.[38] Hegel concluded that in China, as in the Oriental world in general, "there can be no question of philosophy properly speaking,"[39] as the Chinese are "*entirely* wanting in the essential consciousness of the Idea of Freedom."[40]

Hegel saw history as an unfolding consciousness and actualization of freedom of all humankind, and "Asia is severed from the process of general historical development, and has no share in it" until they were drawn into history through its contact with Europe via colonialism.[41] China and other Asian nations "remained stationary and fixed"[42] as "China, Persia, Turkey – in fact, Asia generally, is the scene of despotism, and, in a bad sense, of tyranny."[43] In the lengthy discussion of China in his *Philosophy of*

---

[37] Hegel 1955 [1805]: 121.
[38] Hegel 2001 [1822]: 154.
[39] Hegel 1983 [1837]: C. II.
[40] Hegel 2001 [1822]: 87, emphasis in original text.
[41] Hegel 2001 [1822]: 105.
[42] Hegel 2001 [1822]: 156.
[43] Hegel 2001 [1822]: 179.

History, Hegel reiterated Montesquieu's theme that China had been a land of perpetual Oriental despotism, where "[t]he soil., in which the chief possessions of the Chinese consist, was regarded ... as essentially the property of the State" and all subjects its "serf."[44] The section concluded:

> This is the character of the Chinese people in its various aspects. Its distinguishing feature is, that everything which belongs to Spirit – unconstrained morality, in practice and theory, Heart, inward Religion, Science and Art properly so called – is alien to it. The Emperor always speaks with majesty and paternal kindness and tenderness to the people; who, however, cherish the meanest opinion of themselves, and believe that they are born only to drag the car of Imperial Power. The burden which presses them to the ground, seems to them to be their inevitable destiny; and it appears nothing terrible to them to sell themselves as slaves, and to eat the bitter bread of slavery. Suicide, the result of revenge, and the exposure of children, as a common, even daily occurrence, show the little respect in which they hold themselves individually, and humanity in general. And though there is no distinction conferred by birth, and everyone can attain the highest dignity, this very equality testifies to no triumphant assertion of the worth of the inner man, but a servile consciousness.[45]

The demise of Sinophilia was marked by the tragic ending of the Society of Jesus on the eve of the French Revolution. The Jesuits, who were defeated in the Sorbonne examination in 1700 (see Chapter 2), were able to find their alliance outside the Church among the Sinophiles in the former half of the eighteenth century and gathered public and royal (particularly the French royal) sympathy and financial support. But the rise of radical Enlightenment and the corresponding dominance of Sinophobia threw them into a more vulnerable situation of being attacked by both the Left and the Right, by both the atheists and the Church.

---

[44] Hegel 2001 [1822]: 147–8.
[45] Hegel 2001 [1822]: 156.

The crisis of the French Jesuits first manifested as a financial crisis. By the 1750s, the Jesuits' mission in France was on the brink of bankruptcy with their accumulated debts. The Jesuits were frequently embarrassed by scandals about their involvement in commercial speculation, the most serious being French Jesuit priest Antoine Lavalette's business of a slave plantation in Martinique (1753–1762) and his killing of disobedient slaves.[46] Meanwhile, Jansenism flourished among the wealthy middle class and found protection in the aristocratic *parlement*. Members of the *parlement* and the King grew increasingly intolerant of foreign intervention in France's affairs. They started to complain that the Jesuits were following orders from Rome rather than the French state. This led to an ever louder voice advocating for the dissolution of the Society of Jesus in France. The expulsion of the Jesuits came finally in 1764 when the French king decided to outlaw the Society and confiscate all of its property. It was followed by Pope Clement XIV's suppression of the Jesuit Order in Rome in 1773.[47]

The demise of the Jesuit mission was a final blow to Sinophilia. Jesuit Sinophile writings, which had been circulated as the most authoritative sources and almost the only eyewitness accounts of the superiority of the Chinese civilization for more than a century, lost all of their credibility. This gave way to the travel writings of merchants who were intensely competing with Chinese diasporic traders in the port cities of Southeast Asia and South China. These merchants were hostile to the Chinese and tended to depict them as superstitious, selfish, and hypocritical.[48]

Worse, the Jesuits tried to save themselves by adapting to the Sinophobic atmosphere of the day. In the last compilations of the Jesuit missionary letters from China published between 1776 and 1814,[49] Confucius was portrayed as a distressingly ugly man with a pointed head and dark face, a scraggly beard, and very long fingernails on tiny hands, idly folded (see Figure 4.1). It contrasted

---

[46] Gottschalk and Lach 1973: 120; Thompson 1986: 428–9.
[47] Gottschalk and Lach 1973: 120; Thompson 1986: 432–3; Van Kley 1975: 6–61.
[48] Bien 1986: 364.
[49] Bien 1986: 365.

Figure 4.1 Late eighteenth-century Jesuit portrait of Confucius.
Source: Amiot, Jean Joseph Marie, et al. 1778: 41

sharply with the portrait of Confucius in the Jesuits' earlier classic Sinophilic works, where the Chinese philosopher was portrayed as a good-looking gentleman with a fair complexion, standing elegantly in front of a library filled with books (see Chapter 2).[50] Amid the attack on anything Chinese, European intellectuals' enthusiasm for studying China faded. It was not until the mid nineteenth century that European intellectuals "rediscovered" the Orient and recovered their enthusiasm for studying it through institutionalizing Orientalism as a discipline in the modern university structure. This was known as an Oriental Renaissance, which I will discuss in Chapter 5.[51]

The Political Sociology of the Rise and Fall of Sinophilia

The rise and fall of Sinophilia were, first of all, related to the rise and fall of the popular perception that China was much more advanced than Europe economically and politically. This was grounded on the specific inter-civilizational power relations in the early modern global economy.

In the seventeenth and early eighteenth centuries, Europe was troubled with wars, political upheavals, prolonged economic contraction, and depopulation.[52] China also witnessed political upheavals and economic crises during the mid seventeenth-century dynastic transition. Nevertheless, the upheaval was relatively brief, and the European observers were impressed by the rapid restoration of political stability, prosperity, and population growth under the Manchu rulers, who established the Qing dynasty in 1644.[53] The fine and exotic products from China, predominantly porcelains and silk, that flooded the European markets verified the Jesuits' complimentary reports on China and kindled a widespread admiration for Chinese arts and culture, or what was known as the *chinoiserie*. This popular sentiment created a favorable environment for the dissemination of intellectual Sinophilia.

---

[50] Mungello 1985: 271; Guy 1963a: I; Keevak 2011: Chap. 1.
[51] See Said 1978: 42 and Schwab 1984.
[52] Wallerstein 1980; Stone 1981; Trevor-Roper 1967.
[53] Wakeman 1986; Van Kley 1973; Goldstone 2002; Pomeranz 2000; Hung 2001, 2011: Chap. 1; Rowe 2002.

4 Late Enlightenment Sinophobia

This sentiment evaporated after the mid eighteenth century as the European world economy emerged from the century-long downturn and entered a robust expansion phase. The renewed economic growth was accompanied by successive technological innovations and acceleration of Europe's expansion into the rest of the world, with the British subjugation of India in 1757 as a landmark.[54] The thrust of capitalist growth and colonialism tilted the balance of power between the East and West. It unleashed an optimistic and triumphant sentiment in the nascent bourgeois public sphere of Europe. In this context, the idea of progress, which existed but never took root before the mid eighteenth century, began to dominate. Chinese antiquity, previously regarded as a virtue, suddenly became a vice.

The reversal of the balance of power between the Sinophiles and the Sinophobes was also facilitated by the transformation of the constellations of socio-political forces in Europe amid its capitalist expansion. French historian Louis Dermigny explained the shifting dominance from Sinophilia to Sinophobia in terms of the rising power of the bourgeois class. Dermigny argued that Sinophilia and Sinophobia represented the earlier and later worldviews of the ascending bourgeoisie. The positive image of China was instrumental in the promotion of absolutism and the dismantling of the feudal obstacles to commerce. It was natural for the nascent bourgeoisie to espouse Sinophilia from the seventeenth to the early eighteenth century when their prospects converged with the centralizing monarch. However, after the social power of the bourgeoisie expanded significantly due to the accelerated capitalist growth in the late eighteenth century, their previous alliance with the monarchs became redundant, and they started aspiring to seize state power for themselves. In this context, the philosophers, who served as the spokesmen of the bourgeoisie, abandoned their earlier Sinophilic position and began to attack China alongside absolutism.[55]

This interpretation is insightful but oversimplified, even reductionist. Considering the patronage networks behind many Sinophilic philosophers, we would find it more accurate to classify the Sinophiles as the spokesmen of the absolutist state and

---

[54] see Wallerstein 1989: Ch. 3.
[55] Dermigny 1964: vol. 1; Blue 1999a: 72–3.

the Sinophobes as the spokesmen of the aristocracy and then the bourgeoisie. Most Sinophiles lived off the stipends offered by royal courts. Voltaire depended on intermittent patronage of the French court and then served as the philosopher-poet in the Prussian court of Frederick II.[56] Many other Sinophiles based their livelihoods on the Royal Academies of Sciences under the patronage of monarchs. For example, Leibniz was the founder of the Akademie der Wissenschaften, which was established in Berlin in 1700. Many proponents of a Universal Language in England were members of the Royal Society of Sciences in London.[57]

In contrast, many early Sinophobes were backed by aristocrats in competition with the centralizing monarchs. Montesquieu was himself a provincial nobleman living off his hereditary property. He also inherited the seat in the Bordeaux *parlement* from his family and later became its president. He was a key leader of the French "aristocratic oppositionism" to the absolutist French king.[58] This class interest underlined the advocacy of Montesquieu and many other Enlightenment philosophers with aristocratic backgrounds or patronage for a division of power and a parliamentary check and balance on monarchial power. It was why Montesquieu would denigrate China's political system as grounded on unchecked monarchial power and as a dark example of corrupt and unchecked despotism that Europe should avoid. As such, the Sinophiles–Sinophobes rivalry in the late seventeenth and early eighteenth century was embedded in the conflict between the centralizing absolute monarch and the feudal aristocracy as much as it was a continuation of the seventeenth-century conflict between the Jesuits and the Jansenists and other religious rivals. The prevalence of Sinophilia in the early stage of Enlightenment can, henceforth, be understood in light of the strengthening monarchical order at the expense of the aristocracy in the seventeenth and early eighteenth century, a period when the European interstate system consolidated in the form of rising absolutism.[59]

It was only in the second half of the eighteenth century when the French bourgeois, empowered by the economic boom,

---

[56] Collins 1998: 605.
[57] see Mungello 1985: 183–97.
[58] Collins 1998: 604–5; Anderson 1974: 108.
[59] see Anderson 1974: 15–42; 85–109; Wallerstein 1980: Chs. 3 and 6.

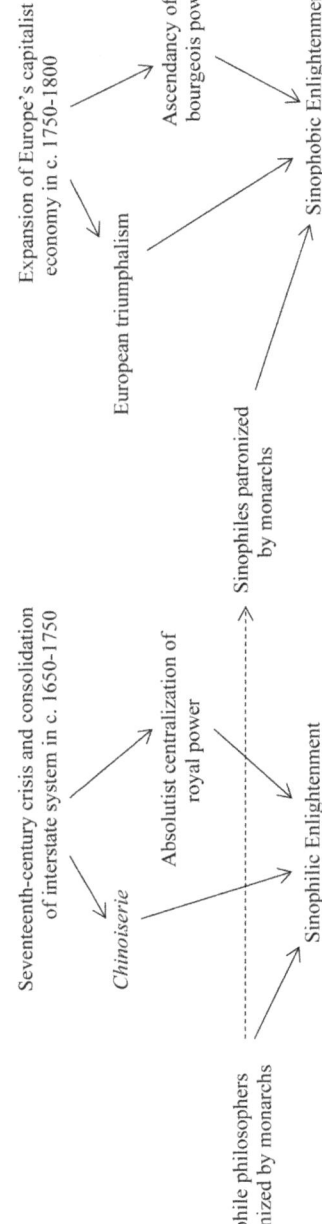

Figure 4.2 Competing philosophical views on China during the Enlightenment

came to intervene actively in the intellectual world as patrons of philosophers. Many late eighteenth-century Sinophobes received financial support from the rising bourgeoisie. For example, Diderot and his fellow Encyclopedists had been hosted continuously by Baron d'Holbach, a wealthy German expatriate in Paris whose family fortune originated in the stock market, and Claude-Adrien Helvétius, who made a fortune in the tax farming business.[60] Tax farmers were among the "wealthiest single group within the French capitalist class" in the eighteenth century.[61] In the particular context of France, the rising financial power of the bourgeoisie vis-à-vis the declining courtiers in patronizing intellectuals was further enhanced by the fiscal crisis of the Bourbon dynasty following France's defeat in the Seven Years' War (1756–1763).

While Sinophilic thinkers in the early Enlightenment believed in deism and were aligned with the absolutist state, Sinophobic philosophers during the radical Enlightenment were mostly atheistic. They were shrouded in the ideology of progress and popular sovereignty against the absolutist state, despising any unchecked despotic power grounding its authority on religious tradition. The Sinophiles–Sinophobes rivalry, and the latter's triumph in the late eighteenth century, was entangled with the conflict between the absolutist state and the contentious bourgeoisie. The final dissolution of Sinophilia went hand in hand with the demise of royal absolutism unleashed by the French Revolution.[62]

In sum, the changing relative dominance of the Sinophiles and the Sinophobes was not only a function of the evolving debate and competition between the two camps of polarized philosophers. It was also shaped by Europe's rising relative economic prowess, which shaped the popular perception of Europe's standing in the world vis-à-vis China. It was further conditioned by the changing balance of power among absolutist monarchs, aristocrats, and the bourgeoisie as patrons of intellectuals. The dynamics underlying the shifting representation of China in the community of philosophers over the eighteenth century are summarized in Figure 4.2.

---

[60] Collins 1998: 606, 608.
[61] Anderson 1974: 110.
[62] Anderson 1974: 109–12.

Part III
INSTITUTIONALIZED ORIENTALISM

5 ROMANTIC SINOLOGY AFTER THE FRENCH REVOLUTION

The expansion of European empires into Asia increased the practical need for training colonial administrators, diplomats, business personnel, and missionaries in the early nineteenth century. The interest in studying Asia revived following the temporary decline in enthusiasm for the East amid the turmoil of the French Revolution and the Napoleonic Wars. With the rise of universities as the new center of knowledge production at the time,[1] the rejuvenated study of Asian civilizations, known as an Oriental Renaissance,[2] was institutionalized as an academic discipline in the university system.

The Colonial Canonization of the East

The emergence of Orientalism as an academic discipline was premised on the assumption that Asian peoples were incapable of studying their own civilizations as scientifically and systematically as Europeans could. Hence, the latter were responsible for documenting these civilizations before they were lost. This fear of the "loss" of these civilizations was associated with the view that all Asian civilizations witnessed a golden age in the distant past before they declined, corrupted, and eventually dissipated.[3]

Though Orientalism resided in the humanities wing of the university's dichotomous disciplinary structure of science and

---

[1] Wallerstein et al. 1996: 6.
[2] Schwab 1984; Bernal 1987: 233–7.
[3] Said 1978: 113–23; Bernal 1987: 235.

humanities, Orientalists emphasized that they used "scientific methods" to codify, classify, and unveil Oriental cultures, societies, and languages in their totality. One means of codifying and classifying Oriental cultures was canonizing the Oriental "Classic Texts." It is a process of selecting certain antiquity texts as representatives of the respective civilization in question. This canonization process was never straightforward and objective but was often shaped by the particular circumstances of the colonial encounter between the Europeans and that particular civilization.

The political nature of the process can be illustrated in the case of the nineteenth century's creation and "enfranchisement" of Hinduism as a coherent, unitary system of beliefs and practices despite sectarian and regional variations.[4] The process heavily involved the British colonial administration, scholars, and missionaries in dialogue with Indian intellectuals. Islam was the state religion of the Mughal Empire before British colonization. Amid the colonialization process, the British administration employed scholars to study Indian culture. They adopted a dualist classification of Muslim and Hindu cultures, with the latter homogenized and sanctified as the authentic Indian culture. A set of ancient Hindu texts were translated and canonized as the "Classic Texts" of the Indian civilization.[5]

This dualist Muslim–Hindu framework overlooked the diversity of the non-Muslim cultures in South Asia. Its adoption had much to do with the British practice of divide and rule. By lumping together all non-Muslim groups into Hindu and bringing forth a colonial legal system based on a "Hindu legal tradition," as revealed in the selectively translated texts, a Hindu majority in India was constructed. Based on this knowledge, the British rulers legitimatized themselves as the patrons of this majority, patrons who drove out the foreign Muslim rulers and recovered the authentic Hindu tradition for the Indians. When European scholars began to work on India in universities, the assumption of Hinduism as the essence of Indian civilization was already in place.[6]

A similar process of canonization took place in other Asian civilizations. By the end of the nineteenth century, this process had

---

[4] Rocher 1993; Pennington 2005.
[5] Rocher 1993: 225–31.
[6] Rocher 1993: 220–5.

been crystallized into the systematic taxonomy of non-western religions as represented in the fifty volumes of *The Sacred Books of the East* compiled by Friedrich Max Müller, a German Orientalist and Indologist who was an authority on comparative religions and comparative philology teaching at Oxford. The compilation was supposed to be a collection of translations of the most representative classical texts of all Oriental cultures. It was enshrined as an indispensable referential instrument of the whole Orientalist enterprise.

Nineteenth-century Orientalism focused on the "religions" of the East, in sharp contrast to the diverse interest in the state, economy, technology, and philosophy of the region in the sixteenth through eighteenth-century European learning of the East, as we have seen in Chapters 3 and 4. What were characterized as religions in the discipline, such as Confucianism and Hinduism, were regarded as philosophies in the earlier period. This changing conception of Eastern thoughts was a continuation of the late Enlightenment view that true philosophy only existed in Europe and that there were only religions or, at most, loose "wisdom" in the Orient. Underlying the European idea of progress was the idea about the evolution of human consciousness – that the human mind evolved from "intuitive" learning, such as religion, ethics, and aesthetics, to metaphysics and, finally, to science.[7] As such, assuming Asian societies stayed at a lower stage of development was tantamount to assuming the people there had no concept of philosophy, economy, technology, and administration. By the nineteenth century, the belief that Europe had any practical thing to learn from Asia had all gone. The result was the reduction of Oriental civilizations to Oriental religions.

The Making of Academic Sinology

Europe's attention to the Chinese civilization revived amid this "Oriental Renaissance." Sinology as an academic discipline started in 1814 when the first Chair of Chinese Language and Literature was established at the Collège Royal (renamed Collège de France in 1870). The canonization of Taoism and Confucianism

---

[7] It is the idea of William Wotton as expressed in his *Reflections upon Ancient and Modern Learning.* (1694). See Spieckermann 1983: 329.

accompanied the disciplinarization of Sinology as the primary objects of study in the field. In the nineteenth century (and to this day), three religions were identified as the defining religions of the Chinese civilization. They were Taoism, Confucianism, and Buddhism. However, Buddhism was regarded as an imported religion and not essentially Chinese. Moreover, it was believed that the Chinese variation of Buddhism was influenced much by Taoism. Thus, Buddhism in China did not receive much attention from nineteenth-century Sinologists, who only regarded Confucianism and Taoism as the essence of Chinese civilization. *The Texts of Confucianism* and *The Text of Taoism* (both translated by James Legge, whose work will be discussed later) were included in the part on China in Müller's *The Sacred Books of the East*.

As we saw in Chapter 2, Confucianism was canonized as the authentic culture of China much earlier by the Jesuits. Confucius and his doctrines were unknown to the West until Matteo Ricci. Marco Polo and other travelers before the sixteenth century had never said a word about it. What was known to the Europeans back then was the existence of Buddhism and other folk religions. Ricci initially mistook Buddhism for the state religion of China, as it was in Japan. He dressed as a Buddhist bonze when he first arrived in China in 1583, but as we see earlier, once Ricci discovered that the literati of the Chinese state adhered to the principles of Confucian thought and that the ruling elite despised Buddhism, as well as other folk religions, he shifted his attention to Confucianism. After that, the Jesuits directed all of their efforts to reading and translating Confucianism's state-sanctioned Classics. With the introduction of the Jesuits-translated Classics of Confucianism to Europe, the Confucianist tradition was accepted as the core of Chinese civilization. The zeal of the nineteenth-century Sinologist, however, lay not on Confucianism but on the newly canonized Taoism.

Before the nineteenth century, the influence of Jesuits' essentialization of Chinese culture as Confucianist was so strong that discussion about Chinese culture, however sympathetic or contemptuous, was indeed about Confucianist doctrines and practices. Some religious sects were occasionally mentioned in the writings of Jesuits and other European travelers. However, none of these sects were understood as unified, legitimate cultural traditions comparable to Confucianism in China. Only in the nineteenth century was

Taoism canonized as an independent Chinese religious tradition of equal or higher importance than Confucianism.

The canonization of Taoism was emblematic of the birth and development of nineteenth-century Sinology. Most founders of modern Sinology were remembered for their contribution to introducing the Taoist canon to the West.[8] The term Taoism was a European invention and was not used until the nineteenth century. Taoism is "a rare example of a subject related to Chinese culture which has, in modern times, received perhaps more attention abroad than in China itself."[9] It is noteworthy that when translating the Confucianist Classics, James Legge got much support from Wang Tao 王韜, his closest Chinese literati friend, and a prominent thinker, reformer, and newspaper publisher in late Qing China residing in British Hong Kong. Wang suddenly became unsupportive and even hostile to Legge when the latter started to translate the "Taoist Classics."[10] Moreover, the European consensus on the existence of a unitary Taoist tradition, which was thought to have originated in Laozi's 老子 (Lao Tzu) *Daode Jing* 道德經 (*Tao Te Ching*, the Book of Way and Virtue) and practiced as a folk religion, was established only in the late nineteenth century after a prolonged debate that lasted for decades.

In China, many temples and monasteries of various religious sects worshiped Laozi, a contemporary of Confucius during the Warring Period (475–221 BCE), alongside a wide array of spirits and gods. *Daode Jing*, a book of doctrines attributed to Laozi, was studied by priests in those temples and monasteries. Jean-Pierre Abel-Rémusat, the French Sinologist who was the first occupant of the chair of Chinese language and literature at the Collège Royal, was among the first to call for serious attention to *Daode Jing* as a classic text of Chinese civilization. A religious doctrine was thought to be behind it, and the task of translating it into European languages was set. In 1823, Abel-Rémusat published a volume at the French Academy of History and Philosophy titled *Mémoire sur la vie et les opinions de Lao-tseu* (Memoir on the Life and Opinions of Lao-tsue) (Paris, 1823), in which he asserted:

---

[8] Schipper 1995: 467.
[9] Schipper 1995: 467.
[10] Schipper 1995: 471.

The book of Lao-tzu is not easy to understand, because the obscurity of the subject matter is compounded by the conciseness of its antique prose and by a vagueness which sometimes renders the style very enigmatic indeed.... It would be a major feat if someone could translate this text completely and explain it in connection with the doctrine it contains.[11]

In the book, Abel-Rémusat followed the Jesuits' line of interpreting Confucianism and maintained that *Daode Jing* mentioned a monotheistic God several times, hence proving that the ancient Chinese and Laozi were aware of the Holy Trinity. Abel-Rémusat applied the standard Orientalist assumption about Eastern religious development from the pure to the corrupt to the newly identified (or invented) tradition of Taoism. According to Abel-Rémusat, doctrines in the *Daode Jing* represent a "sublime philosophy" that "breathes mildness and goodwill." The folk religions observed in modern times as part of the Taoist tradition could be traced back to the doctrines, though superstitions had corrupted them over the centuries.[12] He believed that the degeneration of Taoism started in the first century and was caused by the influence of Buddhism. Since then, Taoism has grafted monasteries and nunneries onto itself, as well as idolatrous images and rituals like Buddhism.[13]

Stanislas Julien, Abel-Rémusat's student and successor at Collège Royal, published a full translation of *Daode Jing* in 1842. Prior to this full translation, Julien published a selective translation of a chapter in 1835 under the title *Le livre des récompenses et des peines: en chinois et en français; accompagné de quatre cents légendes, anecdotes et histoires, qui font connaître les doctrines, les croyances et les moeurs de la secte des tao-ssé* (The Book of Rewards and Punishments: In Chinese and French; Accompanied by Four Hundred Legends, Anecdotes, and Stories, Which Make Known the Doctrines, Beliefs, and Customs of the Taoist Sect) (Paris, 1835). In the preface, he wrote:

> [I am] to spend my time in making a complete translation of a book which has been spread throughout China since

---

[11] Quoted in Schipper 1995: 468.
[12] Girardot 1992: 189.
[13] Girardot 1992: 191.

several centuries and which has had millions of readers. The commentary, written by a learned *tao-shih* [priest in sects worshiping Laozi], and the numerous legends and anecdotes which are transmitted from generation to generation, express a form of Morality in action which makes us understand in a very instructive way the doctrines, creeds and customs on which we had, until now, but very vague and incomplete ideas.... I have been afraid, by omitting even a single one of them, to suppress a precious document on the history of the human mind.[14]

As such, Taoism was codified into a coherent tradition unifying ancient texts and contemporary living traditions.

The canonization of Taoism was completed by James Legge, the first occupant of the chair of Chinese language at Oxford University, which was established in 1876. He was regarded as "the single most important figure contributing to the late Victorian invention of 'Taoism' as a reified entity located 'classically' and 'essentially' within certain ancient text or 'sacred books.'"[15] In 1883, Legge published an influential article entitled "Tao Teh King" in the *British Quarterly Review*. In the article, he summed up interpretations of Taoism by earlier Western scholars and offered his view. For the first time, Legge argued that *Dao* (*Tao*) should be translated into "Course," which means the course of nature and the right course for individuals and government. *Daode Jing* was translated into "The Sacred Text of the Right Course and Its Characteristics." In 1891, Legge published *The Texts of Taoism* as volumes 39 and 40 of Müller's *Sacred Books of the East*. Besides *Daode Jing*, several texts by Zhuangzi 莊子 (Chuang Tzu), a philosopher younger than Laozi, and commentaries of several more recent Chinese writers were included. The collection of texts included was thereafter regarded as the Classics of Taoism until today.

However, the canonization of Taoism was not without objection in the beginning. Sinologists constantly confronted the contention that Taoism as a coherent tradition did not exist at all, that Laozi was no more than a fabricated figure created in the Han

---

[14] Quoted in Schipper 1995: 469.
[15] Girardot 1992: 188; 2002: 419–34.

dynasty (202 BCE–8 CE), and that *Daode Jing* was a late Han forgery. The integrity of Taoist texts and thoughts was questioned. This skepticism was best represented in the article "The Remains of Laotzu" in the *China Quarterly Review* in 1886, authored by Herbert A. Giles, a Cambridge Sinologist who co-invented the Wade–Giles system of romanizing Chinese characters with Thomas Wade. It triggered a debate between Legge and Giles in a subsequent journal issue. This explains why, in the "Introduction" of *The Texts of Taoism*, Legge dedicated many paragraphs to evidence showing the authenticity of Laozi and *Daode Jing*.

In retrospect, the nineteenth-century canonization of Taoism was very successful. Few would now challenge the coherence of Taoism as a tradition. Its success and the attention it commanded in nineteenth-century Sinology should not be taken for granted. Underlying the presumed centrality of Taoism in the Chinese civilization is the apparent incompatibility between the established understanding of Confucianism and the "Europe/rationality/science–Orient/superstition/religion" dichotomy as the foundational assumption of Orientalist scholarship. Though the worship of ancestors promoted in Confucianist Classics had been attacked as superstitious rituals since the Rites Controversy, such worship was insufficient to justify characterizing Confucianism as a superstitious religion instead of a philosophy. The canonization of a Taoist tradition, more closely associated with worshiping idols and conducting supernatural rituals in temples and monasteries, filled this gap. Taoism was increasingly regarded as more foundational to Chinese civilization than Confucianism toward the turn of the twentieth century.

Romanticism and Orientalism

Besides the practical need for training diplomats and colonial officials amid Europe's geographical expansion into Asia, the growing Romantic movement was another impetus to the revival of enthusiasm for Asia in the early nineteenth century. The Romantic movement took shape in Germany as a reaction to France's radical Enlightenment, which culminated in the French Revolution and the Napoleonic Wars. The Romantics opposed the evolutionist conception of history and indulged in a mystical thirst. They were devoted to the search for childlike innocence and purity in humanity. They sought a reunification of religion, philosophy, and art, which were putatively sundered by modern sciences.[16]

The Romantic movement was connected to the rise of nationalism, which responded to the unifying European identity of Enlightenment philosophy. The Romantics believed reason was inadequate for handling the important aspects of life and morality. They were more concerned with the local and the particular rather than the global and universal.[17] Many Romantics, with their quest for spirituality, painstakingly looked into Eastern cultures in "a search for childlike innocence, a vision of wholeness, a yearning for the recovery of what the poets and philosophers of the period felt the age had lost, namely a oneness with humankind and a oneness with nature."[18]

Idealization and admiration of Oriental antiquity, which radical Enlightenment thinkers despised, resumed among the Romantics. Though resisting the evolutionist ideology of the day and restoring the time-consciousness that presumes the ancient was superior to the modern in certain respects, this Romantic reaction was not a complete comeback of the pre- and early Enlightenment privileging of antiquity. Rather, the Romantic and evolutionist worldviews shared the notion of "childhood versus adulthood" in the development of culture. The Romantic Orientalists searched for some lost qualities of humanity's childhood in the Orient to supplement European modernity. With their supposedly more mature and superior minds, the Europeans shouldered the responsibility of studying the childlike peoples in the East and rescuing the treasures in their cultures that the natives could not preserve.

The rise of Romantic Orientalism first emerged in the German study of the Indian civilization and later branched out to the study of other civilizations.[19] As a reaction to radical Enlightenment centered in Paris, the Romantic movement found footing more predominantly in Germany, England, and Holland than in France. As a result, the emergence of Orientalist scholarship driven by

[16] Clarke 1997: 55–6; Schwab 1984; Bernal 1987: 19–20; Marchand 2009: 53–101.
[17] Bernal 1987: 19–20.
[18] Clarke 1997: 55–6.
[19] Schwab 1984.

Romanticism was the strongest in the former three nations. As we shall see, despite Paris being the center of previous Sinophilia and establishing the first chair of Sinology, most other representative Sinologists in the nineteenth century originated or taught in Germany, England, and Holland rather than in France.

The Romantic Orientalists defined all non-Western civilizations as world religions and presumed that they existed in their most ancient, purest forms. As discussed earlier, they constructed a taxonomy of Oriental religions. They canonized Oriental "Classic Texts," crystallizing into the fifty volumes of *The Sacred Books of the East* compiled by Friedrich Max Müller (1823–1900). The claim that one could understand the totality of an Eastern civilization by understanding a few civilizational "sacred texts" is as reductionist and erroneous as saying one can understand the totality of Western civilization by reading the Bible alone.

Müller's view on non-Western civilizations took shape when he studied Sanskrit at the University of Leipzig. In 1844, he established an intimate relationship with F. W. J. Schelling, a leading German Romantic contending that the human race shared a primitive unity and that the origins of the European culture can be traced back to Indian antiquity.[20] Under the strong influence of Schelling's theory, Müller objected to the evolutionary perspective on human history and suggested that history was a process of degeneration and the struggles against it.[21] He argued that all religions – Christian and Oriental religions alike – developed from a common root that was primitive, rational, and monotheistic in nature. He claimed in a lecture in 1870 that "if we all but listen attentively, we can hear in all religions a groaning of the spirit ... a longing after the Infinite, a love of God."[22] It followed that to unveil God's purpose, one had to study not one but all religions of the world, especially those in their most ancient forms.

In tandem with Müller's search for a common root of religion was a philological movement proposing that all human languages shared a single origin. Gustaaf Schlegel (1840–1903), Joseph Edkins (1823–1905), and August Schleicher (1821–1868) were

---

[20] Clarke 1997: 63–4; Trompf 1978: 14–16.
[21] Trompf 1978: 56, 71.
[22] Müller 1882: 13–14; See also Trompf 1978: 70; Clarke 1997: 132–4.

representative figures of this movement. They put forth the theory that there were two phases in the development of human languages. The first phase was a progressive evolution from monosyllables to fully developed inflection, and the second phase was a decline from the pinnacle of the first phase. Some suggested that English and other modern European languages were in the declining phase. In contrast, the Chinese language was in a more primitive stage of development and had not yet entered the declining phase. Hence, Chinese was the key to deciphering the highest form of human languages.[23]

These two theories of world religions and languages resurrected the seventeenth-century conception that non-Western civilizations were fundamentally unified with the Western ones. They also partially revived the time-consciousness that privileged the past over the present. However, the nineteenth-century Romantics' admiration of the East also manifested key differences from the admiration among the eighteenth-century Enlightenment thinkers. While Enlightenment thinkers were rationalists who claimed to find a superior form of rationalism in the East, or China in particular, the Romantics were anti-rationalists. They claimed to find the antidote to rationalism in Eastern spirituality.[24]

Institutionally, the International Congress of Orientalists was founded in 1873 and met every two or three years. Each Congress was divided into panels according to geographical areas. The purpose was to let the specialists of different areas acquaint themselves with one another's works and keep up with the latest trends within the Orientalist profession at large. It marked the full consolidation of Orientalism as an academic field.

Sinophilic Déjà Vu

Romanticist influences were everywhere in early Sinology, with James Legge and J. J. M. de Groot being two leading authorities in nineteenth-century Romantic Sinology. While James Legge was the representative of the tradition of textual criticism in the

[23] Pulleyblank 1995: 343–4.
[24] See Levenson 1968: xxviii–xxix.

discipline, de Groot, a Dutch Sinologist teaching in Leiden and Berlin, represented the ethnographic tradition.

James Legge's Translation of Chinese Classics

James Legge was a Scottish missionary who worked in Hong Kong, Macao, and Guangzhou (Canton) from 1843 to 1873. In 1861, he published his translation of the Confucian Classics as a series of *Chinese Classics*. It was thereafter regarded as the most authoritative translation of the works of Confucius and his disciples. Herbert A. Giles, a Sinologist specializing in Chinese literature and the Professor of Chinese at Cambridge University contemporaneous to Legge, praised Legge's contribution by saying, "[Legge's] translation of the Confucian Canon has helped many a weaker brother to a right understanding of a most difficult text – a point the latter might otherwise never have reached; ... Legge's work is the greatest contribution ever made to the study of Chinese, and will be remembered and studied ages after."[25]

Joseph Edkins, a missionary, philologist, and another leading Sinologist of the day, also highly regarded his translation as having "marked an epoch in the history of Sinology." In 1876, a Chair of Chinese Language was established at Oxford University, and Legge was appointed its first occupant. Later, Legge turned his attention to Taoism and published his translation of the Taoist Classics as *The Texts of Taoism* in 1891.

The launch of Legge's Sinology career was marked by his involvement in the "term question." The "term question" emerged among Protestant missionaries in 1843. It resembled the Rites Controversy between the Jesuits and their enemies in the seventeenth-century Catholic Church.[26] In 1843, fifteen Protestant missionaries met in Hong Kong to discuss the Chinese Bible versions and to work out a revised and more authoritative version. A debate arose as to the choice of the right term to be used for "God." Legge contended that "God" should be translated into *Shangdi* 上帝 (*Shang Ti*), a term frequently mentioned in the Confucian Classics. Legge's suggestion faced strong opposition from the missionaries

---

[25] Giles 1914: 116 and 346, see also Ride 1960: 21.
[26] See Chapter 2.

who held that Chinese philosophy was atheistic or animistic. The debate became known as the term question. James Legge's daughter summed up the debate concisely:

> [The term question] is the longest and the most embittered controversy in which he was ever engaged, a controversy with certain missionaries who did not think of the root ideas of the old Chinese religion as he did. Nominally it related to the question whether they [the Chinese] had any word that could be used to translate the idea of God: really and substantially it concerned whether they had any idea of God at all. And he maintained they had.[27]

The religious concern behind the contention that the ancient Chinese believed in God was well reflected in a letter that one of Legge's supporters wrote to support him in 1850:

> My dear Legge,
>
> You can be of good service in revising the sheets of our translation which I will do my utmost to have forwarded regularly to you. Your labours in this controversy are not ended. Go to it. The enemy has waxed more imprudent, for I can't use any more fitting expression. If that were all, you had better treat them as children. But it is not the missionaries of this generation that you are to work for. It is the future upon which your work will tell – future missionaries – the future Church in China. May God help and bless you in it.[28]

While the idea that the ancient Chinese believed in God faced stiff resistance in the missionary circle of the time, it was widely accepted in the Orientalist establishment in the scholarly world. Max Müller, the leader of Romantic Orientalism, allied with Legge publicly on the issue. In 1880, the *Chinese Recorder and Missionary Journal* published a letter addressed to Müller and signed as "Inquirer" to denounce Legge's and Müller's views. The "Inquirer" stated that *Tian* (*Thien* in the letter), meaning the physical sky, was worshiped by Confucius and contemporary Chinese alike. He argued that it

---

[27] Legge 1905: 68.
[28] Quoted in Legge 1905: 70.

was a piece of strong evidence that the Chinese did not have the idea of a personalized God but chose the material and visible sky as their chief God. James Legge refuted the letter in a later issue of the journal. He insisted that in the Confucian texts, *Tian* did not mean the physical sky but the personalized Supreme Being, also referred to as *Shangdi*.[29] Legge's idea of the Chinese belief in God extended to his interpretation of *Daode Jing*. In his 1883 article "Tao Teh King" mentioned before, he said that God was at least implied by the five or six references to *Tian* (*Thien*, Heaven) and *Tiandao* 天道 (*Thien Tao*, the Way of Heaven) in Laozi's work. In the end, Legge's suggested terms have been adopted in standard Chinese translations of the Bible till today.

Legge's view on Chinese religion was most systematically expressed in his work *The Religions of China: Confucianism and Taoism described and Compared with Christianity* (London, 1880), which was based on his lecture given to the missionaries at the Presbyterian Church of England in the spring of 1880. In the lecture, both Confucianism and Taoism, in their most original and pure form, were said to express a belief in a monotheistic God. Buddhism was only mentioned briefly and was treated as an external source causing the decay of the former two. Legge partitioned the Taoist tradition into two phases, one before the coming of Buddhism and the other after it. Only in the second phase did Taoism begin to degenerate into a polytheism.

Legge compared Confucianism and Taoism with Christianity in the last section of the lecture. Legge concluded that the three religions agreed on three fundamental points. First, all of them believed in a monotheistic God. He asserted that:

> In the book of Isaiah Jehovah says, 'I am Jehovah, and there is none else. There is no God beside me.' The Confucian books do not contain a similar declaration; but we saw how the monotheism of prehistoric time in China has always striven, and not without success, to assert itself against attempts to corrupt it. In Taoism, which is polytheistic, the name of God is of course common; but Lao-tzu himself spoke of God, so far as the term Tien, 'Heaven,'

[29] Legge 1905: 70–2.

> employed in a non-material sense, could do so, and on one occasion he used the name God itself. The existence of God is assumed in the three religions.[30]

Second, the idea of the possibility and the fact of revelation was common to them:

> [T]hat God should speak or make known His will to men did not seem strange to the Chinese fathers, and in the Shih we read that 'God spoke to king Wan,' just as we read in the Old Testament that 'God spoke to Moses.' Hundreds of Taoist tracts also are circulated in China, each one purporting to be the teaching of this god or that, 'to warn,' or 'to advise mankind.' The idea of revelation therefore is held in the three religions.[31]

At last, all three of them held the idea of the supernatural, as Confucius "thought they [the ever-changing phenomena of the material universe] were produced by the mysterious spiritual operation of God."[32]

According to Legge, the belief in the existence of God was not only manifested in the ancient texts but could also be found in the emperor's prayers in his time.[33] Monotheism had been preserved as it "has always striven, and not without success, to assert itself against attempts to corrupt it."[34] One source of this corruption is Buddhism.[35] After a thorough comparison, Legge tried hard to establish equality between Christianity, Confucianism, and Taoism:

> [The] divine stamp on Christianity must not be supposed to imprint the brand of falsehood on other religions. They are still to be tested according to what they are in themselves.... It must be borne in mind also that when we have concluded that Christianity is the revealed religion, this does not relieve us from the task of searching the scriptures diligently, and finding out their meaning by all legitimate

---

[30] Legge 1976 [1880]: 245.
[31] Legge 1976 [1880]: 246.
[32] Legge 1976 [1880]: 248.
[33] Legge 1976 [1880]: 23.
[34] Legge 1976 [1880]: 245.
[35] Legge 1976 [1880]: 182.

methods of criticism and interpretation. The books of the Old and New Testaments have come down to us just as the Greek and Roman and Chinese classics have done, exposed in the same way to corruption and alternation, to additions and mutilations. The text of them all has to be settled by the same canons of criticism.[36]

Furthermore:

During my long residence among the Chinese, I learned to think more highly of them than many of our countrymen do; more highly as to their actual capacity, and more highly as to their intellectual capacity.[37]

The works of Max Müller influenced Legge's idealizing disposition toward Confucianism and Taoism. Legge and Müller knew each other in 1875. Müller's influences on Legge were well reflected in Legge's *The Religions of China*, in which Legge explicitly cited and followed Müller's methodology of comparative philology and religion. It was also under the encouragement of Müller that Legge decided to teach at Oxford.

As discussed earlier, Müller contended that human history was a history of degeneration and the struggle against it. All religions – from Christianity to idolatrous religions alike – developed from the same primitive, natural, and rational religion that shared the common love of God. Hence, the premise of his *Sacred Books of the East* project was that one should discover God's purpose by studying all religions of the world, especially the religions in their most ancient form. Müller translated the ancient Indian book Rig-Veda himself for the project. In it, he claimed to find a religion in a state of primitive purity and possessed conceptions of the deity "purer and better" than the "savage" communities of today.[38] Under this Romantic Orientalist premise, Legge followed the footsteps of the Jesuits and "discovered" God in the ancient texts of Confucianism and Taoism, even though his fellow Christian missionaries detested such discovery.

---

[36] Legge 1976 [1880]: 286–8.
[37] Legge 1976 [1880]: 308.
[38] Trompf 1978: 71.

De Groot's Ethnography of Chinese Religions

In a different tradition, de Groot was trained at Leiden University and was a student of Gustaaf Schlegel (1840–1903), one of the founding fathers of nineteenth-century Sinology and the first Chair of Chinese Language and Literature at Leiden established in 1876. After finishing his studies, de Groot joined the Dutch colonial service and worked in Amoy (present-day Xiamen 廈門) in 1877–1878 and 1886–1890. He conducted systemic ethnographic observations of the Chinese folk religious practices in Amoy. He compiled his findings into the *Les fêtes annuellement célébrées à Émoui (Amoy) – étude concernant la religion populaire des Chinois* (The Annually Celebrated Festivals in Amoy [Xiamen] – A Study of the Popular Religion of the Chinese) (Paris, 1886).

De Groot returned to the Netherlands in 1890 and shifted to an academic career. In 1891, he was appointed Chair of Ethnology of the Dutch East Indies at Leiden University. There, he published his six volumes, *The Religious System of China: Its Ancient Forms, Evolution, History and Present Aspect. Manners, Customs and Social Institutions Connected Therewith* (Leiden, 1892–1910), which are considered "monumental" works of the study of Chinese folk religion and Taoism.[39]

After the death of Schlegel, de Groot was appointed to the Chair of the Chinese Language at Leiden in 1904. In 1912, he accepted an appointment at the University of Berlin and became the Chair of Chinese there. Also, in 1912, he published the *Religion in China: Universism – A Key to the Study of Taoism and Confucianism* (New York, 1912), based on his lectures delivered in the US in 1910–1911 for the American Committee for Lectures on the History of Religions. This work was an ambitious attempt to account for all Chinese official and folk religions comprehensively. It was to give "a key to the study of Taoism and Confucianism ... No such key has yet been offered."[40] Maurice Freedman, one of the most authoritative scholars of Chinese religion in the late twentieth century, regarded de Groot as one of the most important "sinological-sociological" contributors to the study of Chinese religion and "the

---

[39] Freedman 1979: 356; Schipper 1995: 473.
[40] de Groot 1912: vi.

first to use the sociological methodology to study Chinese religion in the 20th century."[41]

De Groot's early view on China was represented in his *Les fêtes annuellement célébrées à Émoui* (Paris, 1886). The book mostly described his ethnographic obversions of grassroots religious practices in Xiamen. In its Chapter 4, he raised the level of discussion to the general state of religion in China as compared to Europe. He found in China the spirit of tolerant humanism that Christian Europe lacked and that it should emulate. He asserted that throughout China's long history, the tradition of Confucianism, Taoism, and Buddhism peacefully coexisted, and it was in sharp contrast to the obsessions with dogmas and inter-sectoral strife in the Christian tradition in Europe:

> The morality of Confucianism, Taoism, and Buddhism was good. It was based, in all three cases, on the principle of human self-improvement ... [T]he three sects could only unite, bound together by this sacred principle of love for humanity, which they shared. However, in our civilized West, far from serving as the foundation for all religion and morality, this principle has only recently begun to be recognized and preached by a small group of individuals as the sole rational foundation upon which human life should be based ... [T]he three religious systems of China do not rely on divine revelation – that is, deception. They have not needed the ecclesiastical prestige that religious falsehood depends on; in short, dogmatics are unknown to them. ... Consequently, they have never forged authoritarian religious systems around such books, as has been done with the Bible and the Quran.[42]

Unlike Europe, which had been bounded by a tyrannical and corrupt class of priests, China never let a clergy or church institutions dominate its people throughout its history:

> The clergy in China has never achieved prestige or power. Its influence has never led to the creation of a pariah class

---

[41] Freedman 1979: 355; Schipper 1995: 472.
[42] De Groot 1886: 721; translation by Google and ChatGPT.

or sects akin to the Thugs or Stranglers. It has not maintained Suttee practices or incited the people to undertake fanatical pilgrimages, much less crusades. Any systematic incitement to religious hatred, partisanship, or intolerance has always been foreign to China.... National education in China has not been entrusted to religion but to philosophy. Confucius and Mencius are the two great philosophers whose teachings have shaped the nation.... Based on this, the Chinese should not be considered morally inferior to Europeans.[43]

After all, the superiority of China's morality and politics originated in the belief in human's good nature in Chinese philosophy, which is in sharp contrast with the belief in original sin in Europe. Europe has just started catching up with China's moral superiority:

> The conviction that humans are inherently good, preached for over two thousand years in China and universally accepted in this empire as beyond dispute, seems at last to be gaining adherents in the part of the world where we reside. These adherents are to be found among those who have freed themselves from ecclesiastical dogma. Europeans who still adhere to the concept of original sin and the corruption of human nature rely solely on coercion to compel individuals to practice personal and social virtues. They know only how to threaten with hell and the wrath of higher powers.[44]

Unlike James Legge, who saw China as a superior practitioner of God's morality, De Groot saw China as a model of religious tolerance and secular liberalism for Europe.[45]

De Groot's sympathetic attitude toward China resulted from the influence of Gustaaf Schlegel, de Groot's teacher and predecessor at Leiden. As a founding father of modern Sinology, Schlegel was not only the first professor of Chinese language and literature in Leiden but also the co-founder of *T'oung Pao*, which

---

[43] De Groot 1886: 738; translation by Google and ChatGPT.
[44] De Groot 1886: 717; translation by Google and ChatGPT.
[45] see also Freedman 1979: 357.

has been one of the most authoritative journals of European Sinology since its inauguration in 1890. Schlegel's most important contribution to Sinology is his study of Chinese phonology. His most well-known book, *Sinico-Aryaca, ou, Recherches sur les racines primitives: dans les langues Chinoises et Aryennes* (Sinico-Aryaca, or, Research on Primitive Roots: in Chinese and Aryan Languages) (Batavia, 1872), was a study of Malay, Siamese, languages of Formosa (Taiwan), and Chinese in search of cognates within and between these languages and other Indo–European languages.[46]

Schlegel was a leader of the nineteenth-century philologist movement that proposed all human languages shared one origin. Besides Schlegel, Joseph Edkins (1823–1905) was another leading figure in the movement. In his *China's Place in Philology: an Attempt to Show that the Languages of Europe and Asia have a Common Origin* (London, 1871), Edkins compared words in Chinese, Tibetan, Mongol, Hebrew, and others, with words with similar meanings in Latin, Greek, Sanskrit, and modern Indo–European languages to show their common origin. As we have seen, Schlegel, Edkins, and August Schleicher, another leader in the movement, went further to suggest that world language development constituted two phases: a phase of progressive evolution followed by a phase of degeneration. They argue that European languages were in the declining phase, while the Chinese language was still in its primitive form. Hence, it was superior and still in its progressive evolutionary phase.[47]

This movement in philology was a revival of the seventeenth- and eighteenth-century theory of Primitive Language and Universal Language, which proposed that the Chinese language was either the original human language spoken by Adam or the key to the search for a common human language.[48] As such, it is natural that de Groot, who worked under the influence of Schlegel, would think that Chinese civilization had the same origin as the European civilization, and Europe had a lot to learn from it.

---

[46] Pulleyblank 1995: 344.
[47] Pulleyblank 1995: 343–4.
[48] See Chapter 3.

6 SCIENTIFIC-RACIST SINOLOGY IN THE AGE OF EMPIRE

The turn of the twentieth century was the heyday of European colonialism. Eric Hobsbawm characterized the four decades between the Berlin Congress and World War I (1875–1914) as the "Age of Empire."[1] By this "Age of Empire," all corners of the world had been subjugated under Western empires in one way or another. The term "Imperialism" was first used positively in the 1870s and became a popular vocabulary in the 1890s. The social democrats in Europe advocated solving social problems at home by intensifying the exploitation of the colonies. Rulers of European nations began calling themselves emperors.[2]

Scientific-Racist Turn in Orientalism

In the Age of Empire, white supremacy and racism became the popular ideology of the day. This ideology was first fully articulated by the widely circulated works of Arthur de Gobineau, a French aristocratic author known today as "the Father of Racism." His *Essai sur l'inégalité des races humaines* (Essay on the Inequality of Human Races) (Paris, 1855) was translated into different Western languages and became a sensation across the Atlantic in the late nineteenth century up until World War II. He discussed and propagated the pseudo-science that different human races constituted different

---

[1] Hobsbawn 1989.
[2] Hobsbawn 1989: 56–83.

"sub-species" – "White," "Yellow" (subdivided into Mongols and Malays), "Negroes" and "Redskins" – with different skull sizes and levels of intelligence.[3] While the designation of the "Malays" coincided more or less with today's classification of the Polynesians, the category of the "Mongolian race" was a nineteenth-century invention that lumped together all Chinese, Mongols, Japanese, and Koreans into one single biological-racial category (see Figures 6.1 and 6.2).

Gobineau advocated total segregation between the "Aryan" white race and the "colored races." He saw the "brutish hordes of the yellow race" that were "dominated by the need of the body" as a peril and disease threatening Western civilization.[4] He revived medieval Western fear of the Mongol invasion by warning that an influx of the "yellow" horde would destroy Western civilization, presaging the concept of the "yellow peril."[5]

Within the circle of colonial administrators, colonial discourses underwent a significant transformation in the 1890s. They abandoned the original doctrine of assimilationism, which defined colonialism's goal as enlightening and civilizing non-Western peoples, and started to embrace the doctrine that colonized peoples were mentally and physically inferior and incapable of being civilized. The assumption was that the "dark races" were going to become extinct in the struggle for existence, and imperial exploitation and segregation needed no moral justification.[6]

Under the prevalent racist ideology, academic institutions at the turn of the twentieth century saw the dominance of Darwinian evolutionism. By the 1880s, Darwin's idea of evolution through natural selection, which began as a controversial thesis after the publication of *The Origin of Species* in 1859, had been elevated to become a biological orthodoxy and extended to conceptualize the competition and evolution of races as human sub-species. By contrast, Darwin's ecological idea about life's diversity and complex interdependence was overshadowed. Darwinist terminology conquered most academic disciplines. The Darwinian ideology gave rise to eugenics in

---

[3] Gobineau 1915 [1855]: 106–40; 168–81.
[4] Gobineau 1915 [1855]: 85.
[5] Gobineau 1915 [1855]; See also Blue 1999a: 78–80; Blue 1999b.
[6] Adas 1989: 318–42.

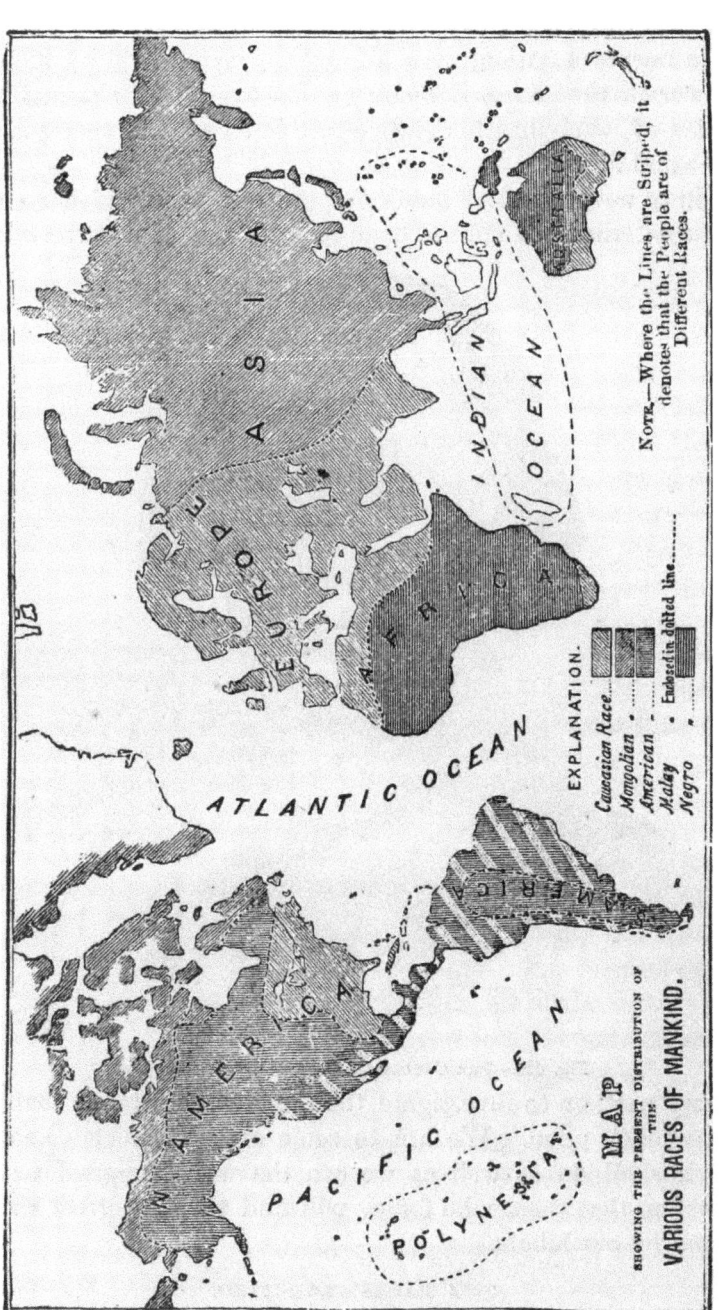

Figure 6.1 Classification and geographical distribution of races, 1894
Source: Well 1894: 380

THE MALAYAN RACE. 385

of which form fig. 484 is an extreme example. Breadth at the base and narrowness at the top distinguish the Mongolian head.

THE MONGOLIAN SKULL.

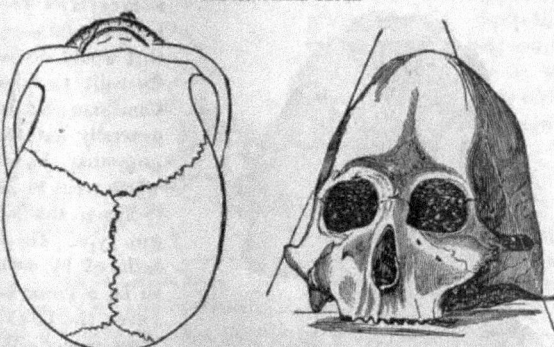

Fig. 483.—VERTICAL VIEW.   Fig. 484.—FRONT VIEW.

Combativeness, Destructiveness, Acquisitiveness, Secretiveness, Cautiousness, and Constructiveness are all generally full or large, while Ideality, Mirthfulness, and Causality are more or less deficient; and we herein see the organic cause of the half-blind but persistent mechanical activity, the tireless, patient industry and the energetic, though instinctive rather than intelligent, pursuit of material ends, which distinguish the race.

Physiognomically, the distinctive traits of the Mongolian are a broad flat face, with the parts imperfectly distinguished; a short, thick, and generally concave nose; small black eyes, the orbits of which rise in an oblique line from the nose to the temple; eyebrows scarcely perceptible; hair coarse, straight, black, and not abundant; beard slight or entirely wanting; and a complexion of tawny olive

III. THE MALAYAN RACE.

This division is generally made to embrace the principal tribes of the Indian Archipelago and all the island of the Pacific, except those which belong to the Ethiopian race. In the form of his cranium, the Malayan shows some of the characteristics of the Caucasian combined with traits which

—17

Figure 6.2 Characteristics and physiognomy of the Mongolian race
Source: Well 1894: 385

6 Scientific-Racist Sinology in the Age of Empire

biology (the word eugenics was first used in 1883), environmental determinism in geography (that climate and geography of a country determined the intelligence and temper of its inhabitants), and Spencerian cultural evolutionism in anthropology and sociology (that human cultures evolved from animism and fetishism to organized monotheistic religions and then modern rationality).[7]

In the hard sciences, racist pseudo-science took hold. In 1894, the prestigious official journal of the Neurological Society of London, *Brain*, published a widely cited article, "Observations on a Chinese Brain." Generalizing from an analysis of less than a dozen samples of Chinese brains, the article concluded that the brain of a Chinese was closer to that of a chimpanzee than a European brain.[8] In the eugenicist literature of the early twentieth century, non-Western peoples were often compared to different kinds of apes. The "dark races" were widely seen as lower kinds of animals.

Besides the great colonial expansion of Europe, the late nineteenth century was also a period when the British world order disintegrated, the Great Depression of 1873–1896 set in, and the inter-imperial rivalry in the West escalated into cutthroat competition.[9] This new geopolitical reality led to the decline of the bourgeois ideals of universal liberalism and rationalism and the rise of ethnonationalism as the reigning ideology of the Great Powers. Under the ethnonationalist ideology, the concept of nation was conflated with the biological concept of race, and the Darwinian tenet of "struggle for existence" was harnessed to justify international aggression.[10] In 1912, German general Friedrich von Bernhardi claimed in his *Germany and the Next War* (which was a bestseller and was translated into several languages) that the survival of the fittest race/nation could only be ensured by the conquest of inferior races and war against rival states. Imperialist policies were regarded as "biological necessities."[11]

These imperialist and ethnonationalist ideologies of the state shaped academic development in the universities. They facilitated the intellectual hegemony of Darwinism by reconfiguring

---

[7] Leaf 1979: 106–39; Driver 1992: 25–7; Hobsbawn 1989: 253; Crook 1994: 6–62.
[8] Bond 1894; Blue 1999a: 81.
[9] Arrighi and Silver 1999: 64–7; 72–9.
[10] Hobsbawn 1989: 101–31, esp. 108; Crook 1994: 63–97.
[11] Romein 1978: 343; Hawkins 1997: 207–9.

state-university relations all over Europe. This was a departure from the early nineteenth century, when the nascent nation-states, still struggling with religious authority and the aristocracy in the name of Reason, allied with the progressive university reformers who espoused the Kantian ideal of universal reason and academic freedom. Without this alliance, the "University Revolution" that enabled the intellectuals to "take control of the immediate conditions of intellectual life" would not have been possible.[12] It was under the resulting atmosphere of academic liberalism that the Romanticist revolt against modernity and the evolutionists in the humanities subjects, including Orientalism, unfolded, as we saw in Chapter 5.

Toward the end of the nineteenth century, the state exalted its willingness and capacity to control university research and teaching, first in post-unification Germany and then in other European countries. Universities were increasingly kept in line with the "national causes" of the states. The cultivation of ethnonational unity replaced the cultivation of free and rational subjects as the animating principle of the university.[13] For example, the German universities, which were internationally recognized as the models of modern research universities through the nineteenth century, were pressured to exclude the *Reichsfeinde* (the "enemies of the Reich," including socialists, progressives, Jews, and other national minorities) during the Bismarckian and Wihelmine periods. The pressure was created through censorship, government funding of research projects, and government control of the hiring or firing of professors.[14] This led to "a progressive shift of professors ... from a stance of independent-minded public leadership to one of acquiescence in the initiatives of the Reich leadership ... [expressing] loyal support of the reigning political notions and ideologies of the Prussian-German state and its domestically conservative, internationally aggressive policies."[15] Consequently, the universities became bastions for advocating hyper-national causes, imperialist expansion, anti-Semitism, and scientific racism.[16] As Max Weber complained

---

[12] Collins 1998: 663; see also Readings 1996: 54–61.
[13] Readings 1996: 61; McClelland 1980: 288–99.
[14] McClelland 1980: 314–21.
[15] McClelland 1980: 314; 319.
[16] McClelland 1980: 319–20.

in 1908: "The 'freedom of science' exists in Germany within the limits of political and ecclesiastical acceptability. Outside these limits, there is none. Perhaps this is inseparably bound up with the dynastic character of our system of government."[17]

In this context of High Imperialism, Romanticism's resistance to evolutionism dissipated, and the Romantic idealization of the East gave way to scientific racism in Orientalist scholarship. Müller's theory of comparative religion was displaced by the evolutionary paradigm, which projected all non-Western religions as primitive, fetishistic, and animistic. Müller abandoned his earlier universalist–humanist stance and shifted to the racist academic discourse. His inaugural speech as the President of the Ninth International Congress of Orientalism (1892) repeatedly invoked Darwin's name. He emphasized that finding the root of the "feeling of strangeness between the East and the West, between the white and dark men, between the Aryan and the Semite" was the fundamental premise of the field.[18] Departing from his earlier theory about the common origins and inherent identity of Eastern and Western civilizations, he now argued that at some point in the pre-historic period, there was a "complete break between East and West," a "break in the triumphant progress of the human race from East to West."[19] This break "determined the course of the principal nations of ancient history as the mountains determine the course of rivers."[20] It followed that,

> [n]o one would in these Darwinian days venture to doubt the homogeneousness of the human species, the brotherhood of the whole human race; but there remains the fact that, as in ancient so in modern times, members of that one human species, brothers of that one human family, look upon each other, not as brothers, but as strangers, if not as enemies, divided not only by language and religion, but also by what people call blood.[21]

The hands of the state's ethnonationalist and imperialist causes in this scientific-racist turn of Orientalist scholarship were evident in

---

[17] Weber 1973 [1908]: 587–8.
[18] Müller 1893: 8.
[19] Müller 1893: 8–9.
[20] Müller 1893: 15–6.
[21] Müller 1893: 8–9.

the inaugural speech. The speech began with a lengthy acknowledgment of royal patrons and governments (including both European and overseas colonial governments) for their protection and support of the Orientalist scholarship.[22] It ended with a frank admission that the ultimate goal of Orientalism was to serve imperial rule:

> England has proved that she knows not only how to conquer, but how to rule. It is simply dazzling to think of the few thousands of Englishmen ruling the millions of human beings in India, in Africa, in America, and in Australasia.... Under the personal patronage of H. R. H. the Prince of Wales, a School of Modern Oriental Studies has at last been established at the Imperial Institute ... [W]e want help, we want much larger funds ... [F]ar higher interests than the commercial supremacy of England are at stake. The young rulers and administrators who are sent every year to the East, ought to be able to keep up much more intimate relations with the people whom they are meant to rule.... [With this intimate relation,] there would have been no Indian Mutiny.[23]

Müller spoke of the great division of humanity into "the fates of the Aryan and Semitic races, as compact confederacies before their separation into various languages and historical nationalities" as the first epic of ancient history in the 1892 speech.[24] Likewise, in his inaugural speech to the Royal Asiatic Society in 1891, he recounted the great separation of the Aryan and Semitic peoples in ancient history and how the Aryans "constituted a Unionist-League embracing the greatest nations of history, and made them all conscious of a new nobility in thought and word and deed, the nobility of the ancient Aryan brotherhood," with their languages and cultures constantly advancing through the principle of "the survival of the fittest."[25] He then went on to argue that China constituted a totally isolated civilization radically different from the Aryans and the Semites. As such, "there are no intellectual bonds that unite us with ancient

[22] Müller 1893: 1–2.
[23] Müller 1893: 35–7.
[24] Müller 1893: 58–9.
[25] Müller 1891: 802.

6 Scientific-Racist Sinology in the Age of Empire

China. We have received nothing from the Chinese. There is no electric contact between the white and the yellow race."[26]

Sinology, as a subfield of Orientalism, inevitably underwent a similar shift from Romanticism to scientific racism. It came to emphasize the irreconcilable difference between Eastern and Western civilizations and the latter's supremacy. Such a shift was manifested in the radical changes in Legge's and de Groot's views on Chinese religions within their careers.

Sinophobic Revival in Sinology
James Legge's Turn against China

Legge's drastic turn of attitude toward Chinese religion was expressed in his "Critical and Exegetical Notes Prolegomena," added to the 1893 edition of *The Texts of Confucius*, as well as in the introduction of *The Texts of Taoism*, published in 1891. It is striking to contrast Legge's later views on Confucianism and Taoism with his earlier views in *The Religions of China*, which were discussed in Chapter 5. In 1893, Legge no longer held the idea that Confucius believed in a monotheistic God. He thought that Confucianism was "unreligious" and "antagonistic to Christianity" and that "when Christianity has prevailed in China, men will refer to it as a striking proof how their fathers by their wisdom know neither God nor themselves."[27] He reconciled with his old opponents – the "Inquirer" with whom he had debated in 1880 – to attack the view that the term *Tian* in the Confucian text referred to a personalized God, "as by his frequent references to Heaven, ... he [Confucius] gave occasion to many of his professed followers to identify God with a principle of reason and the course of nature; so, in the point now in hand, he has led them to deny, like the Sadducees of old, the existence of any spirit at all."[28]

Legge stated that "deceitfulness" and "insincerity" were the inherent ethos of the Chinese as compared with the "benevolence"

---

[26] Müller 1891: 808.
[27] Legge 1893: 55.
[28] Legge 1893: 100.

and "reciprocity" among the Christians.[29] He attributed the Chinese corrupted soul to nothing more than the core teachings of Confucius, particularly his ignorance of God:

> [T]he guilty party must bear his own burden, but we cannot but regret the example of Confucius in this particular. It is with the Chinese and their sage, as it was with the Jews of old and their teachers. He that leads them has caused them to err, and destroyed the way of their paths ... But was not insincerity a natural result of the un-religion of Confucius? There are certain virtues which demand a true piety in order to their flourishing in the heart of man. Natural affection, the feeling of loyalty, and enlightened policy, may do much to build up and preserve a family and a state, but it requires more to maintain the love of truth, and make a lie, spoken or acted, to be shrunk from with shame. It requires in fact the living recognition of a God of truth, and all the sanctions of revealed religion. Unfortunately the Chinese have not had these, and the example of him to whom they bow down as the best and wisest of men, does not set them against dissimulation.[30]

In the eyes of Legge in the 1890s, "Confucius did not think of the reciprocity coming into action" in the relationship between men. On the contrary, Confucius "affirmed the duty of blood-revenge in the strongest and most unrestricted terms" and "[r]evenge is sweet to the Chinese."[31] Having said all that, Legge was comfortable concluding that "China was sure to go to pieces when it came into collision with a Christianity-civilized power. Its sage had left it no preservative or restorative elements against such a case."[32]

His view on Taoism likewise underwent a transition from idealization to contempt. In his 1883 article in the *British Quarterly Review*, Legge showed extensive sympathy for the Taoist texts and tried to prove that Laozi believed in God. But in the introduction of *The Texts of Taoism*, Legge asserted that though the concept of a personal God did occasionally appear in *Daode Jing*, it was not to mean

---

[29] Legge 1893: 101, 109, 110.
[30] Legge 1893: 101.
[31] Legge 1893: 111.
[32] Legge 1893: 108.

a Supreme Being comparable with the God in Christianity. Rather, *Dao*, the course of nature, was placed above God.[33] He pointed out that according to Laozi, the genesis of Heaven and Earth was brought about by evolution, not creation. So, Taoism was atheistic. Legge's most severe accusation of Taoism was that, "[according to Laozi,] the cause of the degeneration of the Tao and of all the evils of the nation was attributed to the ever-growing pursuit of knowledge ... We can laugh at this. Taoism was wrong in its opposition to the increase of knowledge. Man exists under a law of progress."[34]

It is hard to believe that James Legge presented here was the same person who delivered *The Religions of China* lecture and wrote the "Tao Te King" in the *British Quarterly Review*. A radical rupture of Legge's view about China had occurred between 1883 and 1891.

De Groot's Reconstruction of Chinese Superstitions

Like Legge, de Groot's disposition toward China had experienced a drastic change by the end of the nineteenth century. The change was much reflected in his influential later works, in his six volumes *The Religious System of China* (Leiden, 1892–1910), and the *Religion in China: Universism – A Key to the Study of Taoism and Confucianism* (New York, 1912). Though de Groot's work came before the publication of Durkheim's *Elementary Forms of Religious Life*, the comparative approach and general methodology employed in these works placed him into the same movement of sociological and anthropological study of non-Western religions as Durkheim.[35]

The Religious System of China is a study of Taoist rituals and customs. De Groot claimed it was the first attempt to introduce "Science" into studying Chinese religions (the word "Science" with a capital "S" frequently appeared in the very short preface of the first volume):

> The method hitherto so generally pursued of widely grasping about the facts in different nation, has rendered no good service to Science. On the contrary, Science has been led

---

[33] Legge 1959 [1891]: 63
[34] Legge 1959 [1891]: 75
[35] Schipper 1995: 472; Freedman 1979: 355–61. According to Freedman, de Groot's "sociology was entirely Durkheimian." (1979: 361) See Durkheim 1976 [1915].

astray by being thus entangled in a mass of confused information.... The reader will, however, soon become aware that the author has followed the beaten track of Science for the study of Religions and Sociology in general.[36]

In the eyes of de Groot, the Chinese were one of the "semi-civilized peoples."[37] The Chinese were traditionalistic and resistant to change. The outlook of China at present would not be different from that in ancient times, and hence:

> [b]y facts produced from both Chinese literature and actual life it will confirm as well as refute many conclusions arrived at by Western authors in the field of Ethnology, Sociology and the Science of Religion. China may, in fact, be considered a valuable touchstone for many of our theories in these branches of science, this being greatly due to its spirit of conservatism, now proverbial, which scarcely ever allows the nation to drop a custom bequeathed to it by former generations. Many rites and practices still flourish among the Chinese, which one would scarcely expect to find anywhere except amongst savages in a low stage of culture.[38]

Chinese culture was represented as a living fossil. The geographical difference between China and Europe was framed as the temporal difference between modern and primitive societies.

With the presumption that China was homogeneous and unchanged, de Groot felt free to analyze the Chinese religious system by cluttering up the findings from his field works and quotations from ancient texts of different ages.[39] He went further to assert that customs and rituals in China had no spatial variation. As such, what he observed in Amoy applied well in other places in China. Chinese culture was simplified as a uniform whole with temporal and spatial homogeneity.

The Religion in China was more ambitious. In the book, de Groot attempted to outline the totality of Chinese civilization and to identify its essence. Contemporary students of Chinese religions

[36] de Groot 1969 [1892]: ix, xi–xii.
[37] de Groot 1969 [1892]: x–xi.
[38] de Groot 1969 [1892]: xi.
[39] de Groot 1969 [1892]: x.

regarded the book as based on speculations and distortions.[40] However, the views presented in it were seen as being one of the most authoritative in his days.

At the outset, de Groot asserted that the three religions of China – Confucianism, Taoism, and Buddhism – were all the same:

> [T]he three religions are the three branches, growing from a common stem, which has existed from pre-historic times; this stem is the religion of the Universe, its parts and phenomena. This Universism, as I will henceforth call it, is the *one* religion of China. As these three religions are its three integrate parts, every Chinese can feel himself equally at home in each, without being offended or shocked by conflicting and mutually exclusive dogmatic principles.[41]

Buddhism is left beside among the three as it "being merely the engrafted branch."[42] Between Taoism and Confucianism, the former is more fundamental, as "Universism was Taoism; the two terms are synonymous."[43] He goes on to say:

> We may thus equally well call Confucianism Classicism, Universism, Taoism. It alone is orthodox, since there is only one Tao in the Universe, and one set of Classics to maintain it among men. Confucianism has reigned supreme in China to this hour. Thus it is that the whole Chinese system of education by classical study virtually stand on the broad of Taoist basis, as does the state machinery in general.[44]

Noticing Confucius was a younger contemporary of Laozi, de Groot also claimed that Confucius "was a good Taoist."[45] These assertions lacked empirical support and careful explanation, but they justified the author's approach of describing the full picture of the Chinese religion using the Taoist texts and the folk religious practices presumed to be rooted in Taoism.

---

[40] Schipper 1995; Freedman 1979.
[41] de Groot 1912: 3.
[42] de Groot 1912: 3.
[43] de Groot 1912: 3.
[44] de Groot 1912: 92.
[45] de Groot 1912: 92.

According to de Groot, the Chinese worshiped the animated Universe as a mystical force. They also worshiped all spirits, gods, and ghosts in this Universe. Taoism worshiped spirits in rocks, hills, rivers, and so on. Confucianism worshiped dead men and their ghosts. These make China "the principal idolatrous and fetish-worshiping country in the world."[46]

De Groot agreed with Legge that Taoism "suppress[es] knowledge and wisdom."[47] We can also find fresh images of China that are not seen in Legge's works. De Groot attributed the Chinese supposed resistance to change and traditionalism to the Taoist belief that there were spirits all over people's environment, and change would disturb them and make them angry. De Groot also mentioned that most Chinese indulged in finding mystical methods to prolong their lives. Therefore,

> [t]he conclusion to be drawn from the history of the development of the Taoist religion is that, in spite of its sublime Universistic principle, it has not been able to rise above idolatry, polytheism, polydemonism, and anthropotheism, but has, on the contrary, systemically developed all these branches of the great tree of Asiatic paganism. The same judgment must be pronounced with respect to the branch of Universism which we call Confucianism.[48]

Most remarkably, de Groot explicitly denounced his earlier sympathetic view on Chinese religions, expressed in *Les fetes annuellement celebrees a Emoui*, discussed in Chapter 5, as erroneous. In *Sectarianism and Religious Persecution in China*, published in 1903, he declared that:

> [W]e approach a great deal near the truth by admitting the Chinese State to be the most intolerant, the most persecuting of all earthy governments; a State which, on account of certain ancient dogmatic principles in the system of political philosophy whereon it is based, could not consistently do otherwise than brandish fire and sword in the face of

---

[46] de Groot 1912: 188.
[47] de Groot 1912: 65–6.
[48] de Groot 1912: 189.

every religious community or sect which, since the days of Confucius, has ventured to make its appearance in China; a State, in fact, which always follows this political line of action with the most scrupulous exactitude, and must a fortiori be hostile to Christianity and the despised "foreign devils" who introduced it.

For many years I also held the comfortable universal belief in China's religious liberty. I even expressed this belief in one of my earlier writings; the few lines written under the influence of that conviction I now openly withdraw. Since then, I have learned to know better, and I hope, through the medium of this book, to succeed in convincing of error my fellow labourers in the field of Sinology, who as yet believe in that religious liberty.[49]

The Zeitgeist of High Imperialism

The shift of Legge's and de Groot's views on China was strikingly coincidental. Some might explain Legge's change by his career change. Before 1876, Legge was a missionary rather than a scholar. Some would argue that missionaries were always less racist and more sympathetic to non-Western cultures than university professors. Missionaries were more remote from the university institutions, which were the major loci of reproducing the discourse of modernity. Second, their assigned duty of converting the native people made them incapable of abandoning the idea that all non-European peoples believed in God and had the potential to be good Christians who could attain the level of civilization of Europe.[50]

Some might also explain the case of de Groot's shift by his career shift, for he had not shifted to an academic career and remained a colonial official until 1890.[51] His view changed between 1886, when *Les fetes* was published, and 1891, when *The Religious System of China* was published. Maurice Freedman attributed this change to his "switch to an academic career," as "his manner of

---

[49] de Groot 1903: 3.
[50] Adas 1989: 330–1.
[51] Freedman 1979: 358.

presenting China after his appointment to Leiden reflected the anthropology of the day."[52] The terms "animism" and "fetishism" he used to describe Chinese religions were borrowed from the nineteenth-century anthropological study of primitive tribes. However, the career change could not fully explain his change. De Groot's earlier study of China was closely associated with the dominant philological movement in Orientalist scholarship of the time. He was trained in Leiden as a student of Gustaaf Schlegel in the mid nineteenth century. Likewise, James Legge was not isolated from the world of academic Orientalism before he taught at Oxford. He was working under the encouragement and influence of Max Müller at the very beginning. We have seen in Chapter 5 that Legge's earlier idealizing view that Confucius and Taoist texts carried the belief in a monotheistic God was resisted by his fellow missionaries but supported by most Orientalist scholars, most notably Müller. Therefore, the radical shift in their view can hardly be explained by their career shift to academia.

There must be another common factor that contributed to the coincidental change of the attitudes of Legge and de Groot, who did not know each other personally and taught in different nations in 1883–1891 and 1886–1891, respectively. The answer lies in the rise of scientific-racism and the decline of Romanticism in the academic world during the 1890s. Norman Girardot, an authority on Legge's life and work, did attribute the change in Legge's view to the "public criticism engendered by the new science of religion," which called for "a 'more scholarlike spirit' that did not bow to either the unfounded fears or foolish enthusiasms of the non-academic public over 'Oriental Wisdom'" by the end of the nineteenth century.[53]

Legge's and de Groot's shift in their view on China was part of a larger shift in the disposition of academic Orientalism amid the rising domination of Darwinian evolutionism at the turn of the twentieth century when imperialism and inter-imperial rivalry reached their zeniths. As Girardot notes:

> [There] is the passage from a kind of late, idealistically inclined, nineteenth-century "integral humanism" or

[52] Freedman 1979: 357.
[53] Girardot 1992, 2002.

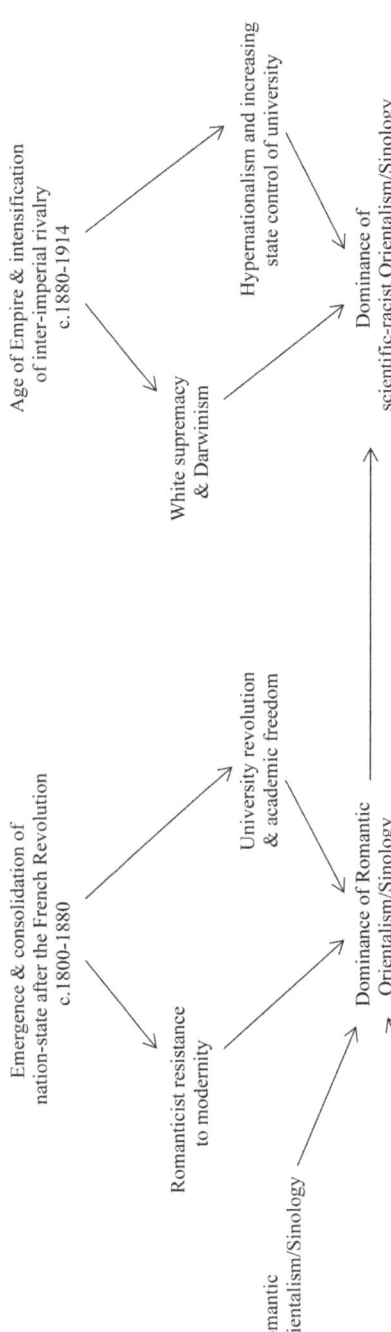

Figure 6.3 Dynamics of changing Orientalism/Sinology in the nineteenth century

"hermeneutics of trust" (exemplified by the innate historical and literary piety of Legge's Sinology and Müller's science of religion) to a more highly specialized, rationalistic, and secularly academic "hermeneutics of suspicion" concerning the integrity of ancient history, text, and authors. Legge is especially interesting because he represents the cusp of this kind of transitional process both with regard to the Western academic study of China and of religion. In many ways this issue comes down to the difference between those holding onto the "enormous antiquity," "purity," "sacredness," or "authenticity" of Oriental texts versus a "higher" critical attitude that demolishes "ancient authority," "sacred books," and "religion" into so many disparate historical and philological fragments.[54]

The dynamics linking the political shift during the age of High Imperialism in Europe and intellectual changes in universities in general and in the field of Sinology in particular are summarized in Figure 6.3.

As we shall see in Chapter 7, Legge and de Groot, as the most authoritative scholars on the Chinese civilization, had their later scientific-racist works cited extensively in Max Weber's *The Religion of China* as a key building block of his vast comparative sociology of religion project. Weber also relied on scientific-racist Orientalist works on other world religions. As such, scientific-racist Orientalist scholarship at the age of High Imperialism became the foundation of Weber's theory about the relationship between cultural characteristics and capitalist development. Such theory gave rise to the postwar modernization school that generated huge academic and policy consequences, as we are turning to in Chapter 7.

[54] Girardot 1992: 190.

Part IV
COLD WAR AREA STUDIES

7 FROM SINOLOGY TO CHINA STUDIES

The early twentieth century saw the rise of social theories that sought to apply systematic, scientific methods to explain social development. One key theme of these social theories was explaining how and why capitalist modernity emerged in the West. This exercise inevitably involved explaining why capitalism did not emerge in the East, particularly in China, which had been widely seen as more economically advanced than Europe before the nineteenth century.

Orientalism and Max Weber

Max Weber is one of the most influential social scientists who pioneered this cross-civilizational comparison and explanation of European capitalist development. He explained the rise of capitalism in Western Europe in terms of the particular doctrines of Occidental religion – Christianity in general, and Calvinism as a Protestant sect in particular – in his *Die protestantische Ethik und der Geist des Kapitalismus* (Protestant Ethic and the Spirit of Capitalism) (Tübingen, 1904/1905).[1] After publishing the *Protestant Ethic*, he moved on to study Eastern religions and exposited why they failed to foment capitalist development. The first Eastern civilization Weber engaged with seriously was China. A decade after he published the *Protestant Ethic*, he published *Konfuzianismus*

[1] Weber 1992 [1905].

und Taoismus (Confucianism and Taoism, later as *The Religion of China*) (Tübingen, 1915/1920),[2] followed by *Hinduismus und Buddhismus* (Hinduism and Buddhism, later as *The Religion of India*) (Tübingen, 1916/1921).[3] As we shall see later, Weber saw the Chinese religion as representative of the general "Asiatic religion" that was irrational, polytheistic, animistic, and magic-based, hindering capitalist growth.

According to Weber, certain areas of Western Europe experienced capitalist breakthroughs because of the dominance of Calvinism, a culture with an affinity for rationalism and the capitalist spirit of accumulation. Without a religion favorable to rationalism and the capitalist spirit, China and other non-Western societies were seen as incapable of developing capitalist modernity from within. Weber laid the foundation for later sociological theories and development models focusing on cultural forces. For example, the modernization theory that dominated postwar social sciences in the US explained success and failure in modernization in terms of the presence or absence of certain cultural traits, such as "achievement motivation" and "work ethic." At the height of the Cold War, this theory dominated Washington's foreign policy approach to promoting development and fighting communism in the developing world.[4]

By today's standard, Weber's analysis of Asian religions – particularly Chinese – is feeble. It is obvious that Weber's generalization of all Chinese cultures into Confucianism and, more fundamentally, Taoism is problematic. Western academia has learned of the many variations and factions of orthodox and heterodox ideologies in different times and parts of China.[5] Suppressing all these variations and portraying the Chinese culture as a homogeneous, timeless whole, in contrast to the nuanced treatment of the many changes and sects within Christianity, manifests fundamental methodological flaws. His argument about the unity between Confucianism and Taoism and the subordination of Confucianism to Taoism is ludicrous in light of today's knowledge about Chinese religions.

---

[2] Weber 1951 [1915].
[3] Weber 1958 [1916].
[4] See Gilman 2003; Lantham 2000.
[5] Ter Haar 2017; Ownby 1999; Wakeman 1998; Yang 1997; Yü 2021 [1986].

In earlier times, Weber's theory would not have seemed convincing to European intellectuals, either. As we saw in Chapters 2, 3, and 5, from the seventeenth-century Jesuits to the eighteenth-century Sinophilic philosophers and the mid nineteenth-century Romantic Orientalists, Asian cultures, especially Chinese culture, was thought to be superior, or at least not inferior, to the Western one. There had not been a consensus recognizing Taoism as China's representative, coherent, and root religion until the late nineteenth century, as described in Chapter 6. More importantly, the Chinese cultural system had often been conceptualized as rationalist and monotheistic, sharing basic values with Christianity before the late nineteenth century, in opposition to Weber's assertion that it was animistic, polytheistic, and magic-prone.

The question is why Weber could formulate his comparative study of China and Europe by resorting to one particular portrayal and reification of the religion in China and elsewhere without hesitation and why he succeeded in convincing his contemporaries and in establishing his works as the authority for his times and for the decades to come. The answer lies in the late nineteenth-century consensus in the field of Orientalism that we examined in Chapter 6. Weber's comparison and theory were built upon many assumptions and the selective, distorted knowledge in the field that was regarded as authoritative in his time.

Weber's Theory of Religion and Capitalism

Influenced by the idealist tradition of German philosophy, Weber explained the rise of capitalist modernity in the West in terms of a specific value system of Europe, that is, Calvinism, which was outlined in his *The Protestant Ethic and The Spirit of Capitalism*. He contended that capitalism hinged on the spirit of reinvesting business profit rather than consuming it, making money for the sake of accumulating more money.[6]

Weber argued that such spirit was not unique in the West and modern times and could be seen in many ages and cultures. But in nearly all instances, such a spirit was seriously stifled by the

---

[6] Weber 1992 [1905]: 50.

dominant culture that saw such compulsion to accumulate for the sake of accumulating as irrational:

> In fact, the *summum bonum* of this ethic, the earning of more and more money, combined with the strict avoidance of all spontaneous enjoyment of life ... is thought of so purely as an end in itself, that from the point of view of the happiness of, or utility to, the single individual, it appears entirely transcendental and absolutely irrational. Man is dominated by the making of money, by acquisition as the ultimate purpose of his life. Economic acquisition is no longer subordinated to man as the means for the satisfaction of his material needs. This reversal of what we should call the natural relationship, so irrational from a naive point of view, is evidently as definitely a leading principle of capitalism as it is foreign to all peoples not under capitalistic influence.[7]

To Weber, what was unique to modern Europe was that this capitalist spirit managed to break free from the straitjacket of hostile orthodox ideologies to establish a whole new system of capitalist economy. Weber asserted that such a capitalist breakthrough was first made possible in certain parts of Europe where Calvinism prevailed – England, Holland, and Germany.

Many aspects of the Calvinist doctrines favored the growth of the capitalist spirit. Calvinists believed that everybody's chance of having salvation was predestined by God arbitrarily. This belief led to anxiety among Calvinists and urged them to find ways to get a glimpse of God's providence. They believed the way to know whether God's grace was bestowed upon them was to engage in a secular vocation and see if it was successful or not. The world was full of irrationalities, so the children of God should regard themselves as God's tool to transform the world rationally through their vocations. Success in one's vocation meant God's grace had been shed on them.

As the Calvinists thought it necessary to act against one's sin and saw their business as a means to reveal their own chance of salvation rather than to gain material benefits, they would go into an ascetic way of life. As such, the Calvinist businessmen rarely consumed their

---

[7] Weber 1992 [1905]: 53.

profits but accumulated and re-invested them into their business. As they thought it was their responsibility to act against the world's irrationality to please God, they were hostile to magic. They developed a rational way of thinking and actions in place of divination and spells to achieve their goals. This led to a disenchantment of the world. Under the prevalence of such religious ethos, the capitalist spirit of accumulating for the sake of accumulating via rational businesses became the dominant mode of economic activity.

Sources of *The Religion of China*

Weber's *The Religion of China: Confucianism and Taoism* was to discern why the capitalist spirit failed to take hold in China, which was perceived to be the most advanced economy outside of Europe in the early modern world. The book started with a discussion of China's monetary system to show how an elaborate bimetallic monetary order, based on locally minted copper and imported American silver, mediated its advanced market economy. Weber then delved into the political and economic institutions of the Chinese empire. He showed that China possessed both favorable conditions to capitalism, such as the non-existence of feudal estates, and unfavorable conditions, such as the non-existence of autonomous mercantile cities and the dominance of administrative cities. As such, one could not explain capitalism's lack of spontaneous rise in China by looking at institutional factors alone. One has to look beyond political and economic forces and explain the failure of capitalist breakthroughs in China through a cultural or religious approach.[8]

Weber asserted that Confucianism and Taoism constituted a unitary religious tradition, with Taoism representing the more fundamental principles. Hence, Weber spoke of "The Religion" of China in the singular. Taoism as a coherent, unified tradition was a Sinological construction in the nineteenth century.[9] The privileged role of Taoism as the fundamental religion of Chinese civilization was established at the turn of the twentieth century by a generation of scientific-racist Sinologists like de Groot. Here, Weber simply adopted the dominant view of his day, a view that was fiercely

---
[8] Weber 1951 [1915]: 248–9.
[9] See Chapter 5.

disputed before and after his own time. Weber also adopted the popular position since the sixteenth-century Jesuits that Buddhism was an imported religion from India and was alien to Chinese civilization. Therefore, Weber's discussion of Buddhism was placed under his *Religion of India*, together with the exposition of Hinduism, instead of in his *Religion of China*.

Weber investigated the Chinese religious system under the presupposition that the ancients laid it down and that it never changed. This assumption enabled him to freely shift between ancient Classics, writings from different Chinese dynasties, and contemporary observations of Chinese behaviors for evidence supporting his argument.

Weber insisted that neither Taoism nor Confucianism had a concept of a monotheistic God. They both worshiped *Tao*, which meant the natural course of the universe. Hence, in contrast with Calvinism, they had neither the concept of predestination nor the concept of God's grace. On the contrary, they were "universists" and advocated that men should behave according to the world's and society's natural order. It diverged from Calvinism's belief that the world was full of irrationality and that men should act against this irrational world and fight magic with rationality as a way to please God.

To Weber, Taoism was a promoter of magic, while Confucianism had never suppressed it. In fact, most Confucian literati and emperors practiced magic – like sorcery and divination – themselves. So, the two religions could not bring forth a rationalization and disenchantment of worldview and ways of life that Calvinism did. Neither Taoism nor Confucianism had the idea of life after death. Therefore, they could not develop the idea of salvation as the Christians had. This made the Chinese focus only on their present life and eager to find ways, most of the time through magic, to enhance their earthy fortunes and prolong their earthy life.

Weber reckoned that China did not lack businessmen operating in the market economy, but their subsumption to Taoist magic impeded their growth into rational entrepreneurs with ever-growing capital:

> The Chinese petty and middle class business man, as well as the big business man who adhered to the old tradition, ascribed success and failure, like the Puritan, to divine powers. The Chinese, however, ascribed them to the Taoistic

god of wealth. For him success and failure in business were not symptomatic of a state of grace but of magically and ceremonially significant merit or offense, and compensation was sought in terms of ritually "good" words. The Chinese lacked the central, religiously determined, and rational method of life which came from within and which was characteristic of the classical Puritan. For the latter, economic success was not an ultimate goal or end in itself but a means of proving one's self.[10]

In his view, both Taoism and Confucianism were "traditionalist" and "conservative." This made the Chinese resist change and innovation. The Confucian virtue of piety made the Chinese only know about following what their ancestors said. Taoists believed that there were spirits all over the world, and they thought that innovation would provoke these spirits. Worse, Taoism was antagonistic to the accumulation of knowledge and wisdom, as Lao Zi taught that an increase in knowledge would make people deviate from the *Tao*. Such conservatism did not exist in Calvinism.

Also, Taoism and Confucianism did not have the concept of "the brotherhood" of men as Protestantism did. Protestants supposed that all men were sons of God, so men must love each other. However, Confucianism and Taoism only stressed the familial relationship as the world's natural order and that men had to be loyal to the family and the emperor instead of just any fellow man in society. Outside the family, the Chinese were supposedly selfish, distrustful, and hypocritical. This hindered the functioning of the business world, as it required reciprocity and trust between men.

The contrast between rationality and magic constituted the most fundamental difference between Protestant Puritanism and Confucianism/Taoism. Weber concluded that:

> [W]hile Confucianism left untouched the significance of magic for redemption, Puritanism came to consider all magic as devilish. Only ethical rationalism was defined as religiously valuable.... Finally, from our presentation it should be perfectly clear that in the magic garden of

[10] Weber 1951 [1915]: 243.

heterodox doctrine (Taoism) a rational economy and technology of modern occidental character was simply out of the question. For all natural scientific knowledge was lacking, partly as a cause and partly as an effect of these elemental forces: the power of chronomancers, geomancers, hydromancers, meteromancers; and a crude, abstruse, universist conception of the unity of the world.[11]

The perspective and terminology Weber employed to describe Confucianism and Taoism were identical to those from the scientific-racist Sinology at the turn of the twentieth century that we discussed in Chapter 6. Looking at Weber's sources on Chinese religion, it is not surprising to find that he relied exclusively on turn-of-the-twentieth-century Sinological works, with James Legge and de Groot as the most extensively cited ones.

In the first footnote of Chapter 1, the major sources for the book were listed and described in detail. At the end of it, Weber writes, "Only a small portion of the documentary sources and inscriptions have been translated and that is a great handicap for the non-Sinologist. Unfortunately, I did not have an expert Sinologist to cooperate on the text or check it. For that reason the volume is published with misgivings and with the greatest reservation."[12]

Among the Sinological sources, James Legge (1815–1897) and de Groot (1854–1921) were the two he referred to most frequently. James Legge was the first author Weber mentioned in the first footnote of the book:

> The great central works of classical Chinese literature will not be cited separately when reference is made to a passage. They have been translated and edited with textual criticism by J. Legge in the series *Chinese Classics*. Some of them have been incorporated in Max Mueller's *Sacred Books of the East*.[13]

Also,

> At present [in 1920] de Groot's great work on the official religion is outstanding. Cf. his main work, *The Religious*

[11] Weber 1951 [1915]: 227.
[12] Weber 1951 [1915]: 252.
[13] Weber 1951 [1915]: 250.

System of China (dealing thus far mainly with ritual, especially with the rites of death). De Groot gives a comprehensive survey of the religious systems of China in *Kultur der Gegenwart*. For the tolerance of Confucianism, see his spirited polemical treatise "Sectarianism and Religious Persecution in China" ... For the history of religious affairs see his essay in vol. VII of the *Archiv fuer Religionswissenschaft* (1904).[14]

The chapter "Orthodoxy and Heterodoxy" dealt mainly with Taoism and a little bit of Buddhism, and de Groot was quoted extensively. When introducing the sources for Taoism in the chapter's first footnote, Weber wrote, "Concerning Taoism, consult de Harlez, and Legge for sources. In general, see the excellent posthumous work of W.Grube, *Religion und Kultur der Chinesen* and especially de Groot's *Universismus Die Grundlagen der Religion und Ethik, des Staatswesens und der Wissenschaft Chinas* (Berlin, 1918)."[15]

In the rest of the chapter, de Groot appeared in over half of all footnotes. With his heavy reliance on James Legge and de Groot's later works as authoritative sources on China, it is not surprising that Weber's view on China was little more than a replication of the turn-of-twentieth-century scientific-racist Sinological view of China.

After *The Religion of China*, Weber worked on *The Religion of India*, covering Hinduism and Buddhism. His analysis of Confucianism and Taoism became a template. What applied to Taoism also applied to Hinduism and Buddhism, according to Weber. At the end of the book, he concluded by generalizing a thesis on the "General Character of Asiatic Religion." China was at the center of such generalization, as Weber asserted that "[f]or Asia as a whole China played somewhat the role of France in the modern Occident. All cosmopolitan 'polish' stems from China to Tibet to Japan and outlying Indian territories."[16] Therefore,

> This most highly anti-rational world of universal magic also affected everyday economics. There is no way from it

---

[14] Weber 1951 [1915]: 251.
[15] Weber 1951 [1915]: 290.
[16] Weber 1958 [1916]: 329.

to rational, inner-worldly life conduct.... All this [spells for different purposes] was either in the gross form of compulsive magic or in the refined form of persuading a functional god or demon through gifts. With such means the great mass of the aliterary and even the literary Asiatics sought to master everyday life.[17]

Though the specific and distorted views on Chinese religions in the scientific-racist Orientalist enterprise at the height of imperialism dissipated with the collapse of Nazi eugenics and the disintegration of European empires in the postwar era, their influences lived on via Weber's cultural theory of capitalist development, a theory that those views inspired and informed. Weber's theory was elevated to become a universal scientific theory, presumably transcending its sources and becoming the foundation of US Area Studies and US policy of development promotion in the decolonizing and developing world after World War II.

Modernization Theory and Cold War China Studies

After the traumas of fascism and the two World Wars, Social Darwinism and scientific-racism ceased to be the mainstream of Europe's academic world. The pre-1890 Romanticist tone revived in European Sinology. Admiration of Chinese antiquity once again became the ethos of the Sinologists. The Romanticist underpinnings of the discipline – that studying the Orient was essential for complementing problematic Western modernity and that the study was a responsibility of Western scholars for the world's sake – reappeared. This description of the field by Dutch Sinologist Kristofer Marinus Schipper, a leading scholar of Chinese religions in Europe, is common:

> Why should we study China? You can use botany as an analogy. Each culture is like a specie of plant; it has strong points and weak points different from the others. The same kind of plant will weaken after a while if it's not cross-fertilized to improve the next generation. The botanists of

[17] Weber 1958 [1916]: 336.

the world keep a gene bank to preserve seeds that may or may not be needed now, because you never know what problems may come up with varieties that are flourishing now, and they might be needed later. But the first step of cross-fertilization is to preserve a "pure variety" with its own characteristics. So the study of traditional Chinese culture, in the long view, is really good of world culture. ... Our consensus is: Chinese culture is too serious to be left to the Chinese alone.[18]

Meanwhile, the disintegration of European empires dried up the financial resources of the Orientalist departments in the universities. The demise of European Orientalism was marked by the postwar dissolution of the International Congress of Orientalists, the organization I discuss in Chapters 5 and 6. Opinions of disbanding the Congresses, as they "no longer serve a useful purpose" under the new geopolitical situation, first emerged among the participants of the Twenty-first Congress in Paris in 1948.[19] In 1973, in the celebration of the 100-year anniversary of the Congress, a resolution was made to bring the Congress to an end. *The Project of Reform of the International Congresses of Orientalist* criticized the "europocentric aspects of studies of Asia, as practiced in the occident in recent generations." The proposal also rejected the "prejudices holding that peoples of Asia were not competent to carry out studies of Asia." As more and more Asians became active in the research on Asian societies, it was an "absurdity" to label the students of Asian civilization as "Orientalists."[20]

The rise of Area Studies in postwar America corresponded to the decline of European Orientalism. US postwar Area Studies, like most social science and humanities subjects in the US at the time, were dominated by Talcott Parsons' theory of structural functionalism and modernization. To Parsons, all social systems were constituted by particular institutions and relationships, as well as values and norms that complement each other's functions, like organs in an organism. As the translator of the first English edition

---

[18] Interview with Kristofer Schipper, Li 1991: 121.
[19] Société Asiatique de Paris 1949: 37.
[20] Filliozat 1975: 57.

of Weber's *Protestant Ethic and the Spirit of Capitalism* (1930), Parson emphasized the imperative of cultural values in hindering or fomenting modernization. Traditional cultures in non-Western countries were always grounded on collectivism, particularism, irrationality, and ascribed status that impeded capitalist economic growth. The key cultural underpinnings of capitalist modernization were individualism, universalism, rationality, and achieved status that had evolved in Europe since the Reformation.[21]

To modernization theorists at the height of the Cold War, the task of Area Studies was to understand non-Western cultures and devise ways to guide cultural changes there to foment new cultural norms compatible with capitalist modernization – yet not so drastic and radical as to create anomie and unrest. Societies that failed to modernize organically would be vulnerable to communism, which was portrayed as a pathological growth path. Such a modernization project was well illustrated in *Harvest*, the widely circulated Chinese-language farmer periodical in Cold War Taiwan. The magazine was founded and funded by the US State Department in the 1950s. It sought to promote modern culture among the peasants by attacking traditional local customs, as shown in Figure 7.1.

The hegemony of the Parsonian modernization theory, hand in hand with the thirst for practical knowledge of different geographical areas given by the practical need to fight communist influences, shaped the formation of US Area Studies. Institutionally, Area Studies were embedded in professional associations (such as the Association for Asian Studies, founded in 1941 and publishing the journal *The Far Eastern Quarterly*, which later became *The Journal of Asian Studies*) and university programs financed by big corporations and government funding. Intelligence agencies also maintained front organizations offering research grants or fellowships to fund academic research in different geographical areas. The Asia Foundation and the National Student Association are two examples.[22] Such organizations have financed the early research of many well-known scholars.[23] The Area Studies establishment

---

[21] See Parsons 1991 [1951], 1971.
[22] Holmes 2020:8–9, 16; Price 2016:165–94; Price 2024.
[23] Holmes 2020; White 2014.

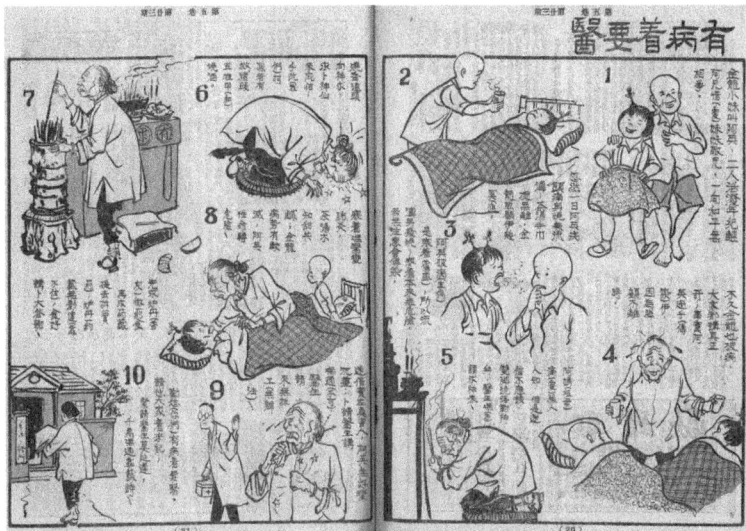

Figure 7.1 Promoting modernization and attacking local traditions in Cold War Taiwan.
Harvest is a widely circulated farmer magazine in Taiwan financed by US development aid and founded in 1951 by the USIS Field Director in the Republic of China, Robert Sheeks, a student of Fairbank. With Taiwan as a bulwark against communism in Asia, the US-funded magazine was a key vehicle promoting cultural changes assumed to be preconditions of modernization. Besides practical knowledge of new agricultural technologies, lifestyle advice, recipes, and light literature, the magazine also featured many contents attacking local customs as irrational superstitions. This cartoon, published in 1955, was about a grandmother resorting to Taoist magic instead of a doctor's visit when her grandchildren got a common cold. The cold deteriorated and caused their lives. The magazine issues in the 1970s and after, nevertheless, manifested a localization turn with a more celebratory tone on local customs, religious or otherwise.
Source: *Harvest* 1955: 20–21 (with permission of Harvest Publishing Group)

developed under the support and influence of what Bruce Cumings called the "state/intelligence/foundation nexus."[24]

The trajectory of the founding of US Area Studies was well outlined by Norman Brown, a founder of South Asian Studies

---

[24] Cumings 1998.

in the US and the president of the Association for Asian Studies in 1960:

> In the United States it seemed obvious that to win the [second world] war and the peace afterwards it was necessary to have the cooperation of the Oriental peoples, and the many wartime agencies began to recruit personnel acquainted with the Oriental world, its varying political structures and changing social institutions, its aspirations, its present economic capability and latent potentiality, the peoples' behavior pattern, their modern languages...
>
> To many persons in the United States during the war years and the years following it was evident that there was a need for the national education system to expand so as to include study of the modern Orient. The great philanthropic foundations took the lead, first the Carnegie Corporation of New York, then the Rockefeller Foundation, and a few years later the Ford Foundation when it was established. The immediate need which the foundations saw was to cultivate oriental studies in the social sciences fields – economics, politics and government, international relations, the behavioral sciences.... The United States Congress also in time came to see the importance of such studies and enacted legislation to support them.[25]

What was said about World War II equally applied to the Cold War.

Postwar US Sinology, as a part of Area Studies, was known as China Studies. The field was constructed under the leadership of John King Fairbank, who founded the "Harvard School" and put the field under the domination of his "impact-response" model.[26] Informed by the modernization theory, the model's basic claim was that the Chinese traditional culture impeded modernization in East Asia, and the region's modernization could only be a response to an external stimulus that dismantled the straitjacket of Chinese traditional culture and institutions. The impact from outside was the only hope of progress, if any.

---

[25] Brown 1971: 32.
[26] For an example, see Fairbank 1953; Fairbank et al. 1965.

The relationship between modernization theory and China Studies was not one-way. China Studies, as constructed by Fairbank and reflected in his masterpiece, *Trade and Diplomacy on the China Coast* (Cambridge, MA, 1953),[27] contributed to the general modernization theory by providing an implicit example of modernizing transformation without colonial violence.[28] In the nineteenth and early twentieth centuries, China's treaty ports, especially Shanghai, were presented as utopian communities representing the promise of a modernized China. The fact that China was never formally colonized lets Fairbank depict the modernization process as peaceful, natural, and harmonious. This made China not just one of the ordinary examples of modernization theory. Instead,

> the "China" of structural-functionalism is the instantiating trope for the theory generally. Without their version of "China," structuralism and modernization theory would have lacked proof of their claim that cultural transformation could occur "naturally" without revolution, and that would certainly have robbed social science theory of its potential to counter the powerful Marxisms of Lenin, Stalin, and Mao.[29]

In the 1940s and 1950s, US–China Studies also saw works that were less tied to the modernization school. Owen Lattimore's works, which examined how Chinese civilization evolved and was shaped constantly by its interaction with Central Asian nomadic peoples at the frontier, constituted a competing paradigm that avoided the Eurocentrism of the Fairbankian impact-response model, which assumed China's stagnation before Western imperialism injected the seeds for change.[30] But this alternative paradigm was eclipsed by the impact-response model after Lattimore was questioned and then sidelined under McCarthyism with allegations that he was a Soviet sympathizer or even a Soviet spy.[31]

---

[27] Fairbank 1953.
[28] Barlow 1997; see also Esherick 1972; Farquhar and Hevia 1993: 486–94.
[29] Barlow 1997: 393–4; cf. Lele 1993.
[30] Lattimore 1940, 1950.
[31] see Rowe 2007; Newman 1992.

Postwar China Studies, like many other US Area Studies, was located mostly in social sciences, predominantly in the study of politics, sociology, economics, and social psychology, focusing on China's modernization dynamics. It was in contrast with the humanities identity of postwar European Sinology that focused on the "timeless" canons of "pure" Chinese culture, just as the Romantic Sinology in early to mid nineteenth-century Europe. The "impact-response" model and the modernization theory were not totally alien to European tradition. They could be regarded as a continuation of the turn-of-twentieth-century scientific-racist Orientalism in Europe, with the Weberian social theory as a bridge. The temporal discontinuity between Romantic Sinology and scientific-racist Sinology in nineteenth and early twentieth-century Europe was, therefore, translated into a transatlantic cleavage between European Sinology and US–China Studies in the second half of the twentieth century. In 1991, the then-president of the European Association for Chinese Studies, Erik Zürcher, remarked, "[T]he new emerging forces [US China Studies] (often trained in political science and economics rather than brought up with the Four Books) accusing traditional Sinologists [in Europe] of being petrified and antiquarian, and Sinologists branding the contemporary China experts as superficial and politicized."[32]

The tension between European Sinology and US–China Studies also created pressure for European Sinologists to stay relevant under the hegemony of US academia by catching up with the social sciences. The social scientific approach to the study of China and the attention to contemporary China was spreading to Europe. An example of Europe's introduction of US-style China Studies was the setup of the "documentary and research center for contemporary China" in the Sinological Institute at Leiden University, one of the oldest Sinological centers in Europe, in 1968. As recalled by Erik Zürcher, the founder of the center,

> The only thing that became quite clear [during my stay in People's Republic of China in 1964] to me was that my training in classical sinology had not equipped me with the tools to interpret what I saw around me, and that it would

[32] Idema 1991:9; see also Idema 2023.

be worthwhile, indeed imperative, to widen the scope of Chinese studies at home.

Back in Leiden, the response to the idea of drawing contemporary China into the sphere of Oriental Studies was not really enthusiastic. In those years, Asian studies as concentrated in the Faculty of Arts were going through a period of what may be called "post-colonial depression." In the past, most of them had been directly or indirectly related with the colonial administration in the Dutch East Indies, or with the curriculum set up for the training of colonial officials ... [A]ll this meant that Oriental Studies were by no means antiqurian or strictly philological ... For obvious reasons this had changed in the early 1950s, at least in the Faculty of Arts. Contemporary developments in what came to be called "the Third World" were largely left to the departments of sociology, anthropology and political science, and in those areas the University of Amsterdam far outshone Leiden. Then came the "Ten Years of Turmoil", starting with the "Cultural Revolution," and with the wisdom of hindsight we can say that that cataclysm has given the push needed to add a "contemporary wing" to the Sinological Institute (and I think that the same happened elsewhere in Europe, where one contemporary China center after another was set up).[33]

As such, modern China Studies informed by social scientific paradigm superseded, at least supplanted, traditional Sinology across the Atlantic.

The Unintended Openness of Area Studies

Despite the links between Area Studies and the Cold War establishment, as well as Parsonian social sciences, the institutionalization of Area Studies led to some unintended consequences, which sowed the seeds for transforming the Western study of Asia that, on the one hand, superseded Orientalist stereotypes, and posed a challenge to the universalist social sciences on the other.

---

[33] Zürcher 1994: 3–5.

Although US Area Studies was always under the social scientists' leadership, the fields became a possible locus of interdisciplinarization and overcoming the "Imperialism of departments."[34] The institutions of Area Studies "offered a rare venue where one could see what a historian thought of the work of an economist, or what a literary critic thought of behavioralist sociology."[35] Second, the application of social scientific theory and methods gradually dissolved the Orientalist reduction of non-Western civilizations into ancient religions and texts. In the case of China Studies, different branches covering a wide range of areas like kinship, urban systems, market structure, demography, foreign trade, science and technology, and imperial jurisdiction blossomed in the 1950s and 1960s. Religion was no longer the privileged area, and ancient texts were no longer the privileged objects of investigation, as in nineteenth-century Sinology.

This diversification of disciplinary approaches to China's past and present, first in the US and then in Europe, led to a more nuanced, multifaceted, historicized understanding of China that overcame the Orientalist reification of Chinese civilization. Germinating as early as the 1930s and 1940s, this diversification of approach was spearheaded by the works of China scholars who were from different disciplinary backgrounds and had no traditional Sinological training but worked on China. The movement back and forth between new social science methods and China Studies at the fringe of Sinology led to the plurality of new insights and perspectives that dissolved the hold of the reductionist Orientalist paradigm.

One example is John Lossing Buck, an American agricultural economist who helped establish the Department of Agricultural Economy at the University of Nanking (Nanjing) in the 1920s, with the sponsorship of US Churches.[36] During his tenure at Nanking University, he and his students adopted new approaches in the study of the Western farm economy to conduct a large-scale survey of tens of thousands of peasant households across China. This research resulted in the *Chinese Farm Economy* (Chicago, 1930),

---

[34] Fenton 1947: 26, 45; see also Palat 1996; Cumings 1998.
[35] Cumings 1998: 24.
[36] Turvey 2019.

which surveyed 2,866 farms, and the three-volume *Land Utilization in China* (Chicago, 1937), which surveyed 16,786 farms.[37] Buck's dataset is still an authoritative source on China's agronomy, illuminating the distribution of land fertility, land tenure, land size, land productivity, and different kinds of economic activities in the Republican period (1911–1945).[38]

Other pioneering research of that era was the ethnographic research of Mongolia by Owen Lattimore, an American Sinologist without formal doctoral training, represented by his *The Inner Asian Frontiers of China* (Boston, 1940), which I discuss in the last section.[39] Lattimore's works show the interaction of climate, economy, people's movement, and politics across cultural and ethnic borders at the northern and western edge of Chinese civilization. He showed that China's history, long before its conflict with Western powers, was far from stagnant. Han Chinese's interactions with the non-Chinese people in Central Asia through trade, cultural diffusion, and wars provided the impetus to sociopolitical change and institutional evolution of premodern China. Lattimore's approach challenges Fairbank's later impact-response model, which portrayed Chinese civilization as stagnant before interacting with Western maritime power in the nineteenth century. Later, Lattimore extended his perspective to the geopolitics of the early days of Cold War Central Asia in his *Pivot of Asia: Sinkiang and the Inner Asian Frontiers of China and Russia* (Boston, 1950). In retrospect, he rightly saw the contradiction between the Xinjiang population's identification with the Soviet Central Asian republics and Communist China's compulsion to absorb the area and anticipated ensuing tension between the USSR and the People's Republic of China.[40]

In the postwar era, G. William Skinner, trained in anthropology and initially focused on Southeast Asia, applied the novel method of spatial analysis of marketing activities to analyze the geographical structure of marketing networks in late imperial China and discovered autonomous economic cycles of eight physiographic

---

[37] Buck 1930, 1937.
[38] E.g., Arrigo 1986.
[39] Lattimore 1940.
[40] Lattimore 1950: 219–22.

macro-regions of China.⁴¹ Besides these works, Mark Elvin's use of the method of demographic-economic history to study the long pattern of Chinese development in the last two thousand years (1973), the discovery of Joseph Needham, who was a chemist by training and profession, about China's technological and scientific progress in premodern times (1954), and Chang Chung-li's 張仲禮 (1955) and Ho Ping-ti's 何炳棣 (1962) application of social stratification analysis to unveil the function of the gentry class and pattern of social mobility in late imperial China, Fei Xiao-tong's 費孝通 (1953) sociological investigation of China's rural social structure and the influence of the Confucianist ethic represent some of the best-known efforts in applying scientific or social scientific methods to transcend traditional Sinological mode of inquiry in the mid twentieth century.⁴²

Within Fairbank School, some of Fairbank's own students advanced his impact-response model by bringing in more dynamic views of the development of Confucianist traditions. For example, in the late 1950s and 1960s, Joseph Levenson's trilogy, *Confucian China and Its Modern Fate* traced the development of Confucianism in the Ming-Qing period before "Western impact," such as the adoption of Buddhist aesthetics in Ming Confucianism and rise of Qing empiricism. Levenson looked at Confucianism's post-1850 development not as a simple replacement of Confucianism by Western values but as a complex process of accommodation and hybridization with the long-term persistence of some Confucianist elements.⁴³ Benjamin I. Schwartz, another student of Fairbank, advanced the impact-response framework by emphasizing neither Western canons nor Chinese scholars' introduction of those canons into China was monolithic. Focusing on the late nineteenth-century translation of T. H. Huxley, Stuart Mill, Herbert Spencer, and Adam Smith into Chinese by Yan Fu嚴復 (Yen Fu), Schwartz showed how Chinese reformists selectively imported Western thoughts that highlighted survival, strengthening, and development of the nation and sidelined the Western thoughts that stressed individual liberty against

---

⁴¹ Skinner 1977.
⁴² Elvin 1973, Needham 1954, Chang 1955; Fei 1939, 1953.
⁴³ Levenson 1968; Cohen 2010: 27–30, 61–71.

the state.⁴⁴ This work, together with Schwartz's earlier study on Mao's indigenization of Marxism–Leninism, illustrated the twists and turns as well as the Chinese agency in the "impact-response" process.⁴⁵

From the 1970s onward, a new generation of US–China scholars, many of whom were students of John King Fairbank, challenged Fairbank's modernization paradigm more openly. They looked at China's crisis and transformation in the nineteenth and twentieth centuries as a result of the internal dynamics of Chinese history rather than simple reactions to Western impact. For example, Paul A. Cohen and Philip Kuhn traced the waves of China's modern rebellions to the eighteenth-century demographic explosion following a long period of stability and the introduction of the New World Corps that fueled the growth of landless, barely surviving vagrants disconnected from stable lineage organizations.⁴⁶ For another example, Philip Huang 黃宗智 employed the thesis of agricultural involution and argued that the demographic expansion in the Qing period enabled the costless addition of agricultural labor. This led to increasing output but falling labor productivity. It resulted in growth without development as an unfavorable condition to capitalist transformation.⁴⁷

During the Cold War, from the 1950s to the 1970s, though social scientists were shut off from mainland China and fieldwork there was impossible, many of them devised methods to get around this challenge. Some conducted ethnography in villages in Hong Kong and Taiwan as accessible samples of Chinese agrarian and lineage communities.⁴⁸ Some interviewed Chinese refugees in Hong Kong and relied on mainland published materials in Mao's China, collected in Hong Kong libraries and archival centers, to research society and politics in Communist China. The most prestigious and massive collection of these materials was at The Universities Service Center, which was set up in Hong Kong by a number of leading China scholars from the US in 1963 with funding from the Carnegie

---

⁴⁴ Schwartz 1964.
⁴⁵ Schwartz 1951.
⁴⁶ Cohen 2010 [1984], Kuhn 1970.
⁴⁷ Huang 1985; see also Huang 1991.
⁴⁸ E.g., Faure 1986, Hayes 1977, Watson 1975, 1983; Hase 2013.

and Ford Foundations. The center was later incorporated into the Chinese University of Hong Kong as The Universities Service Center for China Studies in 1988.[49]

While the introduction of social science paradigms transformed Sinology and China Studies, Area Studies brought the specificity of non-Western social formations into the vision of the universalist social scientists and created the ground for overcoming Western-centrism in social science. In the 1964 annual meeting of the Association for Asian Studies, William Skinner organized a panel on "Chinese Studies and the Disciplines." In his speech titled "What the Study of China can do for Social Science," Skinner pointed out that,

> Social scientists ... have been parochial while claiming universality. They studied Western man and spoke of mankind ... Too much of social science limits its scope of inquiry to Western societies. Researchers in the disciplines shy away from empirical studies outside their own societies, and they are oftentimes unprepared to digest the implications of such "foreign" studies as have been done. And in consequence, theory falls woefully short of universal applicability. If these disciplines are to move away from parochialism toward a universal science of man, we need empirical studies on a large scale in societies outside the Western tradition ... All societies are unique, but some are more unique than others. In my view, China is the most unique of all, by which I mean to say that Chinese society has manifested and now manifests so many exceptional features that social scientists ignore it only at the cost of the universality of their science.[50]

In a similar vein, one of the leading post-colonial critics from India recently traced his critical ideas to the Area Studies training he received in the US during the 1960s:

> [There are] often noted links between the Cold War, government funding, and university expansion in the organization

---

[49] E.g., Chan 1985, Walder 1986; For a history of the Universities Service Center for China Studies, see Vogel 2016; see also Alford 2006; Cohen 2015; Shambaugh 2023.
[50] Skinner 1964: 518.

of area-studies centers after World War II. Nevertheless, area studies has provided the major counterpoint to the delusions of the view from nowhere that underwrites much canonical social science. It is this aspect of my training that compelled me to situate my genealogy of the global present in the area I know best: India.

...The area-studies tradition is a double-edged sword. In a society notoriously devoted to exceptionalism, and to endless preoccupation with "America," this tradition has been a tiny refuge for the serious study of foreign languages, alternative worldviews, and large-scale perspectives on sociocultural change outside Europe and the United States. Bedeviled by a certain tendency toward philology (in the narrow, lexical sense) and a certain overidentification with the regions of its specialization, area studies has nonetheless been one of the few serious counterweights to the tireless tendency to marginalize huge parts of the world in the American academy and in American society more generally.[51]

Institutionally, the rise of Area Studies changed the "demography" of faculty in the history and other social science departments. The traditional and Western social science disciplines were "corroded" by Area Studies, as the number of faculty specializing in non-Western areas in those departments had increased since 1945.[52] Faculty originating from the cultures they studied also increased and broke down the traditional Orientalist mode of "Westerners studying the East," strengthening the immunity to the violence of convenient simplification in the field.[53] To be sure, the production of Orientalist knowledge had involved Chinese scholars since the Jesuits and the Enlightenment. Jesuits relied on the assistance of converted Chinese Christians in their translation and interpretation of the Chinese Classics.[54] The Physiocrats once brought Chinese students to Paris, trained them in Western academic methods, handed them questions, and asked them to collect information when they were back in China (see Chapter 3). James Legge collaborated with Chinese scholar

---

[51] Appadurai 1997: 16–17.
[52] Wallerstein 1997: 219–20.
[53] See Huang 2000.
[54] Hosne 2014.

Wang Tao in British Hong Kong in his translation of the Confucianist Classics, though Wang broke with Legge after protesting (to no avail) Legge's later attention to Taoism, which Wang insisted was not central to Chinese civilization and was embarrassing.[55] However, in such co-production relations, the Chinese scholars' role was subservient to their European counterparts, who dominated the agenda, approach, and perspectives. The entry of the generations of Chinese scholars who were trained in Western social scientific or humanities methods, approaching the study of Chinese history and society from multiple homegrown perspectives, and became scholars in their own right and superseded the role of native informants in the mid twentieth century changed those dynamics. The works of Yü Ying-Shih 余英時, Ho Ping-ti, Chang Chung-li, Tsou Tang 鄒讜, and Philip Huang, who became leading scholars in US–China Studies, are cases in point.[56]

The blossoming of China Studies in other Asian societies, first and foremost Japan, in the postwar era, and the translation of their works into Western languages also contributed to the erosion of Western-centrism in old Sinology and the social sciences.[57] Without the missionary complex of Western Sinologists among the Jesuits and nineteenth-century missionary scholars, and culturally more proximate to China, Japanese Sinologists employed social scientific tools for analyzing class, economic development, and world-system to delve into the socio-economic dynamism of Song 宋 and Ming-Qing China, as well as trade and diplomatic inter-connections among Asian states before Western imperialism.[58] Some Japanese Sinologists concurred with Owen Lattimore's perspective about the Central Asian sources of dynamism in Chinese history and examined the Eurasian origins of key institutions and political structures in Qing China. These Japanese works traveled to American and European academia and helped advance the diversity in perspectives and methods in Western China Studies.[59]

---

[55] See Chapter 5.
[56] Chang 1955; Ho 1962; Huang 1985; Tsou 1963; Yü 1967.
[57] See Fogel 2023. See also Cassel 2023 for Sinology in European countries that never had a colonial empire in Asia.
[58] Iiyama 2023; Hamashita 2008.
[59] See Crossley 1997, 1999; Elliot 2001; Dunnell et al ed. 2004; Perdue 2010; Rawski 1998, 2015; Rowe 2010.

7 From Sinology to China Studies

The multi-disciplinary study of non-Western civilizations alone is not a sufficient condition for undermining ethnocentric universalism in social science. We have seen that Weber's Eurocentric sociology was based on his comparative studies of non-Western societies, too. The social and intellectual turbulence in the US and Europe in the 1960s significantly contributed to the field's transformation. With the rise of the anti-war movement in the 1960s in US universities and the spread of Maoism to Western campuses, a new generation of Area Studies scholars came of age in the context of intellectual radicalization. The increasing popularity of Marxian concepts and theories was a common phenomenon across social scientific disciplines. It led to the rise of social history in the history profession and the canonization of Marx as a key theorist in history, political science, and sociology in the 1960s and 1970s.[60]

In Asia Studies in general, and China Studies in particular, a group of young scholars sympathetic to the peasant revolutions in China and Southeast Asia tried to bring together their anti-war, anti-colonial politics and their academic passion against the establishment Area Studies to build networks of scholars (such as the Committee of Concerned Asia Scholars) that cultivated new critical analysis of Asia and China.[61] Since the 1960s, Marxian perspectives on Asia and China have no longer been confined to academic discussions in Communist-bloc countries and among fringe radical intellectuals. They became increasingly prevalent in the mainstream study of China and Asia. As in the cases of many other social scientific paradigms, the legitimization of the Marxian paradigm opened up new agendas and perspectives, refreshing the analysis of many old problems (e.g., why capitalist modernity did not emerge in China spontaneously).

This input of new methods, approaches, questions, and perspectives, on top of the entry of Chinese scholars as a force in its own right to the field, led to the de-Orientalization of China Studies. As we saw in Chapters 5 and 6, the problem of Orientalist paradigms in Sinology is never about the accuracy of particular representations and interpretations of certain aspects of the Chinese civilization.

---

[60] Sewell 2005: Ch. 2.
[61] See Lanza 2017; for a collection of their original essays, see Friedman and Selden eds. 1971 for example.

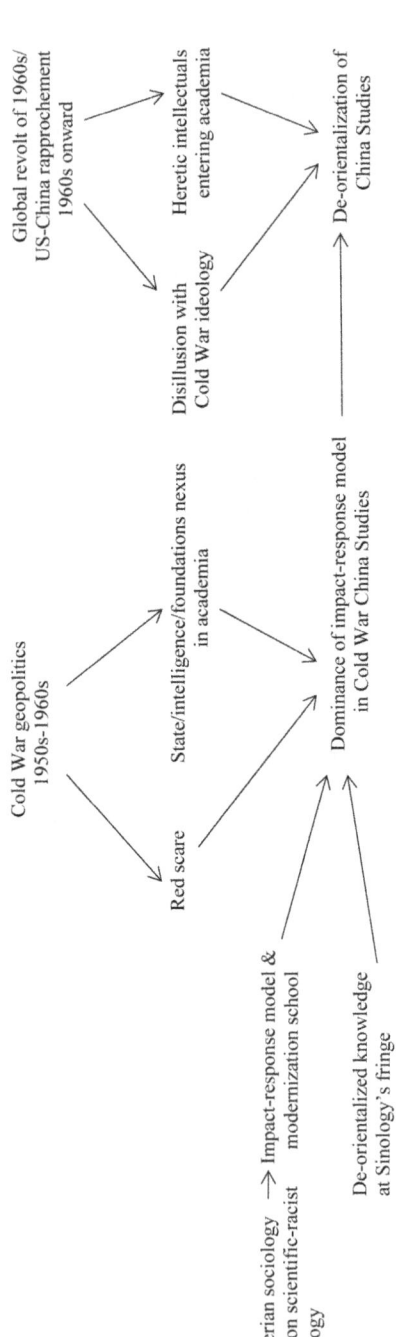

Figure 7.2 From Cold War China Studies to de-Orientalization of China Studies

Orientalist scholarship is problematic because of its reductionism and essentialism, that is, its urge to construct highly generalized, ahistorical knowledge about the Chinese civilization from very particular, local knowledge, as driven by certain religious, ideological, and political premises. As such, the pluralization of methods and perspectives since the early and mid twentieth century, as well as the maintenance of an expanding academic space allowing the coexistence of and dialogues among these methods and perspectives since the 1960s, eroded the reductionist and essentialist urges in the field and fomented the emergence of a more multifaceted, reflexive understanding of Chinese history, economy, society, and politics open to constant contestation. The dynamics of de-Orientalization of China Studies is summarized in Figure 7.2.

Though the introduction of the Marxian approach in the study of Chinese history and society in Western academia at the height of the Cold War contributed to the pluralization and de-Orientalization of the field, the approach itself, when tied too closely with the political and ideological agenda of the Communist bloc, could also introduce new biases and prejudices originating from the sources that Marx relied on in the formative years of his ideas. Such biases and prejudices helped create political and humanitarian disasters when Asian state builders internalized them and turned them into action. These biases and prejudices also seeped back into Western academia to undermine the de-Orientalization of knowledge production. This problem of Marxian Orientalism is what I now turn to.

8 THE "ASIATIC MODE OF PRODUCTION" MYTH

Weber's analysis of Asia in comparison to Europe started with a focus on China. He then extended the insights from China to India and other Asian cultures to generalize a theory about "Asiatic religion." In contrast, Marx's analysis of the "Asiatic mode of production" was anchored on his examination of Indian society. The insights on India were then extended to his discussion on China and other Asian societies.

Marx's Oriental Despots and Communal Villages

Marx first articulated his analysis of India and China in his comments on current political affairs written for the *New York Daily Tribune* in the early 1850s. In the widely cited article "The British Rule in India" (1853), he put forward his thesis on the Asiatic mode of production regarding Indian society for the first time.[1] To Marx, Indian society was constituted of isolated, self-contained, and self-governing village communities. Each community was grounded on communal property and combined agriculture and handicraft industry. Private property and individual freedom were non-existent, and these communities showed no connection with one another. This Asiatic form made India vulnerable to foreign invasion and the tyranny of the "Oriental despot" that extracted surplus from a myriad of village communities and organized hydraulic works and other

[1] Marx 1853a.

8 The "Asiatic Mode of Production" Myth

public infrastructure essential to Asia's agriculture, given the continent's geography and climate. In Marx's own disdainful words:

> These two circumstances – the Hindoo, on the one hand, leaving, like all Oriental peoples, to the Central Government the care of the great public works, the prime condition of his agriculture and commerce, dispersed, on the other hand, over the surface of the country, and agglomerated in small centers by the domestic union of agricultural and manufacturing pursuits – these two circumstances had brought about, since the remotest times, a social system of particular features – the so-called village system, which gave to each of these small unions their independent organization and distinct life ... we must not forget that these idyllic village-communities, inoffensive though they may appear, had always been the solid foundation of Oriental despotism, that they restrained the human mind within the smallest possible compass, making it the unresisting tool of superstition, enslaving it beneath traditional rules, depriving it of all grandeur and historical energies.[2]

To Marx, the lack of private property and dynamic class conflicts deprived Asiatic societies of any dynamics of change. Hence, these societies had not changed since "time immemorial."[3] The despotic state's relation with the villages was no more than tax and corvee extraction. Rulers came and went, and the structure of the villages remained perennially the same. These "semi-barbarian, semi-civilized [village] communities" gave man an "undignified, stagnatory, and vegetative life" and man "fell down on his knees in adoration of Kanuman, the monkey, and Sabbala, the cow."[4] While the impetus of change was non-existent from within, British colonial rule and British manufactured imports became a necessary evil that brought "the only social revolution ever heard of in Asia." As such, "whatever may have been the crimes of England, she was the unconscious tool of history in bringing about that revolution."[5]

---

[2] Marx 1853a: para 10, 13.
[3] Marx 1853a: para 8, 9, 11.
[4] Marx 1853a: para 11, 12.
[5] Marx 1853a: para 14.

In 1853, Marx also wrote "Revolution in China and in Europe," published about ten days prior to "The British Rule in India" at the *New York Daily Tribune*. Marx did not delve into China's social structure in the China piece as he did for India. But he adopted the same perspective that Chinese society has been stagnant and asleep in "hereditary stupidity" since time immemorial.[6] British products and British cannons during the Opium War of 1839–1841 forced isolated China into contact with the world and shattered its perennially stationary social system, bringing China into the world history of progress:

> All these dissolving agencies acting together on the finances, the morals, the industry, and political structure of China, received their full development under the English cannon in 1840, which broke down the authority of the Emperor, and forced the Celestial Empire into contact with the terrestrial world. Complete isolation was the prime condition of the preservation of Old China. That isolation having come to a violent end by the medium of England, dissolution must follow as surely as that of any mummy carefully preserved in a hermetically sealed coffin, whenever it is brought into contact with the open air.[7]

In a later piece, "Trade with China" (1859) at the *Tribune*, Marx more explicitly described China's social structure as composed of self-contained, isolated village communities, as in India. The difference between China and India was that in China, the British lacked the administrative and political means that they possessed in India to dismantle the self-sufficient village communities:

> Quite apart from the opium trade, which we proved to grow in an inverse ratio to the sale of Western manufactures, we found the main obstacle to any sudden expansion of the import trade to China in the economical structure of Chinese society, depending upon the combination of minute agriculture with domestic industry. ...
> It is this same combination of husbandry with manufacturing industry, which, for a long time, withstood,

---

[6] Marx 1853b: para 4.
[7] Marx 1853b: para 7.

and still checks, the export of British wares to East India; but there that combination was based upon a peculiar constitution of the landed property which the British, in their position as the supreme landlords of the country, had it in their power to undermine, and thus forcibly convert part of the Hindu self-sustaining communities into mere farms, producing opium, cotton, indigo, hemp, and other raw materials, in exchange, for British stuff. In China the English have not yet wielded this power, nor are they likely ever to do so.[8]

Marx attempted to generalize further and theorize his ideas about the Asiatic mode of production in the *Grundrisse*, in which he tried to systematically explain Asian stagnation in contrast to the dynamic Western social transformation from antiquity to feudalism when state, communal, and individual property led to contradictions and conflicts that drove history forward:

Amidst oriental despotism and the propertylessness which seems legally to exist there, this clan or communal property exists in fact as the foundation, created mostly by a combination of manufactures and agriculture within the small commune, which thus becomes altogether self-sustaining, and contains all the conditions of reproduction and surplus production within itself. A part of their surplus labour belongs to the higher community, which exists ultimately as a person, and this surplus labour takes the form of tribute etc., as well as of common labour for the exaltation of the unity, partly of the real despot, partly of the imagined clan-being, the god. Now, in so far as it actually realizes itself in labour, this kind of communal property can appear either in the form where the little communes vegetate independently alongside one another, and where, inside them, the individual with his family work independently on the lot assigned to them. The Asiatic form necessarily hangs on most tenaciously and for the longest time. This is due to its presupposition that the individual does not become independent vis-à-vis the commune; that there

---

[8] Marx 1859: para 1, 14.

is a self-sustaining circle of production, unity of agriculture and manufactures, etc.[9]

Marx's depiction of Asian societies as grounded on self-sufficient and self-governing village communities with communal property, in combination with an overarching Oriental despot ruling and expropriating from a vast ocean of isolated villages, is partly a replication of Hegel's description of Oriental despotism.[10] Hegel's notion about a dynamic, constantly changing West based on individual freedom and a constant Orient in lack of individual spirit, exacted by tyrannical despots, and "severed from the process of general historical development," coincided with Marx's thesis about the Oriental despot in his conceptualization of the Asiatic mode of production.[11]

Hegel had not discussed the village society in Asia. Marx adopted the conception that autonomous villages were the fundamental units of Indian society from the *Fifth Report from the Select Committee of the House of Common on the Affairs of the East India Company*, published by the British Parliament in 1812. This report, regarded as the foundation of "the modern [Western] understanding of agrarian India," was cited by Marx extensively in his "British Rule in India."[12]

As contemporary India scholars pointed out, the knowledge about Indian agrarian society in the *Fifth Report* was constructed out of a particular political context: the ongoing debate in London about the British administration of India.[13] Before the 1790s, the East Indian Company subcontracted revenue collection to *zamindars*, local chieftains ruling large areas. After the Company established direct administration of India, it appointed military officer Thomas Munro as the revenue administrator. It also tasked him with surveying and reporting about the conditions of India's agrarian society.

Munro and other revenue officers advocated that the British authorities should directly collect revenue from individual villages and bypass the *zamindar* middlemen. As such, the Company could

[9] Marx 1973 [c. 1857]: 473, 486.
[10] See Chapter 4.
[11] Hegel (2001 [1822]): 105; see also Chapter 4.
[12] Ludden 1993: 260; see also Krader 1975; O'Leary 1989.
[13] Ludden 1993.

raise more tax with lower tax rates. However, such a proposal for reform confronted fierce resistance from the Company's Board of Directors, who preferred to maintain the status quo. To advance his cause, Munro compiled a report emphasizing that autonomous village communities, which were self-sufficient, held communal property and functioned as "little republics." He argued that they were always the basic administrative units in India and that these communities had been tyrannized and usurped by tax middlemen and chieftains as representatives of the Mogul Emperor (i.e., the Oriental despot). In this light, advancing British interests and protecting the rights of the village communities coincided, and both hinged on eliminating the tax middlemen.[14]

Munro's portrayal of Indian agrarian society as constituted by self-sufficient and self-governing communal villages was intended to strengthen the case that the Company should regard villages as the basic units of administration and direct taxation.[15] Munro's report was the basis of the *Fifth Report*, which shaped Marx's understanding of Indian and Asiatic society.

In the 1850s, Marx's depiction of the Asiatic mode of production came with the Hegelian disdain of the history-less Orient. Kevin Anderson researched Marx's later, mostly unpublished, writings from the 1870s onward. He discovered that Marx's view on the Asiatic form shifted from disdain to hope, if not admiration. In their earlier writings on Russia in the 1850s, Marx and Engels saw Russia's tsarist regime as an exemplar of the Oriental despot grounded on isolated, autonomous communal villages lacking private property, as in India and China.[16] Russia's Asiatic characters originated from the Mongol invasion that enslaved the Muscovy, nurtured the despotic Tsarist regime, and set Russia's history apart from Europe thereafter.[17] Marx saw the Tsarist Oriental despot as a reactionary force threatening Western Europe's revolution.[18]

But by the 1870s, Marx had become increasingly influenced by the Russian populists (the Narodniks), with whom he

---

[14] Ludden 1993: 259–60.
[15] Ludden 1993: 260; see also Stein 1989.
[16] Anderson 2010: 43–4.
[17] Anderson 2010: 47–8.
[18] Anderson 2010: 43–50.

was in close correspondence regarding the Russian translation of his works. In his later writings, Marx believed the communal villages were internally equalitarian and could play a positive role in resisting the advance of capitalism in Russia and the rest of Asia. They could even constitute the building blocks of a transition to socialism and spark a world revolution if such communities were put under the leadership of the revolutionary proletariat with the support of the Western working class.[19] Anderson attempted to exonerate Marx from Eurocentrism and Orientalism by highlighting his transformation from despising to admiring the Asiatic communal form.

However, whether Marx despised or admired the Asiatic communal village is not the most important question. We saw in Chapters 1–6, time and time again that the fundamental pitfall of Orientalist knowledge is not its disdain of Asian cultures and societies but its essentialist and distorting conceptions of them. Many times, such Orientalist conception came with romanticization and admiration. Marx's more positive assessment of the Asiatic communal forms reminds us of the Romantic Orientalists' condescending admiration of a rustic, pure, and rural Orient imagined to be unspoiled by modern industrial civilization. In fact, the Russian populist intelligentsia's admiration of the communal villages was a direct outgrowth of Europe's Romanticist movement in the early nineteenth century. The image of the Russian and Indian countryside as a land of egalitarian village communes originated from the fantasy about the Eastern countryside in the writings of German Romanticists in the early nineteenth century.[20] As Lenin pointed out in his critique of the Narodniks, both European Romanticists in the 1820s and Russian populists in the 1890s grounded their arguments on a reactionary fantasy and utopian idealization of rural small producers as a contrast to capitalism.[21]

We know from today's historiography that this Romanticist conception of rural India and China, and elsewhere in Asia, was at most pure fantasy and at least oversimplification. Early modern India, China, and Russia saw extensive and deep development of the market

[19] Anderson 2010: 196–236.
[20] Dennison and Carus 2003; Dewey 1972.
[21] Lenin 1972 [1897].

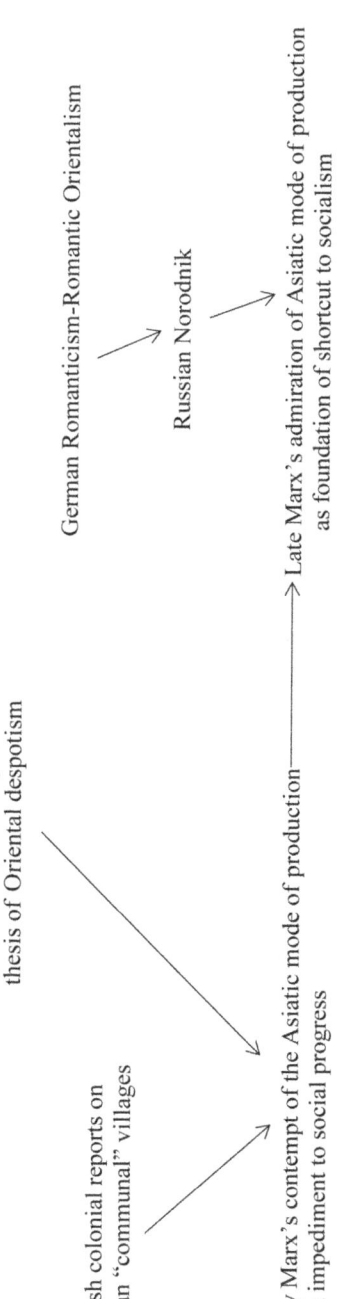

Figure 8.1 Sources and changes in Marx's view of the Asiatic mode of production

economy that integrated the most remote villages into regional and empire-wide market networks.[22] As Perry Anderson (1974) noted, Marx's notion of the Asiatic mode of production, however disdainful or admiring, has been based on a "village myth" and "blending features found in distinct social formations into a single, blurred archetype."[23] The sources and evolution of Marx's views on the Asiatic mode of production are summarized in Figure 8.1.

According to Lenin, the Russian populists' romanticization of the Russian communal villages led to their failed revolutionary program, as the peasants were never as enthusiastic about overthrowing the Tsar as they fantasized. At the height of the Cold War, the continuous fantasy about perennial Asiatic communal villages led to a Marxist Orientalism that contributed to some of the most horrific political and human catastrophes in the twentieth century, as well as to new biases in the academic study of Asia and China, as we will see.

The Bolsheviks' Asia Question

Lenin subscribed to Marx's earlier disparaging view on the Asiatic form and Oriental despotism. He attributed Russia's backwardness to its "Asiatic" characters and asserted the task of the proletariat revolution was to shed Russia of such characters and not to build upon the Asiatic communal villages as the Narodniks advocated. Throughout Lenin's writings, "Asiatic" was frequently used as a derogatory rhetorical device against the Tsarist status quo of Russia. "Asiatic police tyranny," "Asiatic censorship," "Asiatic conservatism of the autocracy," "autocracy's Asiatic savagery," "Asiatic barbarity," "Asiatic philistinism," "slave, Asiatic, tsarist Russia," "Asiatic barbarism," "Asiatically corrupt Russian officials," "the accursed canker of Asiatic tyranny," and "Asiatic despotism" were just a few examples that Lenin used to attribute everything wrong about Russia to Asian influences.[24] To Lenin, the social formations of Imperial Russia and China showed more similarities than differences under the same fabric of Oriental despotism,

---

[22] Skinner 1977, Perdue 2010, von Glahn 2016, Braudel 1992: Ch. 5, etc.
[23] Anderson 1974: 494.
[24] Rahman 2008: para 24.

as "[t]he Chinese people suffer from the same evils as those from which the Russian people suffer – they suffer from an Asiatic government that squeezes taxes from the starving peasantry and that suppresses every aspiration towards liberty by military force."[25]

This Russian Communists' disapproval of everything Asiatic originated from Montesquieu, Hegel, and early Marx. It continued after Lenin's death. In the post-Lenin power struggle, opponents of Stalin mobilized the fear of Oriental despotism against Stalin by attributing his character to his childhood in Georgia, which had been at the Russian Empire's Islamic frontier and influenced by Muslim cultures. The Communist Party Central Committee allegedly claimed in 1925 that "you can expect anything from that Asiatic[Stalin]." Bukharin simply referred to Stalin as the "new Genghis Khan."[26] Trotsky's biography of Stalin started with a lengthy chapter on the Asiatic influence of Georgia on Stalin's childhood. The chapter opened with the following lines:

> The late Leonid Krassin, old revolutionist, eminent engineer, brilliant Soviet diplomat and, above all, intelligent human being, was the first, if I am not mistaken, to call Stalin an "Asiatic." In saying that, he had in mind no problematical racial attributes, but rather that blending of grit, shrewdness, craftiness and cruelty which has been considered characteristic of the statesmen of Asia. Bukharin subsequently simplified the appellation, calling Stalin "Genghis Khan," manifestly in order to draw attention to his cruelty, which has developed into brutality.[27]

Stalin himself was not shy about admitting his Asiatic character. He allegedly told a Japanese diplomat in the 1930s that "Russia is an Asiatic country, and I myself am an Asiatic."[28]

After Stalin consolidated his power and commenced his Great Purges and agricultural collectivization, the Left Opposition in exile, led by Trotsky, immediately portrayed such developments as a tragic revival of the Tsarist Oriental despotism and the oppressive

---

[25] Lenin 1964 [1900]: para 9.
[26] Rieber 2005: 18.
[27] Trotsky 1941: 1.
[28] Time *1956*.

rural communes. To Trotsky and the exiled Left Opposition, the Stalin regime was a resurgent Asiatic mode of production in the guise of communism, and Stalin was a reincarnated Oriental despot. In response, Stalin labeled the theory of the Asian mode of production heterodox and no more than Marx's immature, erroneous thoughts that he never fully developed nor published. Stalin dictated the orthodox historical sequence of primitive communism, slavery, feudalism, capitalism, socialism, and communism as universal stages applicable to all civilizations, and the Asiatic mode of production as a distinct mode diverging from Europe's feudalism simply never existed.[29]

In the late 1920s and early 1930s, Chinese Marxist historians debated whether the notion of feudalism or the Asiatic mode of production would best describe the social formations of imperial China. However, after Stalin's ban on the Asiatic mode of production discussion, the junior Chinese Communist Party (CCP) fell in line and sanctioned such discussion, too.[30] As such, the reference to the Asiatic mode of production disappeared altogether in communist countries and orthodox communist movements around the world. It was left to the Left Opposition and the anti-communist right to use it as a conceptual apparatus to critique the status quo of the Soviet bloc during the Cold War.

In Western academia, the Marxian critique of Soviet communism was more systematically articulated and extended to the analysis of the nascent Chinese Communist regime in the 1950s in Sinologist Karl Wittfogel's *Oriental Despotism: A Comparative Study of Total Power* (New Haven, 1957). The work of Wittfogel, a former member of the German Communist Party, who migrated to the US in the 1930s and turned into a staunchly anti-communist scholar in the 1950s, became a classic critic of Communist totalitarianism in mainstream US academia at the height of the Cold War. Wittfogel's thesis about the totalitarian system of vast areas in communist Eurasia was rooted in the Orientalist portrayal of a homogenous, timeless Asian civilization. The constant agricultural need for centralized state power to mobilize labor for large-scale irrigation works, given the geography and climate of those

---

[29] Fogel 1988: 66–7.
[30] See Zhao 1995; Fogel 1988: 67.

civilizations, created a persistent culture of tyranny and servitude. The underpinning message about the impediment of traditional Asian culture and institutions to capitalist modernization converged with the Weberian modernization theory. It pointed to the conviction that eradicating traditional Asian values and institutions and replacing them with modern Western ones was the key to ending backwardness and tyranny. Communism, on the other hand, held back Asian development by reviving the worst of its traditional polity and society.[31]

Wittfogel's view on the civilizational root of modern communist totalitarianism was shared by scholars outside the Marxian tradition, like Étienne Balazs, a Hungary-born French Sinologist who worked closely with Fernand Braudel within the Annales School in post-war France. Heavily influenced by Weber's later work on bureaucracy (instead of his earlier work on religions), Balazs argued that China had long been ruled by a totalitarian bureaucracy that had control of everything and stifled commercial activities, forestalling urban capitalism and individual liberty.[32]

The Romance and Catastrophe of Maoism

Not all Western scholars were critical of the presumed Asiatic mode of production in Asia. With the success of the Chinese Communist revolution as an allegedly peasant-based revolution and the proliferation of peasant revolts across Asia that culminated in the Vietnam War, the romanticization of Asian peasants and Asiatic communal villages as a formidable force resisting capitalism and imperialism, as expressed in Marx's later writings on Asia, saw the revival of its appeal to a segment of leftist intellectuals in the Western academia. This revived fantasy and admiration about the revolutionary communal peasants among Western intellectuals traveled back to Asia and became a potent ideological force shaping the path of Asian revolutions.

In retrospect, we know from plentiful research that the Chinese Communist revolution did not count on the support of the

---

[31] Wittfogel 1957.
[32] Will 2023: 561–4; Balazs 1964.

stereotypical land-tilling peasants, many of whom actually resisted Communist mobilization in the 1920s and 1930s. Resistance from cultivating peasants in lowland, fertile communities forced the CCP to build its rural revolution by recruiting the highly mobile landless vagrants, ethnic minorities (such as the Hakka), bandits, and heterodox religious sectarians in infertile highlands as the main force of its army.[33] But the CCP propaganda that its revolution was a peasant revolution still inspired a generation of Western intellectuals to see Asian peasants, and peasants elsewhere, as agents of revolutionary change capable of bringing down world capitalism.[34] Mao's top-down, rapid rural collectivization despite peasants' initial resistance in the 1950s and the party-state's propaganda about peasants' enthusiasm in surrendering their lots for large-scale People's Communes reinforced many Western leftists' fantasies about peasants' natural propensity toward communism.[35] This presumption about peasants' enthusiasm for communism was shattered only after the scale of the Great Leap Famine in 1959–1961 was fully known to the world and after Deng Xiaoping 鄧小平 abolished the People's Communes under the pressure of entrepreneurial peasants' passive resistance to collective farming.[36]

In the 1950s and 1960s, the Weber-inspired modernization school dominated mainstream Western academia and saw successful development in the non-Western world as dependent on the successful eradication of traditional cultures. The Marxist dependency theory emerged among the radical non-establishment intellectuals in the US and in parts of mainstream academia in France in the 1950s through the 1970s as an antithesis to the modernization school. As represented by Andre Gunder Frank and the radicals gathering around the *Monthly Review* magazine in the US and Samir Amin in the French-speaking world, dependency theorists argued that the underdevelopment of post-colonial periphery countries did not originate from their traditional culture but stemmed from their connection to wealthy core countries. As commerce with and investment from core countries were mechanisms of expropriating and

---

[33] Erbaugh 1992; Perry 1980; Averill 2006.
[34] Page 1975; Wolf 1969; Scott 1976; see also Skocpol 1982.
[35] Deutscher 1955; Bettelheim 1978; Weil 1996; cf. Li 2006.
[36] Raymond, Selden and Zhou 2000; Kerkvliet and Selden 1998; Selden 1994.

transferring surplus from the periphery, depriving the latter of sufficient resources for capital accumulation, developing countries' best chance of successful, autonomous development was to delink from developed countries and attain autarky.[37] Blaming external economic linkages for economic underdevelopment, high inequality, and all other problems in peripheral countries, dependency theorists in the US and South America were less interested in discerning the pre-colonial social formations of the periphery. In contrast, France's dependency theorists spent more effort explaining how the pre-colonial agrarian order, with reference to French Indochina, was distorted by the colonial process and how it could be somewhat restored through delinking. Two examples of French dependency theorists were Hou Yuon and Khieu Samphan. Hou Yuon finished his dissertation, "Le paysannerie du Cambodge et ses projets de modernisation" (The Cambodian peasants and their modernization projects), in economics at the University of Paris in 1955. Khieu Samphan finished his dissertation, "L'économie du Cambodge et ses problèmes d'industrialisation" (The Economy of Cambodia and Its Problems of Industrialization), in 1959, also at the University of Paris. They were both associated closely with Samir Amin, who obtained his PhD in economics in 1957 at the University of Paris with his thesis, "Les effets structurels de l'intégration internationale des économies précapitalistes: une étude théorique et appliquée des mécanismes de transformation des économies précapitalistes en économie capitaliste" (The Structural Effects of the International Integration of Pre-capitalist Economies: A Theoretical and Applied Study of the Mechanisms of Transformation of Pre-capitalist Economies into Capitalist Economies).

Both Hou Yuon and Khieu Samphan were students from Cambodia and were active in the Khmer Students Association in Paris. The Association was a Khmer student wing of the French Communist Party. Over the 1950s, they and Amin became increasingly drawn to the Chinese revolutionary experience and turned to Maoism. After their studies, Hou Yuon and Khieu Samphan returned to Cambodia to join their senior fellow Paris student, Saloth Sâr, also known as Pol Pot, and participate in revolutionary politics

---

[37] Frank 1966; Amin 1957, 1977.

there. Hou Yuon founded the Communist Party of Kampuchea, also known as the Khmer Rouge, and remained its intellectual leader and architect of a revolutionary program until he broke with Pol Pot and was executed in 1975. Khieu Samphan served as the head of state of the Khmer Rouge regime when it was in power 1976–1979. He was Pol Pot's right-hand man until the very end. Both Hou Yuon's and Khieu Samphan's dissertations presented a romanticized view of Cambodian peasants. They presaged the Khmer Rouge's program of radical delinking by destroying the cities and forcefully creating large rural collective farms that combined agriculture and industry. Hou Yuon's dissertation revived the Russian populists' hope about the revolutionary potential of the peasants in communal villages and Marx's later belief that a communist consciousness could develop spontaneously from the collectivist life of the Asiatic peasants.[38]

To Hou Yuon, French colonialism truncated the autonomous agrarian development of Cambodia and disrupted the protective relations and reciprocal obligations of pre-colonial agrarian society in Cambodia. The colonial process established the city–countryside dichotomy, in which cities became the bridgehead of colonial exploitation, subjugated the villages, and expropriated their surplus to be transferred to developed countries. The remedy was to organize peasants into rural collectives and rid society of urban and foreign exploitation. Hou Yuon asserted that fragmentation and individualism of the peasants were not inherent in the peasant mass but were the results of the imposition of the capitalist system since colonization.[39] Despite such imposed individualism, poor peasants had actively participated in occasional or seasonal cooperation, such as collective labor pools and mutual aid, up to Hou Yuon's time. Given Cambodian peasants' historical familiarity with organized, collective labor and readiness to accept united leadership for the nation's common good, the revolutionaries could achieve agrarian collectivization by turning such spontaneous collectivist arrangements into permanent organizations and advancing them with government support.[40]

---

[38] Galway 2019: 138–9; Kiernan 2006; Hou 1982 [1955].
[39] Hou 1982 [1964]: 152, 159–60.
[40] Hou 1982 [1964]: 140–1; Galway 2019: 140–5.

8 The "Asiatic Mode of Production" Myth

Khieu Samphan's dissertation saw the city–countryside dichotomy and the exploitation of the latter by the former as the root cause of underdevelopment in colonial and post-colonial Cambodia. Khieu Samphan claimed that the advanced handicraft industry had already developed in the villages before French colonialism, only to be destroyed by Cambodia's trade with Western countries that allowed cheap European manufactures to flood the local market.[41] Contrary to academic findings about the mobility and connections between actors in the urban and rural worlds of colonial and post-colonial Cambodia,[42] Khieu Samphan doubled down on the ossified dichotomy between an enslaved countryside and parasitic cities by arguing productive labor of agriculture and industry existed only in village communities. In contrast, all activities in the cities – including commerce, finance, and administration – were unproductive labor "add[ing] no value to the society."[43] Khieu Samphan concluded that "the greater the reduction in numbers of [unproductive] individuals concerned with general social organization, the greater the number who can contribute to production and the faster the enrichment of the nation," presaging the Khmer Rouge's policy of evacuating cities and sending urbanites to rural labor camps.[44]

The notion of an ideal agrarian social order before colonialism was repeated in Samir Amin's assertion that in pre-colonial Cambodia, "exploitation of some by others was, if not non-existent, at least marginal."[45] The sharp rural class division developed only after capital from core countries recruited the upper strata of Cambodian society as their agents to expropriate and suppress the lower strata. To Amin, as to Hou Yuon and Khieu Samphan, the ideal village collectives could be restored and developed once Cambodia cut off outside linkages by depopulating the parasitic cities connecting the country to exploitative foreign capital. During the brief period of Khmer Rouge rule in Cambodia, known as Democratic Kampuchea (1976–1979), Hou Yuon's and Khieu Samphan's radical vision of delinking became a reality through the forced evacuation of cities

---

[41] Khieu 1976 [1959]: 11.
[42] Kalab 1968; Ebihara 1973; McIntyre 1996: 756.
[43] Khieu 1976 [1959]: 9; McIntyre 1996: 747; 755–8.
[44] Khieu 1976 [1959]: 9.
[45] Amin 1978: 75.

and rapid rural collectivization that integrated both agriculture and industry in large collective farms, which were run by the state like labor camps. Even though Hou Yuon was persecuted at the beginning of the Khmer Rouge regime and Khieu Samphan was little more than a loyal executioner of Pol Pot's orders,[46] their visions of a socialist Cambodia had laid the ideological foundation of the Khmer Rouge's policy long before Pol Pot's "Year Zero," the tabula rasa year of New Cambodia declared in 1975. Seeing Pol Pot's "Super Great Leap Forward" to autarky and massive collectivization as an implementation of his proposal outlined in his dissertation some two decades ago, Khieu Samphan hailed Pol Pot's policy as a way to make Cambodia "the first nation to create a completely Communist society without wasting time on intermediate steps."[47]

Moreover, the Pol Pot regime emphasized its goal of reviving the glory of the medieval Khmer Empire between the ninth and fifteenth centuries. The regime's propaganda frequently invoked the large territory and advanced productive forces in the Empire. The Democratic Kampuchea's national anthem sang of the glory of "the times of Angkor" (the Empire's capital). The Orientalist myth about the Khmer Empire inspired the Khmer Rouge's obsession with irrigation work. The regime mobilized rural forced labor to construct large-scale dams and canals that were expected to significantly elevate agricultural productivity. One of the regime's central slogans was, "With water we have rice, with rice we have everything."[48] The regime's English propaganda brochure showcasing its achievements opened with a saturation of images of the ancient Angkor Wat and newly built irrigation infrastructure.[49] In retrospect, those irrigation works were wasteful and destructive. They were the main sources of starvation and death by hard labor.[50]

Khmer Rouge's obsession with state-directed irrigation originated largely from the works of French Orientalist Bernard Philippe Groslier.[51] In the 1950s, Groslier led the excavation

[46] I am thankful to Andrew Mertha for bringing my attention to Khieu Samphan's actual role in the Khmer Rouge regime. See Mertha 2025.
[47] Cited in Galway 2022: 181.
[48] Kiernan 2001: 194.
[49] Democratic Kampuchea 1977.
[50] Tyner et al. 2018; Himel 2007.
[51] See Locard 2015.

8 The "Asiatic Mode of Production" Myth

and study of the Angkor Wat and drew on Wittfogel's thesis on Oriental Despotism to formulate his theory of the "Angkorian hydraulic city." According to this theory, the prowess of the Khmer Empire hinged on the state's centralized labor mobilization for massive hydraulic works that increased the agricultural productivity of arable lands to three to four harvests a year.[52] Groslier's claim about three to four harvests a year at the height of the Khmer Empire was grounded on one single unverified source from a Chinese diplomat in the Mongol Empire who visited the Khmer Empire in CE 1296–1297.[53] That source contained a mix of facts, exotic fantasies, and unchecked hyperbolic claims by natives. For example, the source also claimed the Khmer Emperor had to have sexual intercourse with a nine-headed snake monster every night. Natural disaster would ensue if he missed one night of sex with the monster.[54]

Groslier asserted that the decline of Cambodia after the fifteenth century was rooted in the Siamese invasion that destroyed its centralized power, leading to unrecoverable dilapidation of irrigation networks and a reduction of annual harvests from up to four crops to one crop.[55] Into the late 1970s, Groslier moderated his earlier theory with newer data and argued that the Angkorian irrigation works only increased arable lands but not their productivity, which was never more than one to two crops a year.[56] His earlier theory, however, had already become a powerful myth that helped precipitate the Khmer Rouge catastrophe. Khmer Rouge's utopian vision of self-sufficient, productive rural collectives enabled by mega hydraulic infrastructure built by massive labor mobilized by the state was visualized in the emblem of the Democratic Kampuchea (see Figure 8.2).

Marxian anthropologist Kathleen Gough argued that although the Khmer Rouge's policy was "Maoism carried to the nth degree," "the system that Pol Pot actually imposed was a form of the Asiatic Mode of Production, based on the Khmer Empire of the

---

[52] Groslier 1958: 108–12; Groslier 1956: 24–5.
[53] Groslier 1958: 111; Zhou n.d. [c. 1297]: agriculture section, paragraph 1.
[54] Zhou n.d. [c. 1297]: palace section, paragraph 1.
[55] Groslier 1958: 117–18.
[56] Kiernan 2001: 189–90; Peycam 2010: 161, 168; Groslier 2007 [1979].

Figure 8.2 National Emblem of the Democratic Kampuchea (1975–1979). It is a representation of the utopian vision of the Khmer Rouge regime as a romanticized revival of Marx's Asiatic mode of production: A rural collective that combines agriculture and industry, both enhanced by hydraulic infrastructure constructed by centralized state power.
Source: Public domain

ninth to fifteenth centuries."[57] But as we have discussed, the Asiatic mode of production was little more than an Orientalist construction by Western intellectuals that attracted either contempt (early Marx, Lenin, Trotsky, and Wittfogel) or admiration (late Marx, Russian populists, Maoists, early Groslier) over the years. The Khmer Empire was, in actuality, cosmopolitan, commercialized, and well-connected to the outside world through trade.[58] What the Khmer

[57] Gough 1986: 15, 16.
[58] Hall 1975.

Rouge attempted to do was build a highway to modernity by turning a romantic fantasy of the past into a reality of the present. As such, Western Romanticist views on Asian communal peasants and the Oriental despot helped instigate one of the most horrific genocides in modern times through the ideas and actions of the Paris-educated Khmer intellectuals-turned-revolutionaries.

Asian Peasants in Western Academia

To be sure, the Romanticist idealization of the Asian revolutionary peasants inspired by the Chinese and Vietnamese revolutions was not confined to the Maoist intellectuals radicalized in Paris. Hou Yuon's and Samir Amin's conception of never-changing and autonomous pre-colonial Asian villages grounded on communal reciprocity and minimal class division was shared by the thesis of the "moral economy of the peasants" in mainstream academia in the West.[59] According to this thesis, Indochina's perennial "subsistence ethics" based on an equilibrium of the benevolent and reciprocal patron-client relations, which guaranteed the subsistence of the peasants in bad times, had been eroded by the expansion of the commercial economy and state centralization with an increasing tax burden since the establishment of Western colonial rule. The resulting insecurity and periodic subsistence crisis pushed the peasants to rebellions, which converged in anti-capitalist and anti-colonial revolutions. This thesis was soon extended to the analysis of peasant revolutions or movements in China, India, and beyond.[60]

This romanticization of the pre-colonial Asian countryside as a perpetual, stable, and benign Shangri-la of communal life was disputed by many in-depth works on the pre-colonial histories of Asia. For example, Michael Adas drew on many of those historical works, including his own, to reject the "moral economy of the peasants" thesis. He found that the thesis, though focusing on Southeast Asia, was, in fact, grounded on studies outside of Southeast Asia,

---

[59] Scott 1976.
[60] Wolf 1969; Migdal 1974; Marks 1984; cf. Popkins 1979; Adas 1980; Polachek 1983.

especially China. The evidence needed to support the thesis simply does not exist:

> Scott's approach to the subsistence ethic also overstates the degree to which communal harmony and cohesion dominated village life in the pre-colonial era. Anthropological evidence drawn from many areas supports the contrasting paradigm of the peasant village ... that deep and bitter factional divisions have been a central feature of village life. These divisions have led not only to quarrels and periodic outbursts of violence within the village; they have rendered the peasant community vulnerable to exploitation by regional bureaucrats and the landed gentry. Scott's emphasis on communal homogeneity and solidarity also obscures significant differences in social and economic status that existed within the peasant village long before European colonizers arrived on the scene.[61]

The notion of a homogenous and harmonious pre-colonial countryside had been further refuted by more recent research showing that the extensive commercialization and state centralization in early modern China and Southeast Asia reached the remotest villages and created significant fluidity, mobility, perils, as well as long-distance urban–rural and transnational networks.[62] But back in the 1960s through the 1970s, when the generation of young, anti-war intellectuals finished their PhDs and started to populate mainstream academic institutions, the romanticized view about an egalitarian and communal Asian peasant standing up against world capitalism and US imperialism became increasingly prominent in the Western academia.

More recent research has found that the Communist revolution in China and Southeast Asia succeeded not because of the bottom-up support of the revolutionary causes by the revolutionary peasants, as asserted by Communist propaganda and Western interpretations of those Asian revolutions as peasant insurrections.

---

[61] Adas 1980: 527; Adas 1980: 528, 529 for the reliance on data and thinking from China research.
[62] Hung 2011; Buoye 2000; Marks 1998; Li 1998, 2024; Li and Cooke 2004; Reid 1988.

Instead, they were more a result of the effective Machiavellian maneuvering by the revolutionary elite to take advantage of the social and political crisis of the time. It has been well documented that the CCP's rural power base grew strongest in places where the rural gentry elite was alienated by the Kuomintang 國民黨 (KMT, or Nationalist Party, the ruling party of China from 1927–1949) state's centralizing efforts and shifted their allegiance to the CCP in the 1930s and 1940s when the CCP posed as moderate democratic reformers.[63] In the early 1970s, the Cambodian Communist Party's peasant army grew after Beijing advised Pol Pot to forge a united front with the Cambodian Communists' archenemy, King Sihanouk, who had just been ousted in a coup orchestrated by the US in 1970. With the king as the figurehead, the Communist army attracted many new recruits from the peasants, who thought they were joining a royalist movement to restore the king.[64] In other words, these communist movements successfully built their rural power base not because of any peasants' preexisting affinity to communal socialism but because of the peasants' longing for the restoration of some sort of conservative, hierarchical order after years of sociopolitical breakdown and war. The elite the Communists exploited to attract conservative peasant support, such as China's rural gentry and the Cambodian king, were repressed or eradicated after the Communists seized power.

Under the fervent identification of the idealized revolutionary Asian peasants, many Western intellectuals chose to deny news of the Cambodian genocide as propaganda and lies fabricated by the Western imperialist forces against the nascent revolutionary regime. When Asians spoke or acted in a way that did not fit the Orientalists' romantic stereotype of Asian peasants, the Orientalists, enjoying the Western privilege of deciding what is genuinely Asian, would simply deny them as a false voice orchestrated by Western imperialists. Noam Chomsky, a long-time powerful voice of leftist dissent in the US, even questioned the testimonies of Cambodian refugees about the Khmer Rouge atrocities in condescending and derogatory tones, accusing the refugees of complicity with Western

[63] Xu et al. 2024.
[64] Mertha 2025: Ch. 1.

vested interests in discrediting the "Cambodian revolutionaries" (i.e., the Khmer Rouge) in 1977:

> These reports [by some neglected journalists sympathetic to the Khmer Rouge] also emphasize both the extraordinary brutality on both sides during the civil war [in Cambodia] (provoked by American attack) and repeated discoveries that massacre reports were false. They also testify the extreme unreliability of refugee reports, and the need to treat them with great caution ... Refugees are frightened and defenseless, at mercy of alien forces. They naturally tend to report what they believe their interlocutors wish to hear. While their reports must be considered seriously, care and caution are necessary. Specifically, refugees questioned by Westerners or Thais have a vested interest in reporting atrocities on the part of Cambodian revolutionaries, an obvious fact that no serious reporter will fail to take into account.[65]

Remarkably, many intellectual Maoists who transposed their support of the Vietnamese communist revolution to the support of Mao's Cultural Revolution as two brotherly revolutions against US imperialism in the 1960s were thrown into disbelief and disarray when Mao China aligned with the US and became friendly with Nixon and Kissinger. After visiting China and finding out, through spontaneous conversations, that Chinese peasants were more concerned about economic well-being than revolution, some US Maoists turned rapidly to the right. As Fabio Lanza analyzed, many of these Maoist scholars strived to restore political subjectivity to Asian/Chinese people by shedding positive light on the Maoist revolutionary experience, but they continued to be clouded by the Orientalist legacy. These scholars

> [s]trove to construe the Chinese as active political subjects, they were nonetheless the inheritors of a long history of American orientalism, in which "China" had been constantly figured in terms of passivity and inscrutability .... It is difficult not to see in the very abrupt about-face of *some*

---

[65] Chomsky and Norman 1977: 791.

> concerned scholars ... the lingering traces of an orientalist perspective: China could be loved from a distance as an idealized but ultimately inscrutable whole, just to be abandoned when a closer look showed "her" imperfections, like an elegantly clad foot-bound woman whose deformity, once nakedly revealed, could provoke only absolute disgust. The complete – and literally overnight – shift from all-absorbing passion to absolute disillusion can be explained only once the relationship at stake is not the confrontation with a multitude of complex autonomous political subjects but is reduced again to a gendered object of desire.[66]

The beginning of rural market reform that broke up the People's Communes and unleashed the entrepreneurial spirit of the peasants by the CCP, together with the Chinese invasion of Vietnam in 1979, was the last straw that broke the fantasy about a unitary Asian revolutionary peasantry in solidarity against capitalism and Western imperialism. These developments left many Maoist intellectuals speechless and disillusioned, leading to their exodus from the leftist intellectual camp in the 1980s.[67]

---

[66] Lanza 2017: 110.
[67] Lanza 2017: 143–69.

Part V
SELF-ORIENTALISM

9 SELF-ORIENTALIZING NATION BUILDING

In Chapter 7, we saw how the entry of Chinese scholars helped de-Orientalize China Studies in Western academia after the mid twentieth century. Centuries of Orientalist knowledge had created entrenched stereotypes and biases, positive or negative, that persisted in popular imaginations and political discourses. Political forces and state builders in China have been strategically appropriating fantasies and fears surrounding China in the West to advance their own political projects since the early twentieth century. This strategic, or opportunistic, use of Western stereotypes and biases by the Chinese elite is another reason why Orientalist views of China persisted in the West despite the great advances in de-Orientalization in academia. Chapter 8 discussed how the Marxist revolutionary elite in Asia adopted the Orientalist conception of Asia's past as one of harmonious, communal, and rural societies to construct and legitimize their Maoist project of hyper-rural collectivization. Such social engineering projects, when imposed by a powerful modern state, created large-scale disasters.[1] However, self-Orientalizing nation-state building is not restricted to the communist movement. It is also shared by many conservatives and liberals in China's search for modernity throughout the twentieth century.[2]

In 1911, the Qing Empire collapsed. Han-Chinese provincial military elites declared independence from the Manchu court

---

[1] See Scott 1998.
[2] See Dirlik 1996.

one after the other following the anti-Qing revolutionaries' uprising in the central Chinese city of Wuchang 武昌. The Western-educated revolutionaries, led by Sun Yat-sen 孫逸仙, had been trying to overthrow the Qing government in futility for more than a decade, and they took this opportunity to declare a Republic. The revolutionaries had their stronghold in Guangzhou, just North of British Hong Kong, and were financed by overseas Chinese. But they had practically zero military power. The nascent Republic of China had to ground its existence on the consent of regional warlords, who had evolved from the Qing provincial military strongmen.[3]

The most powerful of such warlords was Yuan Shikai 袁世凱, the Viceroy of Zhili 直隸 – the greater capital region – in the last decade of the Qing Empire. He built and controlled the North Sea Fleet of the Qing. In a bid to win his support for the Republic, Sun and the revolutionaries let him assume its presidency in 1912. But Yuan was dissatisfied with the constraints of the new Republic's constitution, which the revolutionaries devised. Yuan changed the constitution in 1914 to vastly increase the president's power and effectively made him president for life. In December 1915, Yuan replaced the young Republic with a constitutional monarchy by declaring himself the Emperor of a new Chinese Empire. But his attempt faced serious opposition. Provincial armies declared independence and threatened to invade Beijing. Even his loyal army did not defend him. Yuan was forced to adjudicate in March 1916 to restore the Republic. He then died of illness in June 1916.[4] His death and the resulting vacuum in the political center led China into a prolonged civil war among regional warlords, while Sun Yat-sen and his fellow revolutionaries started to receive military assistance from Bolshevik Russia in the 1920s.

Yuan's brief attempt to restore monarchy faced the problem of convincing the ever-growing number of Chinese elite with Western education to support, or at least not fiercely oppose, his reactionary move. Yuan's solution was to hire Frank Goodnow, a founding father of American political science and a renowned scholar of comparative politics who taught administrative law at Columbia University from 1883 to 1914 and was the president of

---

[3] See Zarrow 2005: Part I; McCord 1993: Chs. 1–3.
[4] Jenne 2015; Zarrow 2005: Ch 4.

Johns Hopkins University from 1914 to 1929, to become his constitutional adviser in 1913 and to lead the drafting of a new constitution, making China a constitutional monarchy. Goodnow's intervention in Chinese politics showcases how centuries of Orientalist knowledge about China were used to facilitate the conservative state-building of modern China.

An American Political Scientist and Chinese Monarchists

Yuan's appointment of Goodnow was at the recommendation of Charles Eliot, the former president of Harvard University and a founding trustee of the Carnegie Endowment for International Peace.[5] Goodnow was the first president of the American Political Science Association in 1903. He was not a China expert. His major works were to explain why republicanism and democratic institutions worked in North America while leading to chaos and the dictatorship of military strongmen in South America. He argued that only people with high intelligence could exercise self-determination and uphold a functioning democracy. The reason why democratic institutions could not be sustained in Latin America was that Latin Americans did not possess the necessary intelligence to make such institutions function effectively.[6] His conception of what constituted a people's intelligence was ambiguous. But at his time, it was a common view in the academia that different races possessed different levels of intelligence and that darker and mixed-race people had lower intelligence than white people.[7]

Most US and Western establishment elites shared Goodnow's position that links people's intelligence to democracy at the time. The turn of the twentieth century saw the prevalence of scientific racism that regarded dark-skinned races as genetically inferior. They were supposedly driven by emotion and impulse and less capable of exercising rational decisions than white men. This racist theory was the justification of Western colonial rule or suzerainty in nearly all of the non-Western regions of the world. Domestically,

---

[5] Pugach 1973.
[6] Roberts 2020: 186–7; Kroncke 2012, 2016: 132–57.
[7] See Chapter 6.

this theory also justified the disenfranchisement of non-white population (and women, who were alleged to be less intelligent and less rational than men at that time). Under this racialist view, liberal democracy was essentially a white privilege enjoyed only by white men in majority white nations.[8]

When working as Yuan's constitutional adviser, Goodnow led the efforts to rewrite the Chinese constitution. His advice to Yuan was used by Yuan's allies to persuade the Chinese educated class that only a monarchical system fit China. As Yuan's adviser, he drafted a memorandum to Yuan, who had it translated into Chinese by the Peace Planning Society (Chou'an Hui 籌安會), Yuan's de facto monarchist party. The Chinese translation of the memorandum circulated widely in China in the form of a pamphlet titled *Gonghe yu junzhu lun* 共和與君主論 (On Republic and Monarchy) putatively without Goodnow's consent.[9] In the memorandum, Goodnow reiterated his thesis about the linkage between intelligence and functioning democracy by outlining his analysis of the failure of democracy in Latin America, in contrast to its success in North America. He went on to argue that the Chinese people did not possess the level of intelligence necessary for a republican system. Therefore, China needed an emperor. Yuan's action provoked angry reactions from both the Republican revolutionaries and other regional warlords. Public opinion in the US did not lack criticism of Goodnow's role in dialing back Chinese history by facilitating the attempt to restore the monarchy, as shown in the cartoon (Figure 9.1) that ridiculed Goodnow and Yuan in Baltimore's local newspaper.

Goodnow's discussion of the Chinese people's low intelligence was brief. Apparently, he was not making a genetic argument, as many of his scientific-racist peers did. He asserted that the lower intelligence of the Chinese resulted from a lack of mass education, a lack of experience among the population in large-scale cooperation and participation in national politics, and their being accustomed to autocratic rule. Theoretically, the Chinese people could later develop the intelligence necessary for a democratic system. In his own words,

---

[8] Du Bois 1945.
[9] MacMurray 1915: 49–50.

Figure 9.1 Yuan Shikai and Frank Goodnow as the Walrus and the Carpenter. A Baltimore local newspaper summarized the role of Frank Goodnow, then the president of Johns Hopkins University, in restoring the monarchy in China. The report came with a cartoon depicting Yuan and Goodnow as the Walrus and the Carpenter. It invoked the well-known story of the Walrus and the Carpenter exchanging nonsense and attracting a large following of clueless oysters to listen and follow as if the duo were uttering words of wisdom. After gathering all the oysters, the duo ate them all (Evening Sun of Baltimore, December 14, 1915; Johns Hopkins University Library Goodnow papers).

> China is a country which has for centuries been accustomed to autocratic rule. The intelligence of the great mass of its people is not high owing to the lack of schools. The Chinese have never been accorded much participation in the work of government. The result is that the political capacity of the Chinese people is not large. The change from autocratic to republican government made four years ago was

too violent to permit the entertainment of any very strong hopes for its immediate success.
... [A] monarchy is better suited than a republic to China. China's history and traditions, her social and economic conditions, her relations with foreign powers all make it probable that the country would develop that constitutional government which it must develop if it is to preserve its independence as a State, more easily as a monarchy than as a republic.[10]

This view was far from surprising or radical in Goodnow's time. After all, the disenfranchisement of African Americans in the Jim Crow era of the American South was under the thin veil of a literacy test that made disenfranchisement look like a policy based on education, while it was absolutely based on race.

The brief pamphlet penned by Goodnow did not provide a full analysis of his view of China or the sources of such a view. After Goodnow left China to assume the presidency of Johns Hopkins University in 1914 (while continuing to work for Yuan remotely for another year) and after Yuan died in 1916, he started writing extensively on China. These writings, which included the book *China: An Analysis* (Baltimore, 1926), offered us a fuller view of what informed his belief that a monarchical system was more suitable for China than a republican one. These writings revealed that his analysis of China was mostly drawn from the dominant Orientalist scholarship on China at the time and was much aligned with other social scientists' – including Marx's and Weber's – understanding of China that we discussed in Chapters 7 and 8.

In his more elaborate later writings, Goodnow attributed the lack of education among the masses, the central factor leading to low intelligence in China, to the fundamental faults of China's cultural system. First was Confucianism's adaptive view toward nature and its emphasis on philosophy and literature instead of on science and mathematics. Such emphasis made even the most educated elite lack curiosity and logic.[11] Worse, such an adaptive

---

[10] Goodnow 1915a: 57–8.
[11] Goodnow 1926: 87–8, 171–2, 178.

orientation of Confucianism allowed the prevalence of superstitions of Taoism, which is

> little more than the devices and expedients of a system of magic which in the hands of the Taoist and Buddhist priests alike has been used for the purpose of playing upon the superstitions and fears of the ignorant. A system of philosophy which originally had considerable dignity, has become little more than a scheme of necromancy and geomancy.[12]

More fundamentally, the Chinese language system did not follow any logic, and its reliance on hard memorization preempted the Chinese mental capacity from logical reasoning. It made the promotion of mass literacy difficult and let a small clique of official scholars monopolize reading and writing:

> The important thing is that the [Chinese] written language is not based upon a phonetic alphabet. Each word, ... each simple idea is represented by a particular character which under no circumstances is used to represent any other word or idea. As a result of this peculiarity a tremendous demand is made on the memory of one who learns to read and write.... The Chinese has had, however, to cumber his memory with hundreds if not thousands of symbols whose knowledge must for the most part be arbitrarily acquired. Little if any demand is made on the reasoning powers ... [T]he great mass of the people at the present time are, because of the difficulty of the language, both ignorant and inarticulate.... The great majority of the people are at present at the mercy of the intelligent and designing so far as an education which is based on the ability to read and write might serve as a protection. No wonder that on the one hand they are a prey of a self-seeking priesthood and on the other fall easy victims to the wiles of corrupt officials and petty politicians.[13]

That is to say, the problem of Chinese people's lack of education originated from the very foundation of Chinese civilization: its

---

[12] Goodnow 1926: 119.
[13] Goodnow 1926: 71–5.

cultural values, its psychology, and its language system. Published about a decade after Weber's *Religion of China*, Goodnow's *China: An Analysis* resonated with Weber's and other prominent views on China at the time: that the Chinese culture was fundamentally irrational and magical. Such deep roots of Chinese low intelligence precluded any easy fixes through simply building more schools for the masses.

The book also resonated with the thesis on Oriental despotism or the Asiatic mode of production. To Goodnow, self-sufficiency and communal–familial property of village communities led to the lack of communication and cooperation among its people:

> The population is too scattered, the social groups are too small to make co-operative activity easy. Chinese rural life is particularly hostile to co-operative action on any large scale, because of the self-sufficiency of the rural communities due in its turn to the practical absence of means of communication.... As the means of communication are generally very poor and as the duty of ancestor worship at the family shrine is an imperative one, there is comparatively little migration of population. Large family groups often therefore form the bulk if not the entirety of the population of particular villages. The family system thus often brings about what is really village ownership of property.[14]

This is a continuation of his view expressed earlier in his address to the eleventh annual meeting of the American Political Science Association in 1915:

> In China ... it is the family rather than the individual that counts. It is often the family rather than the individual in which the ownership of property is vested ... The existence of the Chinese family idea, based as it is on ancestor worship, has further had the effect of rendering the population rather stable and immobile with the result of congestion at particular points, and has at the same time made difficult the development of social groups wider in extent than the

[14] Goodnow 1926: 57, 156.

family. The character of the family would thus appear to have hindered the development of social cooperation.[15]

These social conditions, combined with the many cultural traits discussed, "justify if not to produce autocratic government to which all Asiatic peoples are prone."[16] Such a despotic state did not usually interfere with the self-sufficient village communities besides "collecting taxes and administering justice."[17]

Goodnow's use of these views to justify the argument that China needed to continue its autocracy by restoring the monarchy was just the beginning of the liaison between Western Orientalism and reactionary state-building projects among the conservative elite in China. Such liaison recurred throughout the twentieth century and continued into the twenty-first, as we shall see later. This episode illustrates a new mode of co-reproduction of Orientalist knowledge that involved active and somewhat equal participation of Chinese political actors in the twentieth century and beyond.

Orientalist Origins of Cultural Radicalism

While Goodnow and his monarchy restorationist allies harnessed the Orientalist conception of the Chinese civilization to justify their reactionary political project of turning the Chinese Republic back to monarchy, many young intellectuals in China came to understand Chinese civilizations through the Western lens and used the same Orientalist view for their radical agenda.

The May Fourth New Culture movement that started in 1919 was triggered by China's unfair treatment at the Treaty of Versailles. It cultivated a generation of young intellectuals who attributed China's continuous weakness and the strength of reactionary forces despite the 1911 Revolution to the lack of a cultural revolution following the political one. These intellectuals advocated the wholesale importation of Western culture and political doctrines in place of traditional Chinese culture. Reiterating the Western portrayal of Chinese culture as irrational and superstitious,

---

[15] Goodnow 1915b: 214.
[16] Goodnow 1915b: 143.
[17] Goodnow 1915b: 189.

which fomented autocratic rule and isolated communal villages, many May Fourth intellectuals called for total Westernization and the implantation of Western science and democracy as the only way out for China. Marxism was first introduced to the Chinese intellectuals via this movement and directly led to the formation of the Chinese Communist Party (CCP) in 1921.[18]

Goodnow's critique of the Chinese language as the root cause of the low literacy rate, the irrationality of the Chinese culture, and the lack of scientific spirit was a common position among Western scholars of the time. Many May Fourth radicals agreed. Goodnow asserted that Japan's reduction of the use of Chinese characters and turning more to its phonetic alphabet-based language contributed to Japan's successful modernization.[19] This view resonated with many Chinese radicals, who called for reforming the Chinese language as the linchpin toward Chinese modernity. May Fourth intellectuals started abandoning classical Chinese and formulating vernacular Chinese by introducing European-style grammar to Chinese sentence structure. Proposals for simplifying the Chinese characters, abandoning all characters, and turning the language into a romanized, phonetic, alphabet system thrived.[20] The whole generation of May Fourth writers – including Lu Xun 鲁迅, Ba Jin 巴金, and Mao Dun 茅盾 – devoted their literary careers to attacking traditional Chinese cultures as impediments to the progress of the young Chinese Republic.[21]

The most radical intellectuals in the May Fourth movement became followers of the CCP, which supported language reform and cultural revolution as essential to China's quest for modernity. The CCP saw wiping China clean of its traditional cultures through top-down transformation and social engineering as its core task after taking control of state power. And it did after 1949. Though stopping short of completely writing off the Chinese characters and turning the Chinese language into a romanized, alphabet-based language, as was initially contemplated and as Vietnam and Korea achieved, the Communist party-state did succeed in simplifying

---

[18] Chen 2007; Wasserstrom 1991: Part I.
[19] Goodnow 1926: 73–4.
[20] Kuzuoğlu 2023; Tsu 2022.
[21] Goldman ed 1977: 189–232, passim.

all Chinese characters.²² The violent rejection and destruction of structures and artifacts representing traditional cultures during the Cultural Revolution of 1966–1968 was the culmination of the May Fourth call for a total rejection of Chinese traditional culture.²³ The radicals' understanding of Chinese culture was largely a replication of what the simplistic Western Orientalist knowledge projected as China's stagnant and monotonic civilization.

China's liberal intellectuals, who flourished in the 1980s amid the market reform, inherited the May Fourth call to reject Chinese culture. Aspiring to end the one-party dictatorship and introduce liberal democracy to China, many of the 1980s liberal intellectuals saw the one-party authoritarian state as a contemporary reincarnation of Oriental despotism made possible by the traditional, rural-oriented culture of subservience. It was no accident that China's academic discussion of the Asiatic mode of production revived and blossomed in the 1980s.²⁴ Many Chinese historians with liberal political orientation brought back Marx's concept of the Asiatic mode of production. They suggested it was a more accurate description of the Chinese past than the concept of feudalism. They portrayed China's history as perennially dominated by a peasant economy based on scattered self-contained villages. This rural structure enabled the rise of Oriental despotism that continued well into the twentieth century, with an implicit reference to the dictatorship of Mao as a new emperor in Marxist clothing.

Some scholars influenced by this view reiterated the call for total Westernization of Chinese culture as a pathway toward political liberalization. Jin Guantao 金觀濤 and Liu Qingfeng 劉青峰, who were part of a group of intellectuals close to the reformist CCP leader Zhao Zhiyang 趙紫陽, coined the concept of China's "ultrastable structure" grounded on conservative, despotic lineage communities at the bottom and a despotic state at the top.²⁵ According to Jin and Liu, China's despotic state was recurrently rebuilt for thousands of years after each interruption by rebellions and state breakdown, as the blueprint of a despotic state was embedded in

---

²² Kuzuoğlu 2023; Tsu 2022.
²³ See Mitter 2005: Ch. 3.
²⁴ See Brook ed. 1990.
²⁵ Jin and Liu 1984.

each communal village. This thesis is a variant of Marx's Asiatic mode of production view. Jin and Liu argued that China had to modernize by breaking this eternal cycle of despotism through total Westernization from top to bottom of the society. This view later culminated in the popular and controversial TV documentary *River Elegy* (Heshang 河殤), aired on CCTV, China's official TV network, in 1988. The project was orchestrated by the leading liberal intellectuals within the Communist Party close to Zhao Zhiyang, including Jin Guantao. The main argument of the series was that China's problems, from the perceived economic stagnation in the late imperial period to the persistence of authoritarian rule and the lack of individual freedom, all originated from a backward, peasant-based, irrational Confucianist culture that had thrived in isolated inland China. It argued that China must embrace the ocean and Western civilization to break free from this geographically determined conservatism and despotism.[26] Such a thrust toward abandoning the traditional Chinese culture and embracing Western ones was well reflected in the Western-style Goddess of Democracy, a monument modeled after the Statue of Liberty, which protesting students in 1989 erected in Tiananmen Square to symbolize their aspirations. The rest is history.

Cultural Conservativism and Confucian Fascism

On the other side of the same coin, cultural conservatives reacted to the May Fourth radicals throughout the twentieth century to call for preserving traditional Chinese culture. Their understanding of traditional Chinese culture was no less based on Western Orientalist construction of Chinese traditions. Defending Chinese traditions against the attack from the liberals and the communists became the rallying cry of the KMT government led by military dictator Chiang Kai-shek 蔣介石 in the 1930s and 1940s. In 1943, in the middle of the war against Japan, Chiang Kai-shek authored and published *China's Destiny* to outline his vision of a modern Chinese state grounded on China's traditional culture that valued collectivism and subservience to a strong leader.[27] The book was

[26] De Jong 1989; Field 1991; Eng 2019.
[27] Chen 2014; see also Taylor 2011: Chs. 2 & 3.

allegedly ghost-written by conservative historian T'ao Hsi-sheng 陶希聖 (Tao Xisheng). It crystallized the thinking of the most prominent conservative thinkers in China at the time. The book was meant to reject Communism, as the Chiang government had been engaged in a civil war with the CCP until he reluctantly entered a united front with it against the Empire of Japan, which launched a full-scale invasion of China in 1937. More surprisingly, the book devoted a large portion to attacking Western liberalism as well. Reiterating the stereotypical image of traditional Chinese culture as conceptualized since nineteenth-century Western Orientalism, Chiang anchored all of his state-building project on the defense of a monotonous and static traditional Chinese value system echoing the construction by Goodnow and other Western scholars, as well as the radicals calling for abolishing those values.

To Chiang, the essence of Chinese culture was collectivism, which motivated people to "sacrifice their personal interests for the benefit of the whole community" of the village, clan, and nation.[28] To Chiang, the coming of Western imperialist powers and their subjugation of the Chinese economy, society, and politics led to the destruction of such communal spirit and the spread of anomic individualism and selfishness:

> [D]uring the past hundred years, as a result of the oppression of the unequal treaties, the welfare of the agricultural villages declined, while life in the cities became extravagant. As a result, the traditional structure of the family, the village, and the community was disrupted. The virtue of mutual help was replaced by competition and jealousy. Public planning was neglected and no one took an interest in public affairs ... [T]he average citizen became disorderly and lacking in logic, as revealed by his recklessness and dissipation, his stupidity and confusion ... [People] benefited themselves at the expense of others; promoted their private interests and neglected public affairs; and failed to understand the nature of the state or of the nation. They possessed no virtue or righteousness, no sense of thrift or of

---

[28] Chiang 1947 [1943]: 41.

shame. The decline of the nation's virtue could not have been more extreme.²⁹

Chiang asserted that China could only be saved by rejecting Westernization and restoring the traditional virtue of communalism, together with loyalty and obedience to the leader. He attacked Rousseau's theory of the natural rights of man. He claimed Rousseau's advocacy of freedom did not fit China's reality:

> After the conclusion of the unequal treaties, China's academic and intellectual circles lost their self-confidence and blindly echoed foreign theories. As a result, some quoted European theories of the eighteenth and nineteenth centuries to destroy our people's concept of government by law. They came across Rousseau's doctrine of "the natural rights of man" and then maintained that China's Revolution and the European Revolution of the eighteenth and nineteenth centuries were part of the same fight for "freedom." They did not realize that Rousseau's theory did not fit the historical facts ... If we investigate the history of evolution, there is no evidence of man's natural rights as claimed by Rousseau ... The [European] people had long been subject to ruthless absolutism and were suffering deeply from the consequences of lack of freedom. Their only solution, therefore, was to fight for "freedom" in order to eliminate such sufferings ... If we examine the government of China under successive dynasties, it will be observed that it generally adopted a magnanimous attitude toward the people, and that, aside from paying the grain tribute, the people had almost no contact with officials ... The Chinese people had long had great "freedom" and it was not necessary for them to fight for it.³⁰

He invoked a variant of Oriental despotism or the Asiatic mode of production thesis that China's autocratic government has perennially left the village communities untouched except for taxation, making the Chinese society "a pan of loose sand." This echoed Goodnow's description that the communal–familial foundation of Chinese society

---

²⁹ Chiang 1947 [1943]: 88–9.
³⁰ Chiang 1947 [1943]: 209–10.

left its people isolated in pockets, making it difficult to develop a higher order of social cooperation. As such, adopting the Western idea of expanding individual freedom could only increase this malaise and make China weaker and more chaotic. The right remedy for China was to overcome its social disorganization and to unify all people under a strong state and strong leader. Chiang contended that, "To resist foreign oppression, we must curtail 'individual freedom' and form a solid organization, like putting cement into loose sand to make it a solid rock ... '[I]ndividual freedom' of the type of loose grains of sand cannot be tolerated ... We must never permit individual interest to interfere with the common interest of the state."[31]

Such a call to defend a simplistically constructed tradition, which was hinged on collectivism and statism, against the erosion by individualism is far from unique in China at the time. Noticing the resemblance between Chiang's political languages and practices and that of Mussolini and Hitler, historian Frederic Wakeman characterized Chiang's government as a "Confucian fascist" regime.[32] It is in this context that we can understand Chiang's awkward attack on the gypsies as the "most licentious people in the world" and warned that the Chinese people would be despised and discarded like the gypsies had the Chinese continued to disregard traditional culture and disrespect the state:

> We all know that the "freedom" of the gypsies amounts to nothing but indulgence and wandering. Internally, they have no concept of law and no sense of national consciousness, and externally they cannot form into an organized body to protect their own safety. Therefore, they have become the lowest and most backward group in the world, scorned and forsaken by others and mistreated wherever they go. We Chinese citizens cannot adopt the free behavior of the gypsies on the one hand, and on the other, talk grandly about modernization and the establishment of government by law. We must recognize that the state is the source and foundation of ten thousand generations of descendants.[33]

[31] Chiang 1947 [1943]: 209–11.
[32] Wakeman 1997.
[33] Chiang 1947 [1943]: 209–12.

Chiang's *China's Destiny* was published at the height of World War II in 1943 when China was a key ally of the US in fighting fascism. Remarkably, China advisers in the Franklin D. Roosevelt (FDR) government, including John King Fairbank, were exasperated by the book's interpretation of China's history and attribution of all China's ills to Western ideas. Fairbank later described the book's anti-Western, anti-liberal tenets as the "[s]keleton from the Kuomintang closet."[34] In 1943, Fairbank remarked in his diary entry that

> I must say I am appalled after reading more of *China's Destiny*. I never saw such a pernicious use of history for political purposes. Much of the book is in the guise of straight history … The book is a tract unworthy of a statesman, and I can now see why everyone connected with the English translation is having chills and fever.[35]

Chiang's inner circle knew very well the book's content would damage Western countries' support of his regime. The KMT government, therefore, worked hard to prevent the English translation of the book. The Office of Strategic Services (OSS), the US intelligence service at the time, provided a chapter-by-chapter summary of the book for internal circulation within the FDR administration. The secret OSS memo, dated July 15, 1943, and titled "China's Destiny – by Chiang Kai-shek, A Political Bible for the New China," acknowledged that:

> It appears that the Generalissimo [Chiang] was embarrassed by the question of foreign publication of his book. It was written for domestic consumption … The author was probably told that parts of the book would create a bad impression abroad. In America, it would explode the China myth. Specifically, the strictures against liberalism and internationalism would make bad reading, as would the ardent nationalism and the totalitarian position of the Kuomintang … If a foreign edition is authorized, it will doubtless contain significant emendations.[36]

---

[34] Fairbank 1947.
[35] Fairbank 1982: 252–3.
[36] Cited in Reed 2021: 75.

The "China myth" that the OSS memo referred to was the image that the KMT ruling elite and the pro-KMT China lobby in the US had been carefully cultivating in the US for years. It was an image of Chiang Kai-shek, who was baptized in 1930 as a Methodist under the urging of his wife, Soong Mei-ling 宋美齡, and her Methodist family, as a good, benevolent Christian who was leading China to become a populous, powerful Christian nation and a reliable ally of the West in the East.[37] Such a myth resonated with the long-time Western fantasy of Marco Polo, the Jesuits, and nineteenth-century Romantic Sinologists that Chinese morality was aligned with Christianity and that China would soon be converted and become the largest Christian nation on earth.

Chiang and his allies in Washington managed to keep the book's English translation from appearing. Increasingly, US intellectuals, journalists, and scholars became aware of the book and referred to it as Chinese *Mein Kampf*. The call for an English translation grew alongside advocacy for reevaluating US support of the KMT government. In December 1945, after Japan surrendered and the Pacific War ended, US Congressman Hugh Delacy spoke on the floor of the House of Representatives on the Chinese *Mein Kampf*:

> I now have some comments to make upon the lack of democracy under Chiang Kai-shek … It is very odd that his book, which is the *Mein Kampf* of China, called *China's Destiny*, has never been permitted by him to have a single English translation nor has his strict censorship permitted any copy of any translation to come out of that country. It is very odd that no correspondent has ever been authorized to quote a single line from Chiang Kai-shek's book … Some of us [Congressmen] wondered why and we asked the Secretary of State to give us a copy – the State Department copy because they made a translation. The Secretary of State just smiled and said he thought at this moment it might not be wise to make it available.[38]

After all the hassle, the official English translation of the book was published in the US in 1947.

---

[37] Bradley 2015: Ch. 4.
[38] Hugh Delacy, December 7, 1945, cited in Reed 2021: 78.

In this chapter, we saw that both the radical and the conservative intellectuals and elites in twentieth-century China grounded their arguments on their presumption about a motionless, monotonous, traditional Chinese culture characterized by irrationality, rural collectivism, and autocracy. All these characteristics were put under the overarching label of Confucianism. The radicals and the conservatives only differed in whether to abandon or revive such traditions. The problem is that such a simplistic understanding of Chinese civilization is little more than an Orientalist projection. Those radical and conservative intellectuals in China perpetuated old Orientalist knowledge about China to serve the political project of their state-building elite patrons despite the de-Orientalization efforts that were well underway. Their projection of the Chinese traditions was at odds with the historical changes and complex variations of the Confucianist canons. Such changes and complex variations were what the New Confucianists, a group of Chinese intellectuals who attempted to revive the liberal variants of Confucianism and integrate them with Western liberalism, embraced and tried to rescue at the height of the Cold War.

10 CONTESTED CONFUCIANISM

Both the cultural radicals and cultural conservatives in twentieth-century China borrowed from the Orientalist construction of Confucianism by the Jesuits through the nineteenth-century Sinologists.[1] They both grounded their arguments on understanding Confucianism as a monolithic, unchanging doctrine embodied in some ancient classic texts. In reality, Confucianism, just like any ideological system, had been constantly evolving and interacting with other homegrown or imported ideological currents. Such developments were intertwined with imperial China's social, economic, and political developments.

In the mid twentieth century, at the height of the Cold War division, a group of diasporic Chinese scholars attempted to rescue Confucianism from the reification by cultural radicals and conservatives. They attempted to restore the understanding of Confucianism to its full complexity and sought to find ways to fuse it with Western liberalism as a strategy to foster a Chinese cultural renaissance compatible with liberal democracy. It was nothing less than a conscious effort to fight the self-Orientalism of many Chinese intellectuals serving the interests of authoritarian state-builders in the name of preserving or eradicating Chinese traditions. The achievements and failures of this New Confucianism movement still reverberate in the cultural matrix underlying the twenty-first-century China boom.

---

[1] See also Jensen 1997.

Varieties of Confucianisms in Imperial China

From the Song dynasty in the eleventh century to the height of the Qing dynasty in the eighteenth century, China experienced a long process of administrative centralization and commercialization. By the eighteenth century, on the eve of China's direct confrontation with Western imperialist powers, empire-wide commercial networks had reached the remotest corners of the empire. The imperial state had attained administrative penetration into grassroots societies all over the empire to regulate local moral and economic affairs. The state's micromanaging of local grain prices in the eighteenth century illustrates the imperial state's reach.[2] The image of Chinese society as constituted by an ocean of isolated, self-sufficient village communities untouched by the state besides taxation, constructed in nineteenth- and early-twentieth-century Sinological accounts, cannot be farther from reality.

Concomitant to this long-term economic and political change was the changing ideological formations of Confucianism as a state and elite ideology over the centuries. One fundamental tenet of classical Confucianist thought is the principles of filial loyalty (*zhongxiao* 忠孝) and benevolence (*renai* 仁愛). These principles dictate that all familial and extrafamilial social relations must follow a seniority-based hierarchy. Within the family, the juniors had to be docile to the seniors, and the seniors had to nourish the juniors with great care. Applying this to the political relations between officials and their subjects, classical Confucianism suggested that subjects must be respectful and obedient, while officials were obliged to offer paternalist care and fatherly discipline. The same logic applied to the relations between the emperor and officials. Relations among the emperor, his officials, and his subjects were conceptualized as quasi-familial relations resembling those between grandparents, parents, and children.[3]

Classical Confucianism was constituted by no more than an array of moral dictums. Facing strong competition from Buddhist metaphysics imported from India after the eighth century,

---

[2] Hung 2011: Ch. 1; Will and Wong 1991.
[3] Hamilton 1990; Rozman 2003; Hung 2024: 382–90.

Confucianist philosophers were anxious to devise a metaphysical foundation for the classical Confucianist moral dictums. In the eleventh century, the Cheng-Zhu 程朱 School of neo-Confucianism, or the "philosophy of principle" (*lixue* 理學), became the dominant form of Confucianism under state sponsorship. This official neo-Confucianist orthodoxy emphasized that the moral principle (*li* 理) of filial piety, among others, was inscribed in the natural world, waiting to be discovered by the educated elite through rational learning. The elite were then obliged to inculcate these principles upon others via authoritative institutions, such as state academies. The state's educational endeavors were perennial, as eradicating all individual desires incompatible with the *li* was a constant struggle necessary to secure harmony and prosperity.[4] State elites were also obliged to promote the construction of lineage organizations in local societies across the empire. Such organizations could transmit the Confucianist morality of filial piety to youngsters by practicing such morality daily.[5]

The Cheng-Zhu School remained dominant until the late sixteenth century when resourceful private academies thrived with the support of the mercantile wealth in the southern coastal cities of the Ming Empire. Private academies, freed from state control, became the scholarly institutions where literati could contemplate new philosophical tenets outside the Cheng-Zhu orthodoxy.

The Wang Yangming 王陽明 School of neo-Confucianism, or the philosophy of the mind (*xinxue* 心學), became popular among independent-minded intellectuals in the sixteenth and seventeenth centuries. Heavily influenced by the Buddhist concept of self-meditation and enlightenment and expressing populist, liberal tendencies, this new philosophy asserted that the *li* was not inscribed in the natural world but was embedded in the human mind. It did not need to be discovered and imposed by the state elite. However, it could be approached by subjective self-learning and open discussion among free individuals, regardless of class, ethnicity, gender, and level of education. Everyone was equally poised to be enlightened to the *li*. Hence, "the streets are full of sages" (*man jie shi sheng ren* 滿街是聖人). It followed that the state's monopoly of philosophical

---

[4] Liu 1973; deBary 1981: Ch. 21–3.
[5] Faure 2007; Chow 1994: 71–97.

interpretation was illegitimate and that individuals should have the right to freely pursue and debate moral principles.[6]

This school of neo-Confucianism also espoused the horizontal relations of "friendship" (*peng* 朋) among literati as an alternative to the vertical hierarchy based on filial loyalty under the Cheng-Zhu orthodoxy. It promulgated that peer alliances among scholar-officials were politically virtuous, as it helped check monarchical power. Armed with this liberal, populist, and anti-authoritarian ideology, late Ming literati in southern metropolises coalesced around the private academies as public spheres and as quasi-political associations. The allegedly repressive, corrupt, and predatory central government of the time, based on an alliance of the Emperor and inner-court eunuchs, became a target of virulent attacks from these academies. The academies advocated a more decentralized political system based on a federation of self-governing regions. This liberal philosophy helped fuel an array of urban revolts against the central government in the closing decades of the Ming Empire.[7] The Wang Yangming School of Confucianism also developed into more radical variants that embraced the absolute sovereignty of individual minds and a Nietzschian revaluation of all dominant morality and institutions. One such example of radical Confucianism was the "mad Zen" philosophy of Li Zhi (李贄) (See Figure 10.1).[8]

Frederic Wakeman characterized this school of neo-Confucianism as the Chinese equivalent of a bourgeois ideology fostering a cultural revolution. He regarded Wang Yangming's "populist spirit … [can be] compared to qualities of the Protestant Reformation in Europe."[9]

Following the collapse of the Ming dynasty and the founding of the Qing amid urban uprisings, peasant rebellions, bureaucratic infighting, and the Manchu invasion, Chinese literati who defected to the Manchu conquerors blamed the Wang Yangming School for the moral laxity, political chaos, and dynastic breakdown of the Ming. They called for a conservative restoration of the Cheng-Zhu orthodoxy. The new Manchu rulers of China,

---

[6] Wakeman 1972, 1998; Yü 2004: Ch. 6.
[7] Elman 1989; Wakeman 1972, 1998; Masatoshi 1984; Wu 2011; von Glahn 1991.
[8] Perdue 2000; Lee, Paulin 2012; Handler-Spitz et al ed. 2021: 3–14.
[9] Wakeman 1998: 169.

Figure 10.1 Li Zhi (1527–1602), the anarchist neo-Confucianist in sixteenth-century China. Li Zhi, who formulated the "mad Zen" School of neo-Confucianism of the Wang Yangming lineage, was from a Fujian mercantile background with Arab–Muslim heritage. He questioned all authorities and moralities. Some compared him to Nietzsche. The Ming government saw him as too dangerous and arrested him. He committed suicide in jail.
Source: Wikimedia Commons

anxious to win the support of Chinese literati and portray themselves as Confucianist sages inheriting the Mandate of Heaven from the Ming, were happy to follow the defectors' advice.[10] The Manchu Emperors resuscitated the Cheng-Zhu School as the sole legitimate system of morality through a state-sanctioned curriculum and state-sponsored academies in the late seventeenth and early eighteenth centuries. Independent private academies were closed, and the Wang Yangming School of neo-Confucianism was denounced as heresy to be excluded from the curriculum of

[10] Gao 2000: Ch. 4; Wakeman 1998: 173–7; Elman 1989: 402–8.

imperial examination.¹¹ The Qing state achieved more than a simple restoration of the orthodoxy. With its unprecedented capacity to regulate and intervene in society, the Qing state managed to mold social relations after the Confucianist principle of filial piety to an extent unseen in previous dynasties.

With the motto of "governing the heaven and earth through the principle of filial piety" (*yi xiao zhi tianxia* 以孝治天下), the Manchu rulers reinstated the principle that emperor-official and official-subject relations were extensions of father-son relations.¹² Under this filial ideology, the emperor's control of his officials and subjects and governmental provision of welfare to the subjects were framed as the state's exercises of paternalist discipline and benevolent care. In the early days of Manchu rule in the late seventeenth century, the *Xiao jing* 孝經 (Book of Filial Piety), which was believed to be written by Confucius' disciples and stated in the opening paragraph that "[t]he gentleman's service of his parents with filial piety produces a loyalty that can be transferred to the ruler," was the most frequently reprinted Confucianist treatise from the state printing house.¹³ In 1670, the Kangxi Emperor issued the *Shengyu* 聖諭 (Sacred Edict), which was composed of sixteen "politico-moral maxims" aimed to "indoctrinate the masses with the official ideology."¹⁴ The top maxim was to "esteem most highly filial piety and brotherly submission in order to give due importance to all social relations."¹⁵ The imperial state reproduced large volumes of the Sacred Edict to be disseminated to all local governments. County magistrates were required to organize semi-monthly lectures to explain the Edict to local populaces and interpret current affairs in terms of its creeds. County magistrates also assigned local magnates to replicate this lecture in the villages.¹⁶ This practice was not unlike weekly mass in European churches. It was quite successful until after 1850, and "[t]he remarkably prolonged stability of the eighteenth-century reigns may, in some measure, be attributed

---

¹¹ Wakeman 1998: 173–7; Elman 2000: Ch. 7 & 8; Chow 1994: 44–7; Woodside 1990.
¹² Ye 2002: 74–5.
¹³ Ye 2002: 74–5.
¹⁴ Chang 1955: 65.
¹⁵ Translation adopted from Mair 1985: 325.
¹⁶ Mair 1985; Zhou 2006; Chu 1962: Ch. IX.6.

to the effectiveness of formal lectures and informal homilies on the Sacred Edict in propagating a uniform ideology."[17]

To exterminate any remaining influence of the Wang Yangming philosophy that espoused friendship among peer scholar-official as an alternative to filial loyalty to the emperor-patriarch, the Yongzheng 雍正 Emperor authored *Yuzhi pengdang lun* 御製朋黨論 (The Imperial Discourse on Friends and Parties) in 1724. He assigned it as a must-read title among all educated subjects. In the book, the Yongzheng Emperor promulgated that friends, parties, or cliques among literati could be no more than platforms to advance one's selfish interests. A gentleman who placed the common good of the empire above his self-interest should "only have the emperor in his heart," and he should "attune his judgments to the emperor's judgment, not his friends." The book also claimed that once a gentleman became an official, he "gives his body to the throne and can no longer consider the body as belonging to his [biological] father and mother, let alone his friends."[18]

Besides promoting the subjects' filial loyalty toward the throne, the Qing state also continued the early Ming drive to strengthen lineage organizations and regulate intra-familial relations at the grassroots level. These efforts were grounded on the Confucianist conviction that stable families were the most effective bulwark against any immoral and unlawful behaviors, as well as the belief that once people had internalized the filial disposition in their biological family, they would be automatically attuned to the standard of proper behavior toward officials and the emperor as their imagined fathers and grandfather.[19] In the *Daqing lüli* 大清律例 (Great Qing Legal Code), extensive sections were devoted to laws that sanctioned behavior deemed destabilizing to orthodox familial relations, such as extramarital affairs, incest, and homosexuality.[20]

Outside the orbit of Confucianism, other cultural traditions, such as lay Buddhism and other syncretic sectarian religions, grew in tandem with the expansion of the population and commercial activities in the empire. Some studies did point out that the grip

---

[17] Mair 1985: 337.
[18] Yongzheng Emperor 1724, my translation.
[19] Faure 2007: 151–252; Rowe 2002: 529–37; Ocko 1990; Furth 1990.
[20] See Sommer 2000; Shen 2007: Ch. 6, Pt 1.

of the neo-Confucianist orthodoxy loosened gradually during the eighteenth century when worsening social malaises prompted the literati to focus more on finding practical solutions to those problems than purifying society with rigid orthodoxy.[21] However, the orthodoxy's dominance was generally intact during the mid-Qing period.

Under the domination of the neo-Confucianist orthodoxy, the state carefully scrutinized other ideological communities, particularly the Buddhists. Some of these heterodox religious groups were persecuted rigorously for allegedly trespassing the moral boundary defined by the orthodoxy. Through the eighteenth century, the Qing state was increasingly active in investigating the doctrines and practices of Buddhist groups and distinguishing the heterodox ones from the non-heterodox ones. However, drawing the line between the two was very difficult in practice. The state was never hesitant to root out heterodox groups, such as the White Lotus sect, once they were identified. In certain extraordinary times, when the moral legitimacy of the imperial center was in crisis, heterodox Buddhist groups became more capable of recruiting aggrieved commoners, grew in size, and occasionally fostered open rebellion.[22]

Though repressed by the Manchu state, the Wang Yangming School of neo-Confucianism did not completely dissipate. It continued to exist as a subterranean opposition consciousness connected to the hidden Ming restorationist, anti-Manchu ideology among the literati elite. After the empire was rocked by aggravating corruption scandals and large-scale heterodox rebellions at the turn of the nineteenth century, the monarch – Jiaqing 嘉慶 Emperor – contemplated administrative reform. In the early nineteenth century, pro-reform officials started forming factions, transcending the taboo against factionalism imposed by the Yongzheng Emperor. They became increasingly outspoken advocates for a bold administrative revamp.[23] Despite the pertinence of many of these reform proposals and the energy of the growing pro-reform factions, the vested interests' resistance to reform was so grave that most of the proposals were never actualized before time ran out in 1839–1842

---

[21] E.g., Chow 1994: 161–203; Furth 1990; Elman 1984: 1–36: Rowe 2001.
[22] Hung 2011: Ch. 4.
[23] Polachek 1992; Kuhn 2002: 27–53; Gao 2000: 548–78.

when China's humiliating defeat in its clash with the British shattered the fragile legitimacy of the Manchu state.[24]

In the wake of the Qing's defeat in the Opium War with the British, anti-Manchuism, which was hidden among the pro-reform Han scholar-officials before the war, came out into the open. A Qing historian notes that "commencing in late 1843 or thereabouts, a literati-bureaucratic opposition did, in fact, begin to galvanize and acquire a highly visible organizational form: the so-called Ku Yen-wu Shrine Association."[25] It is noteworthy that the association was named after Ku Yen-wu (Gu Yanwu 顧炎武), a seventeenth-century anti-Manchu intellectual who, unlike many other Chinese literati defecting to the nascent Manchu state, steadfastly maintained his loyalty to the Ming dynasty and refused to accept the Manchus as China's legitimate rulers. In the latter half of the nineteenth century, literati broke the taboo imposed by the Manchu ruler by openly discussing the Wang Yangming School of neo-Confucianism again. After the Qing defeat in the Sino–Japanese War of 1894–1895, radicalizing reformist literati like Kang Youwei 康有為 built openly oppositional associations after the model of late Ming private academies. It was the beginning of the end of the Qing Empire.[26]

New Confucianism after Empire

As we have seen in Chapter 9, following the Republican Revolution of 1911 and the New Culture Movement that started in 1919, the intellectual scene of China was divided between the radicals advocating total Westernization and the conservatives trying to defend traditional cultures. Both grounded their understanding of China's traditional culture on the Orientalist projection of a constant, unitary Confucianism.

In 1915, after Frank Goodnow presented a paper reiterating his position that China was unfit for democracy and a monarchy would work better there (see Chapter 9) at the American Political Science Association's eleventh annual meeting, the discussant of the paper, Sudhindra Bose, an Indian scholar teaching at the University

---

[24] Hung 2011: Ch.5 and Epilogue.
[25] Polachek 1992: 206.
[26] Polachek 1992: 205–36.

of Iowa, refuted the idea that democracy did not fit China, and Asia more broadly, by invoking the liberal-democratic traditions within Confucianism:

> I have listened with unusual interest to the learned paper on "Reform in China" just read by President Goodnow. It seems to me, however, that the Occidental people find no end of difficulty in understanding and interpreting our Oriental laws, customs, and institutions. We are told, for instance, that the Chinese like other Asians, who are mainly agricultural peoples, are unfit for representative government. I doubt if this statement can stand the test of adequate proof. Take, for example, the people of China ... had from time immemorial enjoyed local self-government, had been accustomed to "take communal action": they would close up their business and resist the imposition of an unjust tax. It is to be remembered that the powers of the mother of parliaments developed in this fashion. "The financial functions of parliamentary assemblies are always the centre of their action.".... I challenge the assumption that representative forms of government are the monopoly of the West. I resent the implication that the Orientals are in any essential manner different from the Occidentals. We of the East ask only one thing of the West. It is this – that you of the West stay away from us and our problems: leave us to solve our own problems, to work out our own destinies, while you spend your time looking after yours.[27]

A few years after Bose's rejoinder to Goodnow, a group of Chinese intellectuals founded the magazine *Xueheng* 學衡 (Critical Review) in 1922. This group of intellectuals and successive generations of their disciples, later known as the New Confucianists, attempted to chart a middle ground between the cultural radicals and the conservatives by fostering a liberal, modernizing program for China based on a reconstruction of the Confucianist canons. This involved resuscitating the liberal and populist Wang Yangming lineage of

[27] Bose 1915: 224–6.

Confucianism. Aware of the critical reflection of Western modernity in the West in the aftermath of the disastrous World War I, they rejected total Westernization and saw a critical, selective union of Western and Chinese ideational systems as an alternative way for China.[28]

According to one of the leading scholars in this school, Mou Tsung-san (Mou Zongsan 牟宗三), Confucianism was never a static tradition but was ever-mutating in response to external challenges, leading to successive phases of Confucianist development. For example, the challenge of Buddhist metaphysics gave rise to the eleventh-century revival of Confucianism in the form of Cheng-Zhu School and later the sixteenth-century Wang Yangming School as different responses. This resulted in the departure from the original phase of Confucianism and the rise of its second phase in late imperial or early modern China. The second phase was marked by the integration of Buddhist elements into the Confucianist system of thought. The coming of Western modernity in the nineteenth century constituted a new challenge that urged a new round of Confucianist response, leading to the third phase of Confucianist development in the twentieth century. Mou himself worked on a critical union of Confucianist philosophy and Western idealist philosophies of the Kantian and Hegelian traditions as part of Confucianism's third phase response to external shock.[29]

New Confucianist scholars tried to break the Orientalist dichotomy between Chinese communalism and Western individualism by resusitating the Confucianist conception of individual reflexivity, enlightenment, and self-cultivation in the web of communal, social interconnectedness. In 1958, the representative scholars in the New Confucianism movement, including Mou Tsung-san, Hsu Foo-kwan 徐復觀, Carsun Chang 張君勱, Tang Chun-i 唐君毅, having mostly moved to Hong Kong or Taiwan after fleeing the Communist takeover of 1949, issued "A Manifesto for a Re-appraisal of Sinology and Reconstruction of Chinese Culture" to express the common denominator among the many different streams within the movement.

---

[28] See Hon 2015: Ch. 6.
[29] See Chan 2011; Zhu 2021; Tu 2017; Schmidt 2011; Clower n.d.

The Manifesto, published in the January 1, 1958 issue of the New Confucianist magazine *Minzhu pinglun* 民主評論 (Democratic Review), critiqued the Eurocentrism of Western Sinology since the Jesuits:

> [T]he fundamental motivation of the Jesuits was to carry out missionary work in China. Their intellectual strategy in China was to advocate for the Six Classics and Confucian teachings in opposition to the Neo-Confucianism of the Song and Ming periods, as well as to Buddhism and Daoism. Consequently, their introduction of Neo-Confucian thought was not based on an understanding of the natural development of Chinese culture itself but rather approached from the perspective of their missionary agenda ... Chinese and European sinologists have made remarkable and enduring contributions over the past several decades. However, at the same time, we cannot deny that the curiosity of Westerners about Chinese artifacts, along with their efforts to explore, acquire, and transport Chinese cultural relics as research materials was not directly focused on the origins and developmental trajectory of the cultural vitality and cultural spirit of China as a living civilization. This kind of interest, fundamentally, is no different from the interest Western scholars have in investigating the already extinct civilizations of Egypt, Asia Minor, and Persia – traveling everywhere to discover, acquire, and transport the relics of these civilizations.[30]

The Manifesto also critiqued aspects of Chinese culture. It advocated a critical comparison and union between the Confucianist and Western cultural systems. The Manifesto fretted about the failure of homegrown democracy in China and the persistence of monarchial tyranny. It also cherished the democratic values and tenets embedded in Confucianism. It established "democratic nation-building" (*minzhu jianguo* 民主建國) as the political goal of the reconstruction of Confucianism:

> Although China has not yet completed the task of building a democratic nation, we cannot say that the intrinsic

---

[30] Chang et al 1958: 3–4; my translation.

demands of China's political development do not lean toward the establishment of a democratic system. Even more so, we cannot claim that there are no seeds of democratic thought within Chinese culture … In China's political system, the restrictions on monarchical power, which were once solely implemented internally by officials such as chancellors and censors, must evolve into external restrictions imposed by the power of the people.... [T]hrough the development of China's monarchical system and the political resistance and demand against monarchial politics within Chinese culture, China must ultimately abolish the monarchy and move toward the establishment of a democratic system.[31]

In retrospect, the Manifesto was to reconstruct a Confucianist philosophy of embedded individualism that transcended the dichotomy between individualism and communalism, as well as between cultural radicalism and conservatism. The New Confucianist movement, which started in the early twentieth century as a variant of a Han nationalist movement, morphed into a transnational cultural movement that encompassed East Asia and the Chinese diaspora community, or what Arif Dirlik characterized as "borderland Confucianism."[32]

One of the third-generation New Confucianism scholars, Tu Weiming 杜維明, emphasized that Wang Yangming's thought on individuals achieving sagehood through one's reflexivity and actions amid one's interconnectedness to the world, together with one's persistent struggle with dominant social norms illustrated a universal transcendence of the dichotomy between communalism and individualism. Further, he noticed Wang's conception of the union between knowledge and action, as well as his objection to pure learning through books and academic institutions, was the inspiration of generations of revolutionaries in twentieth-century China as well as modernists in Japan:

> The repercussions of Yang-ming's ideas are still evident in China and Japan today: Sun Yat-sen's (1866–1925)

---

[31] Chang et al 1958: 16, my translation.
[32] Dirlik 1995: 230, 271; see also Chan 2011: 278.

doctrine of action, Hsiung Shi-li's (1885–1968) philosophy of mind, and Mao Tse-tung's theory of practice, not to mention Mishima Yukio's ritual suicide that shook the literary world in November, 1970, are all, at least in part, influenced by Yang-ming's mode of thought ... Under his influence, the Confucian Way could no longer be considered a privileged avenue of the literatus. It became, as it was originally meant to be, a way of being human for all ... [W]hat Yang-ming had done to Confucianism was no less profound than what Martin Luther had done to Christianity.[33]

The influence of the Wang Yangming School of Confucianism in the making of Japan's modernity has been apparent.[34] We might even see it as a source of Japan's "honorific individualism" (vis-à-vis possessive individualism in the West) in its transition to modernity.[35]

The New Confucianists objected to both the May Fourth radicals' program of total rejection of Chinese culture that developed into the Chinese Communist movement and the authoritarian conservatism of Chiang Kai-shek's KMT regime. After the Chinese Communist Party (CCP) came to power in mainland China and Chiang's KMT government retreated to Taiwan, most of the New Confucianists chose to move to Hong Kong under British rule to take advantage of the liberal intellectual environment in the colony. They continued developing the New Confucianism project and cultivated new generations of students. Some moved between Hong Kong, Taiwan, and the US academia. The bastion of their intellectual activities in the 1950s was the New Asia College in Hong Kong, which later became a key unit in constituting the Chinese University of Hong Kong, founded in 1963. This New Confucianist movement continued to struggle as a living, developing tradition among the Chinese diaspora communities at the interstices of the Communist government, the KMT government in Taiwan, and Western powers in the mid and late twentieth century.[36]

This movement remained strictly intellectual. The successive generations of its disciples rarely made overt political

---

[33] Tu 1976: ix–x.
[34] See Moore 1973.
[35] Ikegami 1995.
[36] Chou 2012.

comments, except for Yü Ying-shih, who, over time, became a keen anti-authoritarian opinion leader and supporter of democratic movements in Taiwan and Hong Kong.[37] More recently, there have been discussions about how the institutions, norms, and social formations developed in several East Asian democracies, including South Korea and Taiwan, manifest the influence of Confucian communitarianism and meritocratic elitism so much so that their political system could be characterized as Confucian democracy.[38]

In contrast, when China's economic boom under Communist rule was in full force at the turn of the twenty-first century, intellectuals aligned with the CCP authoritarian state blew the trumpet of perpetual Chinese communalism and obedience as the impetus of China's rising power against the hedonist individualism underlying Western decline. This Orientalist dichotomy between individualist West and collectivist East prevailed again despite the New Confucianists decades-long effort to undo such dichotomy.

Post-Cold War Asian Values

With the rapid economic growth of the so-called Confucianist circle, including Japan, South Korea, Taiwan, Hong Kong, Singapore, and part of Southeast Asia in the 1960s onward, a social scientific literature emerged in the 1980s that tried to use these cases of "Asian Tigers" to refute Weber's thesis about the affinity between capitalist growth and Protestantism and the lack of such affinity between capitalism and Confucianism. With the rapid economic growth of China after the 1990s, this literature also expanded to explain China's rise and asserted that Confucianism was a functional equivalent of Calvinism in creating a work ethic essential to capitalist takeoff. As such, Confucianism was the main reason for East Asia's economic success. Such literature usually saw Confucianism as some omnipotent ether that embraced all of East Asia and was defined by some ahistorical cultural traits such as collectivism, family values, obedience to authority, discipline, hostility to individual enjoyment, and so on. Some argued that while the

---

[37] See Yü 2022a & b.
[38] Kim 2014; Fetzer and Sope 2012; Shin 2012.

Confucianist ethic of disciplined hard work was channeled toward seeking excellence in examination in imperial times, it became redirected to entrepreneurial activities after global capitalism incorporated East Asian economies and conferred the Confucianist ethic a new goal for which to strive.[39] Some argued that the Confucianist emphasis on collective goods over individual enjoyment made East Asian capitalism more sustainable and superior to Western capitalism based on individualism, and that Confucianism's emphasis on stable hierarchy and social harmony provided a better framework for efficient market functioning with less social disruption.[40] Some claimed that China's authoritarian system represented the Confucianist ideal of meritocracy and rule by sages that had excelled in bringing prosperity and peace for millennia and were superior to conflict-prone, inefficient Western democracy.[41]

Reducing all societies of the East Asian region to a few fixed Confucianist tenets is problematic and emblematic of Orientalist epistemology. It is particularly so after all East Asian societies had undergone prolonged hybridization of local cultures with foreign ones, including liberalism and Christianity. Whether Japan and South Korea, which both deliberately de-Sinicized and strived to establish their own cultural identities vis-à-vis Chinese Confucianism in the twentieth century, can be regarded as Confucianist is open to question. This culturalist explanation of China's and Asia's rapid economic growth was at odds with the developmental state literature, which saw the guidance of the market economy by institutions of centralized government, instead of any arbitrary cultural tenets, as the origins of successful economic transformation.[42]

Besides academics who sought to explain East Asia's economic dynamism by Confucianism, there was also a revived interest in Confucianism among state elite in the region. Such revival reflected a renewed essentialization of Confucianism that converged with the anti-Western political project to legitimize paternalistic authoritarian rule in Asia. In the 1980s, Mahathir Mohamad of Malaysia and Lee Kuan Yew in Singapore, both authoritarian

---

[39] Redding 1993, Berger 1988.
[40] Poznanski 2017.
[41] Bell 2010, 2016.
[42] E.g., Amsden 1992; Chang 2002; Evans 1995; Haggard 1990; Wade 1990.

10 Contested Confucianism

leaders, asserted that Asian values emphasizing communitarianism over individualism, obedience to authority over individual freedom, work ethic and thrift over consumption underlined the authoritarian capitalism that made Asia thrive. They generalized that these cultural values were shared by all of Confucianism, Hinduism, and Islam. At the same time, conservative scholars in China resisted the call for total Westernization and political opening by the liberal intellectuals in the 1980s by borrowing the "Asian values" idea to argue that strengthening, not weakening, the authoritarian rule of the CCP would warrant social harmony and continuous economic growth. This school of thought was dubbed neo-authoritarianism at the time. It became the monopolistic position of all official intellectuals after the CCP crushed the 1989 democratic movement and the liberal intellectuals behind it.[43]

This justification of authoritarian rule by the self-Orientalizing conception of a perennial and monolithic Asian culture was a repetition of Chiang Kai-shek's Confucian fascism.[44] Just as Chiang's line of thought was aligned with the ideas of many Western scholars like Frank Goodnow, who believed liberal democracy did not suit Chinese culture and China needed to maintain authoritarian rule to warrant stability and economic growth, the late twentieth-century idea of Asian values was echoed by some leading thinkers in the West. For example, in *The Clash of Civilizations and the Remaking of World Order* (1996), Samuel Huntington predicted the end of the Cold War would not lead to the global triumph of Western liberalism as Francis Fukuyama claimed (1992).[45] Instead, it would pave the way for an inter-civilizational conflict grounded on irreconcilable differences among cultural values and political systems.

Huntington argued that the "Sinic" sphere, which valued collectivism and statism, would never see the success of liberal democratizing attempts. This resonates with Goodnow's view about China's incompatibility with liberal democracy. Huntington predicted that such a sphere, empowered by rapid economic growth, would become more assertive and join hands with the Islamic world, which also embraced collectivism and statism and

[43] Thompson 2001; Chia 2011; Sautman 1992.
[44] See Chapter 9.
[45] Huntington 1996; Fukuyama 1992.

enjoyed a demographic advantage to topple Western hegemony. To Huntington, the democracy promotion agenda of the universalist liberals was destined to fail in the Sinic and Islamic worlds, and the West should accommodate a collectivist and authoritarian Asia in international politics while purifying its domestic Christian identity.[46]

With the coming of the China boom and the increasing assertiveness of Beijing's geopolitical posture vis-à-vis the US-led Western alliance, Chinese official scholars became ever more confident in claiming a Confucianist-civilizational foundation of China's authoritarian system. They emphasized the system's superiority in delivering rapid economic growth to stifle internal and external advocacy for liberalization.[47] They spoke of not only a domestic Confucianist authoritarian order but also a Confucianist China-centered tributary system as the new foundation of China's foreign policy.[48] Most of these intellectuals openly embraced and promoted the anti-liberalism and statism of Nazi legal theorist Carl Schmitt.[49]

The world got a first clear glimpse of this Confucian-collectivist self-conception of Chinese culture through the grandiose opening ceremony of the 2008 Beijing Olympics. The ceremony was carefully orchestrated by China's central government and was meant to send a message to the world about a rising China. Accompanying the artistic showcase of a range of real and imagined traditions of China was 2,008 People's Liberation Army soldiers dressed in ancient costumes, playing imaginatively constructed *fou* 缶, an ancient drum instrument, in perfect unison. The movements of the more than two thousand soldier-drummers were carefully choreographed to make large-scale patterns. It was a stunning spectacle of collectivism and centralized coordination in the name of celebrating tradition.[50] Since Xi Jinping took power in 2013, he frequently portrayed the CCP regime as the culmination of China's "unbroken history of more than 5,000 years of civilization."[51]

---

[46] Huntington 1996: 207–45; 301–21.
[47] Dotson 2011.
[48] Zhao 2021 [2011].
[49] Che 2020; Qi 2012; Veg 2020; Mana 2023; Chu 2020; Hung 2022b.
[50] Barmé 2009: 71–2.
[51] Xi 2013, 2023.

This Confucian-collectivist ethos promoted by the Chinese state was most recently manifest during the Covid-19 pandemic in 2020–2022. Beijing resorted to the top-down imposition of complete city lockdowns and termination of all activities to stop the spread of the virus. Such a measure, known as the dynamic zero COVID approach, eventually led to widespread discontent, protests, and an unsustainable fiscal burden on local governments, so much so that Beijing hastily and disorderly ended such an approach in the spring of 2023. However, in the middle of the pandemic, Beijing praised the policy as being superior to the liberal approach in Western countries, which experienced an explosion in case numbers and deaths. Government propaganda blatantly attributed the efficiency and success of the Chinese approach to China's collectivist culture. According to the propaganda, such a collectivist culture and the political system built upon it explain the success of Communist China in all other aspects. As a leading author in the CCP nationalist tabloid newspaper *Global Times* asserted:

> Western media has taken a satirical tone when reporting on the Chinese government's mass mobilization capabilities. Many have failed to understand why the government mobilized millions of people in such a short period and why almost everyone cooperated. The underlying reason is that Chinese culture is collectivist, and such unity strengthens the ability to collaborate and contribute to large-scale movements with greater efficiency. The concept is the polar opposite of what Western society has always been advocating – individualism.... For decades, mass mobilization has been a key advantage of the Chinese system. It has accompanied the Communist Party of China through revolution, state-building, as well as reforms and opening-up.[52]

As such, Beijing's propaganda machine framed the competition and conflict between China and the US/the West as an East–West civilizational conflict between collectivism and individualism. Such framing has its audience outside of China.

---

[52] Wang 2020.

During the early phase of the pandemic, many Western observers praised China's collectivist and even authoritarian approach to containing the outbreak. For example, an American college professor caught in the Shanghai outbreak and quarantined while spending his sabbatical semester there hailed the Chinese approach. He found China's approach that "everyone must accept ... sacrificing [one's] 'rights' for the collective good" was far superior to the Western "*laissez-faire* attitude" and "prioritization of personal freedom." This made him feel safer in China than in the US. With this achievement, he felt perfectly at peace with authoritarian rule, which produced a good outcome of a collectivist spirit, an "all for one and one for all" ethos.[53]

At a more general level, Martin Jacques, who blew the triumphalist horn about China becoming the new ruler of the world, saw that collectivism "goes back to Confucius and runs deep in the Chinese."[54] He also saw the coming dominance of Confucianist collectivism over Western individualism in the world:

> Confucian teachings underpinned the conduct of the state and the nature of Chinese statecraft during the dynastic period and are presently experiencing something of a revival. The continuing influence of Confucian culture is reflected in the highly moralistic tone that the Chinese government frequently adopts in its attitudes and pronouncements. The profound differences in the values of China ... in contrast to those of Western societies – including a community-based collectivism rather than individualism, a far more family-orientated and family-rooted culture, and much less attachment to the rule of law and the use of law to resolve conflict – will remain pervasive and, with China's growing influence, acquire a global significance.[55]

In Putin's Russia, establishment intellectuals increasingly saw the country's fate hinging on the existential choice between the collectivist East and individualist West. Aleksandr Dugin, dubbed "Putin's brain" in finding the theoretical foundation of Putin's

---
[53] Perman 2020.
[54] Jacques 2023: 12.
[55] Jacques 2009: 398–9.

imperial expansion, advocated Russia's delinking from the decadent, liberal, and individualist West to reinstate its Asiatic roots, originating from the Mongol Conquest that allegedly laid the foundation of the Russian Empire as Eurasian and Mongol–Turkic, instead of European.[56] Many mainstream academics in Russia echoed Dugin's views in a more subtle form. For example, economist, mathematician, and Sinophile Vladamir Popov remarked during the Covid-19 pandemic that:

> The main contradiction of the modern era, and indeed of all human history, is not between capitalism and socialism, and not even between authoritarianism and democracy, but between individualism and collectivism ... "Asian values" is the priority of the interests of the community (village, enterprise, nation, world community) over the interests of the individual ... Comparative economic and social dynamics during the COVID-19 pandemic in 2020–21 is another proof of the advantages of the collectivist model ... [I]f Russia ties its fate to China and the new collectivist model, the decline of the West could happen faster than expected.[57]

It is remarkable that such contemporary Orientalist projection of an epic East–West, collectivist–individualist showdown mirrors the Orientalist projection of the showdown between the free Occident and the despotic Orient, as a reenactment of the ancient Greece–Persia War, as imagined by Hegel:

> In the case before us, the interest of the World's History hung trembling in the balance. Oriental despotism – a world united under one lord and sovereign – on the one side, and separate states – insignificant in extent and resources, but animated by free individuality – on the other side, stood front to front in array of battle. Never in History has the superiority of spiritual power over material bulk – and that of no contemptible amount – been made so gloriously manifest.[58]

---

[56] Dmitry Shlapentokh 2007; Klump n.d.
[57] Popov 2021.
[58] Hegel 2001: 276.

The Orientalist, essentialist conception of Chinese or Asian culture and the use of it to justify authoritarian rule vis-à-vis a liberal West is practically and conceptually problematic. In fact, every modern nation experienced a tug-of-war between individualism and collectivism. Notably, the center of twentieth-century fascism, as a form of collectivist, totalitarian system, was 1930s Germany, where liberal philosophers Kant and Hegel used to bring the celebration of Occidental freedom and the critique of Oriental despotism and collectivism to a new height. Taiwan and South Korea, early poster children of Asian values and authoritarianism, have swiftly and spontaneously transitioned to stable, functioning liberal democracies by the turn of the twenty-first century. In the Freedom House's global freedom index, these two liberal Asian countries often rank as high as or higher than many Western countries, including the US.[59] But so far as the problematic frame of Western individualism versus Eastern collectivism served the dominant political projects in both China and the US, as well as in other countries in the intensifying rivalry between political blocs, the frame is more likely than not to gain more ground at the expense of more nuanced analyses and perspectives.

[59] Freedom House 2023.

CONCLUSION
De-Orientalizing Triumph, Re-Orientalizing Perils

In the West, the academic study of China has experienced recurrent pendulum swings between polar opposite views of naïve idealization and racist contempt from the age of Pax Mongolica to the Cold War, while the locus of academic production of knowledge about China shifted from the Catholic Church in the thirteenth through the seventeenth century to the community of philosophers in the eighteenth century, and then to modern universities in the nineteenth and twentieth centuries. These polarized views were not, of course, the only views at any particular time, but they were often the dominant views that leading intellectual figures espoused. Until after the mid twentieth century, more nuanced and complex views about China were often overshadowed. Though the quest for academic knowledge about China has become more nuanced today, simplistic Sinological views from earlier times still underlie popular and political discourses on China.

Eight Hundred Years of Fantasy-Fear Cycles

Mixing up the Mongols, Manchus (or collectively, the Tartars), and Chinese and seeing them as one uniform racial-cultural group since the medieval period, Europeans have made sense of these very distant and very different peoples in terms of either extreme particularism (they are irreconcilable aliens) or extreme universalism (they are the same as us). In the thirteenth century, Marco Polo marveled at the bridges, warehouses, markets, and canals of China under Mongol rule, as well as the benevolent and effective governance of an allegedly Christian-prone Great Khan, with an implicit comparison to the bygone days of Pax Romana. Half a century prior, English Benedictine monk and chronicler Matthew Paris had described the Mongols/Chinese as barbaric, demonic cannibalists. In the seventeenth century, the Jesuits saw the Chinese as monotheists who escaped European-style degeneration to stay true to God's original morality. In the meantime, Jesuits' rivals in the Church saw the Chinese as idol and demon worshippers banished from God's grace. In the eighteenth century, Sinophilic philosophers held China up as a model of rational government, rule of law, respect for human rights, market efficiency, and moral righteousness. At the same time, Sinophobic philosophers described China as an exemplar of Oriental despotism and a decaying civilization. In the nineteenth century, Romantic Sinologists portrayed Chinese Classics texts and cultural practices as embodying the original, innocent, pure God's morality lost in Western modernity. In contrast, scientific-racist Sinologists saw only superstitions, cruelty, and irrationality in Chinese culture.

The competition for attention between rival networks of intellectuals drove recurrent polarization and swings between the two views. The nested fields of institutional politics and political economy shaped the relative prominence of each view. Public sentiments and the dispositions of the social and state elite, as the audience for and financial supporters of most intellectual activities, became the link that transmitted the influences of geo-economic and geopolitical changes to academic knowledge production about China. Different as they may seem, the recurrent idealizing and disdainful knowledge of China shared the same Orientalist epistemology that projected the Chinese civilization as a homogenous, ahistorical whole. As such, the idealizing and disdainful depictions of China supported and reinforced each other. The two views differed in their dispositions toward the very same depiction. For example, the supposed continuity of the Chinese civilization from antiquity was seen as proof of its superiority among the Jesuits, the early Enlightenment philosophers, and the Romantics. The same antiquity was seen as a manifestation of Chinese civilization's inferiority by the late Enlightenment philosophers and the modernists.

After all, the fundamental problem of Orientalist epistemology is not that it is idealizing or demonizing the Orient but in its reification of any non-Western civilization and its compression of vast, complex civilizations into a few "Sacred Books" and sets of religious rituals. Orientalists always tried to project from a specific interpretation of a particular aspect of an Asian civilization valid in a particular time to construct a highly generalized reading of the civilization's totality. For example, the evidence that scholars rely on to construct the thesis about "Oriental despots" or "benevolent and efficient rulers" in China could be true. But instead of carefully examining how those different elements of Chinese history were dynamically combined and related at a given time and space, Orientalist knowledge would exercise its epistemological violence to amplify any of these elements to create an ideal China to be fantasized about or a horrific China to be feared. The result was competition and a shift between the polarized constructions of China and the failure to accommodate any complexities of reality.

Analysts of Orientalist scholarship on Islamic cultures and South Asia notice similar swings between idealization and disdain, too. However, such swings have been the most drastic in the case of China, given that China has been a unique Asian civilization that was never fully subjugated by Western powers and did not engage in military conflict with the West until the mid nineteenth century. Such swings usually had little to do with changes within China. They were often driven by the changing political economy within Europe and Europe's changing geopolitical and geoeconomic relations with China.

De-Orientalization in China Studies

Into the twentieth century, scientific-racist Sinology and scientific-racist Orientalism helped shape the Weberian modernization theory, which became the dominant paradigm underlying US Area Studies at the height of the Cold War. At the same time, postwar Europe saw the revival of Romantic Sinology, though the influence of US-style China Studies with heavy social-scientific underpinning also advanced. The resulting interactions of diverse methods and approaches from different social science and humanities disciplines led to the opening of Cold War China Studies to historical, social, and geographical approaches that transgressed the nineteenth-century Sinological focus on ancient text and religious rituals. Starting at the fringe of professional Sinology, such an opening helped China Studies shed the reductionist and reifying epistemology of centuries of old Sinology. The acceptance of stellar scholars originating from China in Western institutions, as well as input from China Studies scholars in other Asian societies like Japan, also brought in fresh perspectives that contributed to the de-Orientalization of China Studies.

Into the 1960s, anti-war movements in the US and Europe fueled a radical reflection across the social sciences on Western colonialism. Such reflection advanced the self-reflexibility of the field of China Studies. The import of Marxian concepts, hitherto a taboo, in China Studies, as in wider academia, ushered in the flowering of social history and class analysis and further diversified the field. In the 1970s, Nixon/Kissinger's strategic pivot toward Communist China opened up more space for different perspectives and approaches by shedding the field of China Studies of its fear of McCarthyism. It is not an accident that Edward Said found that China Studies was the field that most dramatically rid itself of the old Orientalist epistemology in his time.[1] The opening of China for fieldwork and archival works in the 1980s, combined with intensifying interaction between PRC and Western scholars, accelerated the field's de-Orientalization.

From the 1990s onward, the new global history that sees the early modern world as an integrated global system with connectedness and parallel developments in China, Europe, and other civilizations further delegitimized the treatment of China as an ontologically alien, self-contained entity for inquiry.[2] The rise of New Qing history that emphasized the Altaic origins of Qing institutions revived Owen Lattimore's approach, as well as the approaches of many Japanese Sinologists, that saw the centrality of Central Asia in shaping China's history.[3] The study of China's transformative appropriation of Western concepts and institutions through translation, not as a passive adoption but as a creative process, dismantled

---

[1] Said 1985: 105.
[2] E.g., Atwell 1986, 2002; Flynn and Giráldez 1995; Pomeranz 2000; Wong 1997.
[3] Crossley 1997, 1999; Elliot 2001; Dunnell et al. ed. 2004; Perdue 2010; Rawski 1998, 2015; Rowe 2010.

the impact-response model that saw China's modernization as a simple implantation of Western ideas and institutions.[4] Studying the Chinese diaspora in the transnational economic and social spaces transgressed the nation-state boundary and challenged the national geographical boundary of China Studies.[5] The Inter-Asian perspective that studies China not through the lens of its interaction with the West but from the perspective of its interactions with other Asian civilizations destabilized the Eurocentric East–West framework of comparison.[6] The China Studies community in Australia, which was founded as a European settler colony and increasingly identified itself as a multicultural part of Asia,[7] has called for a "New Sinology" that is grounded on a "robust engagement with contemporary China and indeed with the Sinophone world in all of its complexity, be it local, regional or global" and transgresses the rigid boundary between the study of the past and the present.[8] These are just a few examples illustrating how the advance of new paradigms enabled the academic study of China in Western universities to leave behind eight centuries of Orientalism.

De-Orientalization of China Studies does not necessarily mean the total abandonment of established methods by nineteenth-century Sinologists (such as textual analysis by James Legge and ethnography by J. J. M. de Groot). What is most important is the coexistence and cross-fertilization of different methods and perspectives, old and new, to reveal different aspects of the Chinese civilization. Instead of stamping out inconvenient aspects and facts and privileging others to construct a static understanding of China that serves certain ideological and political purposes, de-Orientalized China Studies accommodates the multiplicity of all the aspects and facts unveiled from different angles and carefully examines the ever-changing inter-relatedness among those different elements to present the Chinese civilization in its full complexity and dynamism. It also refuses to ossify any assessment and analysis into dogmas and maintains an openness to contrasting views and debates.

---

[4] Liu 2000, 2009; cf. Schwartz 1964.
[5] Wang 2002; Shih et al. ed. 2013; Miles 2020.
[6] Saussy 2022; Duara 2010, 2015; Chen and Chua ed. 2015.
[7] Mahajani 1964.
[8] Barmé 2005: 4–5.

Lasting Popular Orientalism

While the nuanced, syncretic, and open knowledge in professional China scholarship slowly reshaped the understanding of China in the general public, the popular stereotypes of China cultivated by centuries of Orientalist knowledge remain stubbornly strong. Jeffrey Wasserstrom noticed that the popular image of China in the US today – which could be extended to other Western countries – was still vacillating between the archetypes of the devilish, manipulative Mandarin in the novel series *Fu Manchu* and the innocent and honest peasants in the novel *The Good Earth*.[9] These two extreme stereotypes originated from eight centuries of pendulum swings between disdain and idealization in Western scholarship on China that we discuss throughout this book. It is natural that a few decades of de-Orientalization in the field of China Studies could not swiftly dislodge these prejudices deeply ingrained in the popular imagination.

This bifurcation between a de-Orientalized academic study of China and a lasting Orientalist popular perception of China is well represented and presaged in the 1930s in the works of American agricultural economist John Lossing Buck (as discussed in Chapter 7) and his wife Pearl Buck (before they divorced in 1933), who authored *The Good Earth*. John Buck's survey of China's farm economy presented a thorough and fine-grained analysis of China's rural economy. His survey data are still regarded by today's economic historians as authoritative and consistent with many more recent findings about the period. However, his wife's much more famous novel *The Good Earth* created an image of an unchanging, harmonious Chinese countryside without class exploitation and abuse by officials. Those were problems only in the cities. In the romanticized countryside, all misfortunes originated from bad weather and family discords, and the honest, hardworking peasants never complained about the social system. It is a world in which, according to one contemporary critic of *The Good Earth*, Mao's revolution was impossible.[10]

While John Buck's nuanced economic survey of China was confined to a small readership of academics, Pearl Buck's *The Good*

---

[9] Wasserstrom 2006.
[10] Hayford 1998: 6.

Earth became a bestseller that earned her a Pulitzer Prize and a Nobel Prize in Literature. The book was remade into a blockbuster movie in 1937 (with all Chinese characters played by white actors). In a speech to urge the American public to support China's KMT government in 1935, Pearl Buck stretched her image of Chinese peasants to emphasize the geo-climatic similarity between China's rural inland and the American heartland. She claimed that American and Chinese farmers shared the same ethos because of this similarity. China was destined to become a great Christian nation affined to the US:

> The lands of the United States and of China are extraordinarily alike – the northern plains in China and our western plains, the deserts of north and west, the rich central plains of both countries, the long seacoast, the vast, long rivers, the bleakness of the north and tropics of the south, the self-sufficiency of both countries, the similarity of the food produced with, I think, the higher honor given to the Chinese cook – here are great similarities, inevitably producing, or so I think, similarities in temperature ... I think we shall find our ideas, even, becoming increasingly like theirs.... In brief, then, our emotions are not so much the result of our ideas or our religion as of the food we eat and the land and the climate in which we live, and because China and the United States are so much alike in these respects, we are very much alike in the way we feel ... The same kind of land, feeding the same kinds of foods, under the same sun and winds, the shores washed by the same seas, will produce the same kind of hearts and minds, however the skins may differ. The skin, the color of the hair and eyes – these are, after all, only a kind of dress given us by our chance parents, and not more important than dress ever is. Inside we have the same heart and lungs, the same organs by means of which we live and feel and are.[11]

After all, *The Good Earth* is a story about a farmer Wang Lun, who started with nothing and became a successful landowner with a thriving (albeit quarrelsome) family through hard work. It is a projection of the image of an upwardly mobile, self-made man living

---

[11] Buck 1970: 78–83.

the American Dream in China. Buck's romantic imagination of China was a rejuvenation of the Jesuits' and Romantic Sinologists' fantasy that the Chinese were all inherently the same as Europeans in their God-inspired morality. It also brought back the Romantic Orientalist fable about Asia's harmonious communal villages (as discussed in Chapter 8).

Concomitant with the popularity of *The Good Earth* was the US and UK's best-selling novel series surrounding the supervillain character of Fu Manchu. From the *Insidious Dr Fu Manchu*, published in 1913, to the *Emperor Fu Manchu*, published in 1959, British novelist Sax Rohmer constructed the character Fu Manchu, who originated from the old Mandarin class of the Qing dynasty and became a criminal mastermind controlling an extended underground empire active in British Asian colonies and in Britain's homeland. Subverting the law and order of the Western world with drugs, assassinations, and enslavement, Fu Manchu was said to be "the head of the great Yellow Movement" and the representative of the "unemotional cruelty of the Chinese."[12] The author was never shy of portraying Fu Manchu as the personification of the yellow peril:

> Imagine a person, tall, lean and feline, high-shouldered, with a brow like Shakespeare and a face like Satan, a close-shaven skull, and long, magnetic eyes of the true cat-green. Invest him with all the cruel cunning of an entire Eastern race, accumulated in one giant intellect, with all the resources of science past and present, with all the resources, if you will, of a wealthy government – which, however, already has denied all knowledge of his existence. Imagine that awful being, and you have a mental picture of Dr. Fu-Manchu, the yellow peril incarnate in one man.[13]

Fu Manchu and the yellow peril, according to the protagonists in the novel, were going to destroy Western civilization and rule the world if kept unchecked, and "his existence is a danger to the entire white race."[14] Reinvigorating the fear of yellow peril and Mongol invasion, the novel series struck a chord in the Western mind.

[12] Rohmer 1913: 120, 168.
[13] Rohmer 1913: 25–6.
[14] Rohmer 1913: 172.

Numerous blockbuster movies and bestselling cartoons were made in the UK and US from the 1920s to 1970s.[15]

After the end of the Cold War and China's full integration into the global capitalist system as a rising power, these extreme views on China returned to popular culture and political discourse. The long cycle of the Western Sinological conceptions of China and their continuation in popular culture and political discourses is summarized in Table C.1.

Orientalism Strikes Back

Since the 1980s, Western media have been packed with jubilant voices celebrating that China, after all, was the same as the West. Western minds were relieved that after the Maoist aberration, China was back to its pursuit of private wealth and political freedom despite the temporary setback in Tiananmen. Political and public opinion leaders kept reassuring us that China would sooner or later become an economically and politically liberal country just like the US.[16] Some went further and claimed that China was not only the same as the West but was doing better and beating the West in its own game. At the height of the China boom, popular literature emerged to hail China's better work ethic, larger respect for meritocracy, and discipline in finance under a never-well-defined Confucianist culture.[17] Books that called for the US and Europe to learn better ways to conduct capitalism from China attracted wide attention.[18]

Though serious academic works showed China's economic success since the 1980s was largely attributable to its participation in the US-led neoliberal global economic order under the guidance of its central and local developmental states,[19] the notion that China represented a distinct model of development superior to the Western one, as manifested in Joshua Ramo's *Beijing Consensus* (as opposed to the Washington Consensus), Martin Jacques' *When China Rules the World*, and Frank Newman's *Six Myths that Hold*

---

[15] See Frayling 2014; see also Kuo and Yeats 2014.
[16] Vukovic 2012: Ch. 1.
[17] E.g., Reid 2013; Teng 2014; Bell 2010.
[18] E.g., Newman 2011; Lee, Ann 2012; Jacques 2009.
[19] Hung 2015.

Back America: And What America Can Learn from the Growth of China's Economy became entrenched in the popular imagination. Many of those works targeted mass audiences instead of academic ones. They lauded China's increasing influence in the world. They asserted that China's increasing footprint worldwide was underlined by its benign intention and capacity to bring peace and development, and they appreciated that China showed the world a better model of capitalist development than the broken Western one. With Ramo being the CEO of Kissinger Associates, Jacques' book being endorsed by many financial writers and outlets, and Newman being a former Deputy Secretary of Treasury under Clinton and having worked for numerous US and Chinese banks, their idealization of China aligned with the economic interests of Wall Street institutions in luring investors' money into China-related investment in the wake of the global financial crisis of 2008.[20]

This idealization of China as a free market paradise in the 2000s invites comparison to the Jesuits' and Romantic Sinologists' view that the Chinese were monotheistic God believers, that they were better than Europeans in practicing God's morality, and that Westerners should emulate the Chinese in different aspects of lives. In previous centuries, the Sinophiles fantasized about China as an exotic, alien land where Christianity as the core Western value excelled. Today's Sinophiles likewise imagined China as a superior practitioner of core Western values, only that free market capitalism has replaced Christianity as that core value.

At the same time, there was a parallel, ascending popular and political discourse that China has been shrouded in a political and economic system alien from the Western one and that the Chinese have always been conspiring to dominate the world and to remake the world after its own image of authoritarianism and collectivism, despite its pretension of abiding by Western values. For example, to excite a perennial China threat perception, Michael Pillsbury, who later became Trump's China adviser in his first administration in 2017–2021, claimed in 2016 that China has been following a plan of a "hundred-year marathon" to dislodge US leadership in the world since the founding of the PRC

---

[20] For a review of Jacques' book in financial outlets, see The Economist 2009 and Pilling 2009 for examples.

in 1949.[21] Everything Beijing did in every historical period was supposedly a carefully calculated step toward the ultimate goal of world domination. The CCP was said to follow the stratagem of Sunzi originating in the Warring Period of the fifth century BCE. Pillsbury warned that China always had a mysterious "assassin's mace" – a concept from Sunzi – that it could deploy at the right time to end Western hegemony in one blow.[22]

Another example is Jon Halliday and Jung Chang's biography of Mao, *Mao: the Unknown Story*, which became a bestseller after its first release in 2005. The book followed a monster troupe after the stereotype of Fu Manchu. It portrayed Mao as a psychologically twisted, cunning, and evil monster dreaming of invading America and becoming a global overlord. Without the support of any credible evidence, the authors claimed Mao told "a small audience … strictly confidentially" including an "elite army group" and "select provincial chiefs" in 1958 that he would "set up the Earth Control Committee, and make a uniform plan for the Earth." He also contrived with Lin Biao a plan to "build big ships, and be prepared to land in Japan, the Philippines, and San Francisco … [i]n 1962."[23] According to the authors, Mao's spirit still defines China's political system and global ambition today. The alleged sources and materials from which the authors made their claims were debunked by China Studies scholars, who found some were outright fabrications.[24]

More recently, China has been lending massively to the developing world. Some of these Chinese loans led to excessive debt distress in Africa and South Asia. Academic works show that China's external lending was a remedy to the overcapacity crisis in China's domestic economy, but it was not well coordinated. The resulting non-performing loans in the indebted countries, much like domestic non-performing loans in China, created major problems for Chinese creditors and the Chinese government, as well as the recipients of these loans in most cases.[25] But after China seized the

---

[21] Pillsbury 2016.
[22] Pillsbury 2016: 134–55.
[23] Halliday and Chang 2005: 426.
[24] See Benton and Lin ed. 2010.
[25] Hung 2020.

strategic port of Hambantota in Sri Lanka following Sri Lanka's failure to repay its loan, a "China's debt trap" narrative, according to which Beijing deliberately made massive, unsustainable loans to developing countries with the intention of seizing their strategic assets when they failed to repay, took off in Western media and establishment political circles. Such a narrative prevailed despite academic findings that the case of Hambantota was an exception rather than the norm of China's external lending.[26] The rapid propagation of this discourse portraying China as an evil mastermind having a long, grand plan to control the world is yet another reincarnation of the Fu Manchu stereotype.[27]

With the US–China economic integration and US–China geopolitical rivalry both intensifying over the last two decades and drawing in other European countries, the extreme fear and fantasy in popular and political discourses about China have been on the rise. Worse, the self-Orientalizing political discourse from China's party-state regime, as we examine in Chapter 10, has continued fueling fear and fantasy in the West. According to CCP official scholars, the Chinese political and economic system was rooted in China's Confucianist civilization, which was fundamentally different from and superior to Western civilization. Some openly suggested that China, equipped with such superior systems, should usurp Western leadership in the world market and the realm of global governance for the good of the world. Chinese official scholars' open advocacy of turning China into a world empire fed the Western fantasy of China as a new benign global overlord or its fear of a new Fu Manchu.[28]

The academic field of China Studies, which has come a long way to de-Orientalize, has so far been largely immune to this escalation of rhetoric. Though the bloom of diverse new perspectives on China continues in academia, promoting nuanced scholarly knowledge and reflexive views on China to the public sphere is becoming more difficult. Such promotion inevitably encounters an uphill battle against media clickbait, politician oratory, Chinese government censorship, and self-censorship that Beijing inspires. Worse, the raw

[26] Brautigam and Rithmire 2021.
[27] Mawdsley 2008.
[28] For the advocacy for China becoming a world empire, see Jiang 2019; for a discussion of China's imperial ambition, see Hung 2022a: 60–1.

fear and fantasy about China still prevail in the popular imagination and have started leaking back into the academic realm. Back in the 1990s, Samuel Huntington claimed in his classic *The Clash of Civilizations* (1996) that countries in the "Sinic circle" – which include Japan, Korea, China, Malaysia, and Singapore – were founded on collectivist Confucianist values fundamentally different from Western–Christian liberalism.[29] He asserted that with their economic ascendancy, the "assertive" Sinic world would inevitably join hands with the inherently "intolerant" and collectivist Muslim world to challenge Western hegemony. He envisioned the next great conflict in the world to be between the Western–Christian world and a Muslim–Confucianist alliance.[30] When rivalry between China and the US (and other Western countries) intensified in recent years, many scholars revived this thesis in one way or another and framed the rivalry as an inter-civilizational showdown between collectivism and individualism, as we discuss in Chapter 10. Most recently, some authors started to speak of an epic "global culture war" with the US leading the bloc with "emphasis on personal dignity" vis-à-vis China leading the bloc that prioritized "communal cohesion."[31]

Amid the intensifying US–China rivalry, it became increasingly common that critique of China's ruling elite, policy, and political-economic system crossed the line and developed into racialized attacks of anything Chinese and fueled the revival of many contemptuous images of China in the public sphere.[32] In response, it became tempting for academics to be nostalgic about the early modern Jesuits and Sinophilic philosophers' fantasies about China as if they could be antidotes to racist biases.[33] However, as we see throughout this book, the embellishing idealization of China was no less dangerous than its disdainful demonization. Though the idealizing accounts did contain some accurate descriptions of China (as did the disdainful ones), their essentializing and homogenizing epistemology, their systematic concealment of inconvenient facts that were at odds with the idealizing image, and their many absurd epistemological premises

---

[29] Huntington 1996.
[30] Huntington 1996: 207–45.
[31] Brooks 2022; see also Levine 2024.
[32] Kim 2022.
[33] Perkins 2004: 199–208; cf. Osterhammel 2018: 482–91.

(such as the idea that ancient Chinese believed in monotheistic God and the Chinese language was the Lingua Adamica lost in the Tower of Babel) was the other side of the same Orientalist coin that underlined a racist understanding of China.

As we have seen in the case of early Republican-era monarchists and in the case of the Chiang Kai-shek regime in the 1930s, Chinese state builders and their subsidiary intellectuals were often involved in the co-reproduction of the Orientalist views of China. They harnessed it to advance their ideological and political projects as they saw fit. In the process, they helped perpetuate Orientalist notions about China in Western popular and political discourse despite the advances in de-Orientalizing efforts in the professional field of China Studies in the last few decades. Ironically, just as the global system of knowledge production became less Western-centric, with greater input and influence of voices from the non-Western world, such politically and ideologically driven self-Orientalism from within China became an ever-greater challenge to the effort of de-Orientalization. Beijing's recent campaign to selectively reinstate some allegedly Confucianist core values – such as filial piety, distaste of individualism, and obedience to authorities – and promote a simplistic view of what constituted the essence of "Chinese culture" is a case in point. The Chinese authorities also encouraged Western academia to stop criticizing China and bring back the bygone "golden age" of Westerners' flattering of China in the times of Marco Polo, the Jesuits, and early Enlightenment philosophers, though such flattering was often grounded on ludicrous fantasy.[34]

For example, the Universities Service Center for Chinese Studies in Hong Kong has facilitated pathbreaking studies of Chinese politics, economy, and society for generations of Western China Studies scholars since 1963.[35] Its vast collections of materials from mainland China at a time when Western scholars could not visit the PRC greatly served the field. After China's opening up, the Center was integrated into the Chinese University of Hong Kong in 1988. It became a venue for scholarly exchange between the PRC and foreign social scientists through its visiting scholars programs,

---

[34] For example, Tan 2024.
[35] See Chapter 7.

seminar series, and many international conferences.³⁶ Following Beijing's imposition of the National Security Law of Hong Kong in 2020 in response to the 2019 uprising, the university decided to close down the Center and fold its collection into the main library's special collections, with some of the most sensitive materials (such as internal reference documents of the Chinese government) now listed as "closed stack" and requiring special request to access.³⁷

As such, one key venue of open, critical exchange between PRC and foreign scholars was terminated. This closure deprived Western China Studies scholars of a long-cherished venue to develop a nuanced, reflexive, and syncretic understanding of contemporary China through lively interaction with Chinese scholars from the PRC. Such a venue became increasingly important when liberal academic space within mainland China shrank in the recent decade.³⁸ Around the same time, in 2023, the Chinese University of Hong Kong Library launched an exhibition, "Bringing Together China and the West: Books of Early Modern Western Sinology," to showcase the library's collection of Jesuit books about China. It celebrated the bygone age of a better and more correct understanding of China by the West. The exhibition's introduction lauded that bygone age was a time when "Chinese and Western scholars interacted and cooperated to gain a mutual understanding of cultures and appreciation of shared humanity that transcends all boundaries."³⁹

The exhibition, of course, did not criticize any of the Jesuits' erroneous biblical premises of their knowledge about China. The Jesuits' outlandish claims that "events of Christian sacred history like the Noachian Flood were recorded in Chinese annals" and that

---

³⁶ Vogel 2016; Shambaugh 2023: 7–8.
³⁷ AAS board of directors 2021; Times Higher Education 2021. For the 2019 uprising and 2020 National Security Law of Hong Kong, see Hung 2022b.
³⁸ The Chinese University of Hong Kong stated that they did not close the Universities Service Center but only restructured them. Besides folding the Center's collection of materials into the university library, it let the University's Institute of Chinese Studies, the activities of which covered mainly linguistic and cultural studies of pre-1949 China, take over the exchange and academic activities of the Center, with scant details (Chan 2020). Time will tell whether the Institute can reproduce the open space of exchange and debate over contemporary China's politics and society at the Center despite the suffocating academic environment under the new National Security Order.
³⁹ Tuan 2023: xii.

Table C.1 *Eight hundred years of fantasy–fear cycles*

Fields	Eras	Sinophilia	Sinophobia
Catholic Scholarship	c. 1240s		Mongols as descendants of idolatrous lost tribes of Israel; they are satanic, despotic and cannibalistic (e.g., Matthew Paris)
	c. 1290s	Mongols as descendants of Three Magi/Prester John; Mongol Khan as effective, benign ruler practicing Christian morality; Mongols ready to be baptized (e.g., Riccoldo, Marco Polo)	
	c. 1650–1700	Chinese knew of monotheistic God and still practice God's morality; Chinese language could be the Lingua Adamica (Jesuits)	Chinese are idolatrous; predestined for hell (Jansenists, Dominicans, Franciscans, [Dutch Calvinists])
Enlightenment philosophy	c. 1740–1760	Chinese as exemplary practitioner of Deist philosophy; model for Europe in administration, morality, economy, liberty (early Enlightenment philosophers e.g., Voltaire, Quesnay)	China as exemplar of Oriental despotism (Montesquieu; Rousseau)
	c. 1780–1800		China as corrupt, stagnant, superstitious, despotic land (late Enlightenment philosophers e.g., Diderot, Kant, Hegel)

Institutionalized Orientalism	c. 1810–1880	Chinese manifest pure spirituality and morality of God uncontaminated by industries and urban lives (Romantic Sinology: e.g., pre-1880 James Legge and de Groot)
	c. 1890–1920	Chinese as the world's principal animists and fetishists, hostile against knowledge and progress, to be eliminated in inter-racial struggle for survival (racist Sinology: e.g., post-1880 James Legge and de Groot)
Modern social theory	c. 1850s	Marx's communalistic Asian peasants poised toward socialism
	c. 1880	Marx's Oriental despots and stagnant societies to receive injection of dynamism by Western colonialism
	c. 1910s	Weber's irrational Chinese/Asiatic religions based on magics
Popular culture	c. 1930s	*Fu Manchu*
Cold War Area Studies	c. 1950–1970	*The Good Earth*
		Modernization school, impact-response model
	c. 1960–present	De-Orientalized China Studies

Table C.1 (cont.)

Fields	Eras	Sinophilia	Sinophobia
Chinese nationalist scholarship	c. 1919–present	Confucian fascism (e.g., T'ao Hsi-sheng for CKS's *China's Destiny*)	Cultural radicalism (e.g., CCP language reform, Lu Xun, Cultural Revolution, River Elegy)
	c. 1920s–present	New Confucianism seeking integration of liberal variant of Confucianism and Western liberalism	
Political discourses disguised as scholarship	c. 1990–present	"China's new Confucianism," "China model," "Beijing consensus"	"Clash of civilizations," "Mao: the unknown story," "Hundred-year marathon," "Death by China"

Chinese classic texts "pointed to the ultimate truth of Christianity" were mentioned in passing in the exhibition without critical comments.[40] In contrast, the Pope's prohibition of Jesuits' participation in Chinese rites worshiping ancestors in 1704 was criticized for making Jesuits' "open-minded approach brought by Ricci and his successors … become the victim of excessive dogmatism and cultural ignorance."[41] The Jesuits' exhilarating, uncritical, and hyperbolic depiction of China was enshrined as a model of the Western study of China, and the exhibition's stated goal was to give "members of the university community and the public at large an opportunity to consider how we might better 'combine tradition with modernity and bring together China and the West.'"[42] The coincidence of the shutdown of the Universities Service Centers for China Studies and the launching of the Jesuits exhibition cannot be more suggestive. A once liberal academic institution that had long served as a key nodal point for open, critical exchanges between Western and Chinese intellectuals and for nurturing de-Orientalizing knowledge of modern China was shunned. Uncritical, flattering views on China, however misleading, were celebrated as the correct form of academic knowledge about China under the new National Security Order.

Having been triumphant in shedding the eight centuries of fear and fantasy, essentialism and reductionism, and the ahistorical understanding of China, the academic field of China Studies is now at a testing time. Standing its ground and advancing de-Orientalization in the field while pushing back the re-Orientalizing tide in popular and political discourses fanned by both Western politicians and the Chinese authoritarian party-state is no easy task. The contempt and naïve idealization of China are two sides of the same coin. The latter cannot be an antidote to the former. Upholding and popularizing a more reflexive, critical, multifaceted, and open approach to China is a necessary endeavor. It is not only essential to the field's future vibrancy but also consequential to the peace and freedom of our global community, which is increasingly menaced by authoritarian advances and intensifying conflict between China and the US-led Western alliance.[43]

---

[40] McManus 2023: 123.
[41] McManus 2023: 124.
[42] CUHK 2023.
[43] For the origins and dynamics of US–China conflict as inter-imperial rivalry, see Hung 2022a.

REFERENCES

Abdel-Malek, Anwar. 1963. "Orientalism in Crisis." *Diogenes* 44: 107–8.
Abu-Lughod, Janet L. 1989. *Before European Hegemony: The World System A.D. 1250–1350*. New York: Oxford University Press.
Adas, Michael. 1980 "'Moral Economy' or 'Contest State'? Elite Demands and the Origins of Peasant Protest in Southeast Asia." *Journal of Social History* 13(4), Summer 1980: 521–6.
Adas, Michael. 1989. *Machines as the Measure of Man: Science, Technology, and Ideologies of Western Dominance*. Ithaca: Cornell University Press.
Alford, Duncan. 2006. "A Bridge between East and West: The Universities Service Centre of the Chinese University of Hong Kong." *International Journal of Legal Information* 34(3): 585–8.
Amin, Samir. 1957. "The Structural Effects of the International Integration of Precapitalist Economies: A Theoretical Study of the Mechanism which Creates so-called Underdeveloped Economies." PhD Thesis, Science Po, Paris.
Amin, Samir. 1977. *Imperialism and Unequal Development*. New York: Monthly Review Press.
Amin, Samir. 1978. "The Lesson of Kampuchea." *Ikwezi*. December 1978. No. 10. 74–6.
Amiot, Jean Joseph Marie, et al. 1778. *Mémoires Concernant L'histoire, Les Sciences, Les Arts, Les Moeurs, Les Usages, &c. Des Chinois*, Vol. 3. Paris: Chez Nyon, Libraire.
Amsden, Alice. 1992. *Asia's Next Giant: South Korea and Late Industrialization*. Oxford: Oxford University Press.
Anderson, Perry. 1974. *Lineages of Absolutist State*. London: Verso.

Anderson, Kevin. 2010. *Marx at the Margins: On Nationalism, Ethnicity, and Non-Western Societies*. Chicago: University of Chicago Press.

Andrade, Tonio. 2008. *How Taiwan Became Chinese: Dutch, Spanish, and Han Colonization in the Seventeenth Century*. New York: Columbia University Press.

Andrade, Tonio. 2013. *Lost Colony: The Untold Story of China's First Great Victory over the West*. Princeton, NJ: Princeton University Press.

Andrea, Alfred J. 2020. *The Medieval Record: Sources of Medieval History*. Indianapolis, IN: Hackett Publishing Company.

Appadurai, Arjun. 1997. *Modernity at Large: Cultural Dimension of Globalization*. Minneapolis: University of Minnesota Press.

Arrighi, G. and B. Silver. 1999. *Chaos and Governance in the Modern World-System*. Minneapolis: University of Minnesota Press.

Arrigo, Linda. 1986. "Landownership Concentration in China: The Buck Survey Revisited." *Modern China* 12(3): 259–360.

Associated Press. 2021. "Biden: China Should Expect 'Extreme Competition' from US." Associated Press. February 7, 2021. https://apnews.com/article/joe-biden-xi-jinping-china-8f5158c12eed14e002bb1c094f3a048a

AAS Board of Directors. 2021. "AAS Letter to the Chinese University of Hong Kong Regarding Reorganization of the Universities Service Centre." Association for Asian Studies. February 9, 2021. www.asianstudies.org/aas-letter-to-the-chinese-university-of-hong-kong-regarding-reorganization-of-the-universities-service-centre/

Atwell, William S. 1977. "Notes on Silver, Foreign Trade, and the Late Ming Economy." *Late Imperial China* 3(8): 1–33.

Atwell, William S. 1982. "International Bullion Flows and the Chinese Economy circa 1530–1650." *Past and Present* 95 (May): 2–16.

Atwell, William S. 1986. "Some Observations on the 'Seventeenth-Century Crisis' in China and Japan." *Journal of Asian Studies* XLV(2): 223–44.

Atwell, William S. 2002. "Time, Money, and the Weather: Ming China and the 'Great Depression' of the Mid-Fifteenth Century." *The Journal of Asian Studies* 61(1): 83–113.

Atwood, Christopher, ed. 2021. *The Rise of the Mongols: Five Chinese Sources*. Indianapolis, IN: Hackett Publishing Company.

Atwood, Chrisopher. 2023. "The Empire of the Great Khan: The Yuan Ulus, 1260–1368." In Michael Biran and Hodong Kim, eds. *The Cambridge History of the Mongol Empire*. Cambridge, MA: Cambridge University Press, 107–180.

Averill, Stephen. 2006. *Revolution in the Highlands: China's Jinggangshan Base Area*. Lanham: Rowman and Littlefield.

Balazs, Étienne. 1964. *Chinese Civilization and Bureaucracy: Variations on a Theme* (translated by H. M. Wright and edited by Arthur Wright). New Haven: Yale University Press.

Barlow, Tani E. 1997. "Colonialism's Career in Postwar China Studies." In Tani E. Barlow, ed. *Formations of Colonial Modernity in East Asia*. Durham: Duke University Press, 373–412.

Barmé, Geremie R. 2005. "Toward a New Sinology." Chinese Studies Association of Australia Newsletter – May 2005 No 31. 4–9.

Barmé, Geremie R. 2009. "China's Flat Earth: History and 8 August 2008." *The China Quarterly* 197: 64–86.

Bell, Daniel A. 2010 *China's New Confucianism: Politics and Everyday Life in a Changing Society*. Princeton, NJ: Princeton University Press.

Bell, Danie A. 2016. *The China Model: Political Meritocracy and the Limits of Democracy*. Princeton, NJ: Princeton University Press.

Benton, Gregor and Lin Chun, ed. 2010. *Was Mao Really a Monster? The Academic Response to Chang and Halliday's "Mao: The Unknown Story"* New York and London: Routledge.

Berger, Peter. 1988. "Peter Berger: What the Eastern World Can Teach the West about Itself" World of Ideas October 13, 1988. https://billmoyers.com/content/peter-berger-transcript/

Bergesen, Albert. 1995. "Postmodernism: A World-System Explanation." *ProtoSociology*, 7: 54–9.

Bergesen, Albert. 1996. "The Art of Hegemony." Sing C. Chew and Robert A. Denmark eds. *The Underdevelopment of Development: Essays in Honor of Andre Gunder Frank*. Thousand Oaks: Sage. 259–78.

Bernal, Martin. 1987. *Black Athena: The Afroasiatic Roots of Classical Civilization I The Fabrication of Ancient Greece 1785–1985*. London: Free Association Books.

Bettelheim, Charles. 1978. "The Great Leap Backward." *Monthly Review* 30(3): 37–130.
Bien, Gloria. 1986. "Chénier and China." In Haydn Mason, ed. *Studies of Voltaire and the Eighteenth Century*. Vol. 242. Oxford: The Voltaire Foundation.
Blue, Gregory. 1999a. "China and Western Social Thought in the Modern Period." Timothy Brook and Gregory Blue eds. *China and Historical Capitalism: Genealogies of Sinological Knowledge*. New York and Cambridge: Cambridge University Press. 57–281.
Blue, Gregory. 1999b. "Gobineau on China: Race Theory, the Yellow Peril, and the Critique of Modernity." *Journal of World History*, 10: 1.
Bond, C. Hubert. 1894. "Observations on a Chinese Brain." *Brain: A Journal of Neurology*, 17: 37–49.
Bose, Sudhindra. 1915. "Remarks on President Goodnow's Paper." *The American Political Science Review*, 9(2): 224–26.
Bourdieu, Pierre. 1988. *Homo Academicus*. Palo Alto: Stanford University Press.
Boxer, C. R. 1969. *The Portuguese Seaborne Empire 1415–1825*. New York: Alfred A. Knopf P.
Bradley, James. 2015. *The China Mirage: The Hidden History of American Disaster in Asia*. New York: Back Bay Books.
Braudel, Fernand. 1992. *Civilization and Capitalism 15th–18th Century III: The Perspective of the World*. Berkeley: University of California Press.
Brautigam, Deborah, and Meg Rithmire. 2021. "The Chinese Debt Trap Is a Myth: The Narrative Wrongfully Portrays Both Beijing and the Developing Countries It Deals With." *The Atlantic* (February 6, 2021) www.theatlantic.com/international/archive/2021/02/china-debt-trap-diplomacy/617953/
Breckenridge, Carol A. and Peter van der Veer, ed. 1993. *Orientalism and the Postcolonial Predicament: Perspectives on South Asia*. Philadelphia: University of Pennsylvania Press.
Bridia, C. de. 1996. [1247]. "Tartar Relation (Historia Tartarorum)." R. A. Skelton, Thomas E. Marston and George D. Painter eds. *The Vinland Map and the Tartar Relation*. New Haven, CT: Yale University Press.
Brook, Timothy, ed. 1990. *The Asiatic Mode of Production in China*. New York and London: Routledge.

Brook, Timothy. 2013. *Mr. Selden's Map of China: Decoding the Secrets of a Vanished Cartographer*. New York: Bloomsbury.
Brook, Timothy. 2023. *The Price of Collapse: The Little Ice Age and the Fall of Ming China*. Princeton, NJ: Princeton University Press.
Brook, Timothy and Gregory Blue eds. 1999. *China and Historical Capitalism: Genealogies of Sinological Knowledge*. New York and Cambridge: Cambridge University Press.
Brooks, David. 2022. "Globalization Is Over. The Global Culture Wars Have Begun." *New York Times*. April 8, 2022. www.nytimes.com/2022/04/08/opinion/globalization-global-culture-war.html
Brown, Kerry and Gemma Chenger Deng. 2022. *China through European Eyes: 800 Years of Cultural and Intellectual Encounter*. Singapore: World Scientific.
Brown, Norman. 1971. "Inaugural Session." In Denis Sinor, ed. *Proceedings of the Twenty-Seventh International Congress of Orientalists, Ann Arbor, 1967*. Wiesbaden: Otto Harrassowitz. 22–34.
Bryan Souza, George. 1986. *The Survival of Empire: Portuguese Trade and Society in China and the South China Sea, 1630–1754*. London: Cambridge University Press.
Bryant, Miranda. 2015. "Lord Alan Sugar: We should all move to China if Jeremy Corbyn becomes PM" *Evening Standard*, Oct 1, 2015 www.standard.co.uk/news/politics/lord-sugar-we-should-all-move-to-china-if-jeremy-corbyn-becomes-pm-a2986136.html
Buck, John Lossing. 1930. *Chinese Farm Economy: A Study of 2866 Farms in Seventeen Localities and Seven Provinces in China*. University of Nanking.
Buck, John Lossing. 1937. *Land Utilization in China*. University of Chicago Press.
Buck, Pearl. 1970. *China as I See It*. New York: The John Day Company.
Büntgen, Ulf. and Nicola Di Cosmo. 2016. "Climatic and Environmental Aspects of the Mongol withdrawal from Hungary in 1242 CE." *Scientific Reports*, 6, 25606 (2016). https://doi.org/10.1038/srep25606
Buoye, Thomas, M. 2000. *Manslaughter, Markets, and Moral Economy: Violent Disputes over Property Rights in Eighteenth-Century China*. New York and Cambridge: Cambridge University Press.

Burr, William. 2010. "The Complexities of Rapprochement" *Procedia: Social and Behavioral Sciences*, 2: 7454–69.
Cameron, Nigel. 1989. *Barbarians and Mandarins: Thirteen Centuries of Western Travellers in China*. New York and Oxford: Oxford University Press.
Carroll, John. 2021. *China Hands and Old Cantons: Britons and the Middle Kingdom*. Lanham, MD: Rowman and Littlefield.
Cassel, Pär. 2023. "Solitary Swedish Sinologists: Three Hundred and Fifty Years of Swedish China Studies." *Journal of Chinese History*, 7(2): 463–89.
Chan, Anita. 1985. *Children of Mao: Personality Development and Political Activism in the Red Guard Generation*. London: Palgrave Macmillan.
Chan, Serina. 2011. *The Thought of Mou Zongsan*. Leiden: Brill.
Chan, Alan K. L. (Provost, CUHK) 2020. "Open letter relating to the Universities Service Centre for China Studies." Chinese University of Hong Kong, December 30, 2020. www.cpr.cuhk.edu.hk/en/press/open-letter-relating-to-the-universities-service-centre-for-china-studies-usc/
Chang, Chung-li. 1955. *The Chinese Gentry: Studies on Their Role in Nineteenth-Century Chinese Society*. Seattle: University of Washington Press.
Chang, Carsun 張君勱, Hsu Foo kwan 徐復觀, Mou Chung san 牟宗三 and Tang Chun I 唐君毅 1958. "為中國文化敬告世界人士宣言——我們對中國學術研究及中國文化與世界文化前途 之共同認識 (A Manifesto on the Reappraisal of Chinese Culture: Our Joint Understanding of the Sinological Study Relating to World Cultural Outlook.) 民主評論 (Democratic Review). 1958, No. 1 https://6744278.s21d.faiusrd.com/61/ABUIABA9GAAgjKz3tgUoxMbrigQ.pdf
Chang, Ha-Joon. 2002. *Kicking Away the Ladder: Development Strategy in Historical Perspective*. London: Anthem Press.
Chartier, Roger. 1991. *The Cultural Origins of the French Revolution*. Durham, NC: Duke University Press.
Chaudhuri, K. N. 1981. "The World-System East of Longitude 20°: The European Role in Asia 1500–1750" *Review* V(2): 219–45.
Che, Chang. 2020. "The Nazi Inspiring China's Communists: A decades-old legal argument used by Hitler has found support in Beijing." *The Atlantic*. December 1, 2020.

Chellaney, Brahma. 2017. "China's debt-trap diplomacy." *Project Syndicate*. January 13, 2017. www.project-syndicate.org/commentary/china-one-belt-one-road-loans-debt-by-brahma-chellaney-2017-01?barrier=accesspaylog

Chen, Kuan-Hsing and Beng Huat Chua eds. 2015. *The Inter-Asia Cultural Studies Reader*. London: Taylor & Francis.

Chen, Xiaoming. 2007. *From the May Fourth Movement to Communist Revolution: Guo Moruo and the Chinese Path to Communism*. Albany: SUNY Press.

Chen Chin-ching. 2014. "The Construction of Modern China: Chiang Kai-shek and His China's Destiny." *Academia Historica Journal*, 42: 31–62.

Chia, Yeow Tong. 2011. "The Elusive Goal of Nation Building: Asian/Confucian Values and Citizenship Education in Singapore During The 1980s." *British Journal of Educational Studies*, 59(4): 383–402. https://doi.org/10.1080/00071005.2011.591288

Chiang, Kai-Shek. 1947 [1943] *China's Destiny and Chinese Economic Theory*. New York: Roy Publishers.

Ching, Julia. 1978. "Chinese Ethics and Kant." *Philosophy East and West*, XXVIII(2): 161–72.

Chomsky, Noam and Edward Norman 1977. "Distortions at Fourth Hand." *The Nation* June 25, 197. 789–94.

Chou, Grace Ai-Ling. 2012. *Confucianism, Colonialism, and the Cold War: Chinese Cultural Education at Hong Kong's New Asia College, 1949–63*. Leiden: Brill.

Chow, Kai-Wing. 1994. *The Rise of Confucian Ritualism in Late Imperial China: Ethics, Classics, and Lineage Discourse*. Palo Alto: Stanford University Press.

Chu T'ung-tsu. 1962. *Local Government in China under the Ching*. Cambridge, MA: Harvard University East Asian Center.

Chu, Sinan. 2020. "Whither Chinese IR? The Sinocentric subject and the paradox of Tianxia-ism." *International Theory*, 14(1): 57–87.

Clarke, J. J. 1997. *Oriental Enlightenment*. London and New York: Routledge.

Clower, Jason. n.d. "Mou Zongsan (Mou Tsung-san) (1909–1995)" Internet Encyclopedia of Philosophy. https://iep.utm.edu/zongsan/#SH2b

Cohen, Huguette. 1986. "Diderot and the Image of China in Eighteenth-Century France." In Haydn Mason, ed. *Studies on*

Voltaire and the Eighteenth Century. Vol. 242. Oxford: The Voltaire Foundation. 219–32.

Cohen, Jerome. 2015. "The Universities Service Centre for China Studies – Present at the Creation." https://static1.squarespace.com/static/55c7279de4b014e7aad20a46/t/596467519f7456b6563f6302/1499752274945/The+Universities+Service+Centre%C2%Aofor+China+Studies%C2%A0%E2%80%93+Present+at+the+Creation_Website.pdf

Cohen, Paul A. 2010 [1984]. *Discovering History in China: American Historical Writing on the Recent Chinese Past*. New York: Columbia University Press.

Collins, Randall. 1998. *The Sociology of Philosophies: A Global Theory of Intellectual Change*. Cambridge, MA: Harvard University Press.

Condorcet, Marie-Jean-Antoine-Nicolas. 1796 [1795]. *Outlines of an Historical View of the Progress of the Human Mind*. Philadelphia: M. Carey.

Couplet, Philippe. 1687. *Confucius sinarum philosophus, sive, Scientia sinensis latine exposita* Parisiis: Apud Danielem Horthemels https://archive.org/details/confuciussinarum00conf/page/n121/mode/1up

Crook, Paul. 1994. *Darwinism, War and History: The Debate over the Biology of War from the "Origin of Species" to the First World War*. New York and Cambridge: Cambridge University Press.

Crossley, Pamela K. 1997. *The Manchus*. Cambridge, MA and Oxford: Blackwell Publishers.

Crossley, Pamela K. 1999. *A Translucent Mirror: History and Identity in Qing Imperial Ideology*. Berkeley and LA: University of California Press.

CUHK 2023. "Bringing Together China and the West: A Symposium to Celebrate the 60th Anniversary of The Chinese University of Hong Kong" CUHK Library www.lib.cuhk.edu.hk/en/about/events/symposium2023/#:~:text=In%20sum%2C%20the%20symposium%20will,together%20China%20and%20the%20West.%E2%80%9D

Cumings, Bruce. 1998. "Boundary Displacement: Area Studies and International Studies during and after the Cold War." *Bulletin of Concerned Asian Scholars*, 29(1): 6–26.

Davis, Walter W. 1983. "China, the Confucian Ideal, and the European Age of Enlightenment." *Journal of the History of Ideas*, XLIV(4): 523–48.

DeBary, Wm. Theodore. 1981. *Neo-Confucian Orthodoxy and the Learning of the Mind-and-Heart*. New York: Columbia University Press.

De Groot, J. J. M. 1886. *Les fêtes annuellement célébrées à Émoui (Amoy) Étude concernant la religion populaire des chinois*. Paris: E. Leroux.

De Groot, J. J. M. 1903. *Sectarianism and Religious Persecution in China: A Page in the History of Religions*. Amsterdam: J. Müller.

De Groot, J. J. M. 1912. *Religion in China: Universism – A Key to The Study of Taoism and Confucianism*. New York: Rnickerbocker Press.

De Groot, J. J. M. 1969 [1892]. *The Religious System of China: Its Ancient Forms, Evolution, History and Present Aspect, Manners, Custom and Social Institution Connected Therewith*. Taipei: Sing Man Press.

De Jong, Alice. 1989. "The Demise of the Dragon: Backgrounds to the Chinese Film 'River Elegy.'" *China Information*, 4(3): 28–43.

De Weerdt, Hilde. 2022. "Modelling Tang Emperor Taizong and Chinese Governance in the Eighteenth-Century German-Speaking World." *Global Intellectual History*, 8(5), 609–35.

Democratic Kampuchea 1977. *Democratic Kampuchea Moving Forward*. Phnom Penh: Department of Press and Information of the Ministry of Foreign Affairs.

Dennison T. K. and A. W. Carus. 2003. "The Invention of the Russian Rural Commune: Haxthausen and the Evidence" *The Historical Journal*, 46(3):561–82.

Dermigny, Louis. 1964. *La Chine et l'Occident : le commerce à Canton au XVIIIe siècle, 1719–1833*. 4 Vols. Paris: S.E.V.P.E.N.

Deutscher, Isaac. 1955. "Can Mao Collectivise Half a Billion Farmers?" *The Reporter*. December 1, 1955. www.marxists.org/archive/deutscher/1955/collectivisation.htm

Dewey, Clive. 1972. "Images of the Village Community: A Study in Anglo-Indian Ideology" *Modern Asian Studies*, 6(3): 291–328.

Diderot, Denis. 1780. "État de la Chine selon ses détracteurs." In Guillaume Raynal, ed. 3e éd. *Histoire philosophique et politique*

des établissements et du commerce des Européens dans les Deux-Indes. Genève: J. L. Pellet.
Dijkstra, Trude. 2021. *Printing and Publishing Chinese Religion and Philosophy in the Dutch Republic, 1595–1700*. Leiden: Brill.
Dirlik, Arif. 1995. "Confucius in the Borderlands: Global Capitalism and the Reinvention of Confucianism." *boundary 2*, 22(3): 229–73.
Dirlik, Arif. 1996. "Chinese History and the Question of Orientalism." *History and Theory*, 35(4): 96–118.
Dotson, John. 2011. "The Confucian Revival in the Propaganda Narratives of the Chinese Government." U.S.-China Economic and Security Review Commission Staff Research Report. www.uscc.gov/sites/default/files/Research/Confucian_Revival_Paper.pdf
Driver, F. 1992. "Geography's Empire: Histories of Geographical Knowledge" *Environment and Planning D: Society and Culture*, 10: 23–40.
Duara, Prasenjit. 2010. "Asia Redux: Conceptualizing a Region for Our Times" *The Journal of Asian Studies*, 69(4): 963–83.
Duara, Prasenjit. 2015. *The Crisis of Global Modernity: Asian Traditions and a Sustainable Future*. New York and Cambridge: Cambridge University Press.
Du Bois, W. E. B. 1945. *Color and Democracy: Colonies and Peace*. New York: Harcourt, Brace & Co.
Du Halde, Jean-Baptiste. 1738 [1735]. *A description of the empire of China and Chinese-Tartary : together with the kingdoms of Korea, and Tibet : containing the geography and history (natural as well as civil) of those countries. Enrich'd with general and particular maps, and adorned with a great number of cuts*. (From the French of P. J. B. Du Halde, Jesuit; with notes geographical, historical, and critical; and other improvements, particularly in the maps, by the translator) 4 Volumes. London: Printed by T. Gardner in Bartholomew Close for Edward Cave. 1738–41.
Dunnell, Ruth W., Mark C. Elliott, Philippe Foret, James A. Millward, ed. 2004. *New Qing Imperial History: The Making of Inner Asian Empire at Qing Chengde* London: Routledge.
Durkheim, Emile. 1976 [1915]. *The Elementary Forms of the Religious Life*. London: George Allen & Unwin Ltd.
Dyer, Thomas G. 1980. *Theodore Roosevelt and the Idea of Race*. Baton Rouge: Louisiana State University Press.

Ebihara, May. 1973. "Intervillage, village–town and village–city relations in Cambodia.'" *Annals of the New York Academy of Sciences*, 220(6): 358–75.

Eidelberg, Martin. 2021. "Reconsidering the Beauvais Workshop's Première tenture chinoise." Watteau and His Circle. watteauandhiscircle.org/Beauvais_Essay.htm#1

Eisenstadt, Shumel N., ed. 2002. *Multiple Modernities*. New Brunswick, NJ: Transaction Publisher.

Eisenstadt, Shmuel N. and Wolfgang Schluchter. 1998. "Introduction: Paths to Early Modernities – A Comparative View." *Daedalus* 127(3), Special Issue on "Early Modernities": 1–18.

Elliot, Mark C. 2001. *The Manchu Way: The Eight Banners and Ethnic Identity in Late Imperial China*. Stanford University Press.

Elman, Benjamin A. 1984. *From Philosophy to Philology: Intellectual and Social Aspects of Change in Late Imperial China*. Cambridge, MA: Harvard University Asia Center.

Elman, Benjamin A. 1989. "Imperial Politics and Confucian Societies in Late Imperial China: The Hanlin and Donglin Academies." *Modern China*, 15(4): 379–418.

Elman, Benjamin A. 2000. *A Cultural History of Civil Examination in Late Imperial China*. Berkeley and LA: University of California Press.

Elvin, Mark. 1973. *The Pattern of the Chinese Past*. Stanford: Stanford University Press.

Eng, Robert Y. 2019. "The Ocean as Metaphor and Avenue for Progress: Views of World History in Chinese Television Documentaries." *World History Connected* 16(2). https://worldhistoryconnected.press.uillinois.edu/16.2/forum_eng.html

Erbaugh, Mary S. 1992. "The Secret History of the Hakkas: The Chinese Revolution as a Hakka Enterprise" *The China Quarterly*, 132: 937–68.

Esherick, Joseph. 1972. "Harvard on China: The Apologetics of Imperialism." *Bulletin of Concerned Asian Scholars*, 4(4), 9–16.

European Commission. 2014. *Joint Statement: Deepening the EU-China Comprehensive Strategic Partnership for mutual benefit*, March 31, 2014. Brussels: European Commission. https://ec.europa.eu/commission/presscorner/detail/en/STATEMENT_14_89

European Commission. 2019. *EU-China – A strategic outlook*. March 12, 2019. Brussels: European Commission. https://

commission.europa.eu/system/files/2019-03/communication-eu-china-a-strategic-outlook.pdf
Evans, Peter. 1995. *Embedded Autonomy: States and Industrial Transformation.* Princeton, NJ: Princeton University Press.
Fairbank, John King. 1947. "Introducing a Skeleton from the Kuomintang Closet." *New York Times*, 9 February 1947, BR3.
Fairbank, John King. 1953. *Trade and Diplomacy on the China Coast: The Opening of Treaty Ports 1842–1854.* Cambridge, MA: Harvard University Press.
Fairbank, John King et al. 1965. *East Asia: The Modern Transformation.* London: George Allen & Unwin.
Fairbank, John King. 1982. *Chinabound: A Fifty Year Memoir.* New York: HarperCollins.
Farquhar, Judith B. and James L. Hevia. 1993. "Culture and Postwar American Historiography of China." *Positions*, 1(2): 486–525.
Faure, David. 1986. *The Structure of Chinese Rural Society: Lineage and Village in the Eastern New Territories, Hong Kong.* Oxford: Oxford University Press.
Faure, David. 2007. *Emperor and Ancestor: State and Lineage in South China.* Alto Palo: Stanford University Press.
Fei, Hsiao-Tung (Xiaotong). 1939. *Peasant Life in China: A Field Study of Country Life in the Yangtze Valley.* London: Kegan Paul, Trench, Trubner.
Fei, Hsiao-Tung (Xiaotong). 1953. *China's Gentry. Essays in Rural-Urban Relations.* Chicago: University of Chicago Press.
Fénelon, François. 1917 [1712] *Dialogues des morts in De l'éducation des filles. Dialogues des morts.* Paris: Émile Faguet. https://commons.wikimedia.org/wiki/File:F%C3%A9nelon_-_De_l%E2%80%99%C3%A9ducation_des_filles._Dialogues_des_morts.djvu
Fenton, William N. 1947. *Area Studies in American Universities: For the Commission on Implication of Armed Services Educational Programs.* Washington, DC: American Council on Education.
Fetzer, Joel S. and Christopher J. Sope. 2012. *Confucianism, Democratization, and Human Rights in Taiwan.* Lanham, MD: Lexington Books.
Field, Stephen Field. 1991. "He shang and the plateau of ultrastability," *Bulletin of Concerned Asian Scholars*, 23(3): 4–13.

Filliozat, Jean. 1975. "Project of Reform of the International Congresses of Orientalists." (English Resume by Daniel Thorner) Committee of the Congress ed. *Le XXIX Congrès International Des Orientalistes, Paris, 1973*. Paris: L'Asiatheque. 57–63.

Finlay, John. 2019. "Henri Bertin and Louis XV's Gifts to the Qianlong Emperor." *Extrême-Orient Extrême-Occident* 43: 93–111.

Flynn, Dennis O. and Giraldez Arturo. 1995. "Born with 'Silver Spoon': The Origin of World Trade in 1571." *Journal of World History* 6(2): 201–11.

Fogel, Joshua A. 1988. The Debates over the Asiatic Mode of Production in Soviet Russia, China, and Japan. *The American Historical Review*, 93(1): 56–79.

Fogel, Joshua A. 2023. "Introduction: National Traditions of Sinology." *Journal of Chinese History*, 7(2): 253–5.

Foucault, Michele. 1984. "What is Enlightenment?" In Paul Rabinow, ed. *The Foucault Reader*. New York: Pantheon Books. 32–50.

François Fénelon. 1917 [1712]. *Dialogues des morts*. Paris: Nelson https://fr.wikisource.org/wiki/Dialogues_des_morts

Frank, Andre Gunder. 1966. *The Development of Underdevelopment*. Boston: New England Free Press.

Frayling, Christopher. 2014. *The Yellow Peril: Dr. Fu Manchu and the Rise of Chinaphobia*. Thames & Hudson.

Freedman, Maurice. 1979. "On the Sociological Studies of Chinese Religions." In Maurice Freedman, ed. *The Study of Chinese Society: Essays by Maurice Freedman*. Stanford: Stanford University Press. 351–72.

Freedom House 2023 Countries and Territories. https://freedomhouse.org/countries/freedom-world/scores

Friedman, Edward and Mark Selden eds. 1971. *America's Asia: Dissenting Essays on Asian-American Relations*. New York: Vintage Books.

Furth, Charlotte. 1990. "The Patriarch's Legacy: Household Instructions and the Transmission of Orthodox Values." In Kwang-ching Liu, ed. *Orthodoxy in Late Imperial China*. Berkeley and Los Angeles: University of California Press. 187–211.

Fukuyama, Francis. 1992. *The End of History and the Last Man*. New York: Free Press.

Galway, Matthew. 2019. "Specters of Dependency: Hou Yuon and the Origins of Cambodia's Marxist Vision (1955–1975)." *Cross-Currents: East Asian History and Culture Review* (e-journal) 31: 126–61. https://cross-currents.berkeley.edu/e-journal/issue-31/galway

Galway, Matthew. 2022. *The Emergence of Global Maoism: China's Red Evangelism and the Cambodian Communist Movement, 1949–1979*. Ithaca: Cornell University Press.

Gao Xiang 高翔 2000. 近代的初曙：十八世紀中國觀念變遷與社會發展 (The Dawn of Modernity: Transformations of Ideas and Social Change in Eighteenth-Century China) Beijing: 社會科學文獻出版社.

García-Herrero, Alicia and Abigaël Vasselier. 2024. "Updating the EU strategy on China: co-existence while derisking through partnerships." Bruegel policy brief. www.bruegel.org/policy-brief/updating-eu-strategy-china-co-existence-while-derisking-through-partnerships

Gilchrist, John. 1969. *The Church and Economic Activity in the Middle Ages*. London: Macmillan.

Giles, Herbert A. 1914. *Adversaria Sinica*. Shanghai: Kelly and Walsh Ltd. https://archive.org/details/adversaria-sinica/page/n5/mode/2up?q=Legge

Gilman, Nils. 2003. *Mandarins of the Future: Modernization Theory in Cold War America*. Baltimore: Johns Hopkins University Press.

Girardot, Norman J. 1992. "The Course of Sinological Discourse: James Legge (1815–97) and the Nineteenth-Century Invention of Taoism." Luk, Bernard Hung-Kay, eds. *Contacts between Cultures*. New York: Edwin Mellen Press. 188–93.

Girardot, Norman J. 2002. *The Victorian Translation of China: James Legge's Oriental Pilgrimage*. Berkeley: University of California Press.

Gobineau, Arthur de 1915 [1855]. *Inequality of Human Races*. (translate by Adrian Collins) New York: G. P. Putnam's Sons.

Goldman, Merle, ed. 1977. *Modern Chinese Literature in the May Fourth Era*. Harvard University East Asian Research Center.

Goldstone, Jack A. 2002. "Efflorescence and Economic Growth in World History: Rethinking the 'Rise of the West' and the Industrial Revolution." *Journal of World History*. 13 (2): 323–89.

Goodnow, Frank. 1915a. "Dr. Goodnow's Memorandum to the President" in Papers relating to the Foreign Relations of the United States, with the Address of the President to Congress. December 7, 1915. File No. 893.01/35. https://history.state.gov/historicaldocuments/frus1915/d47

Goodnow, Frank. 1915b. "Reform in China." *The American Political Science Review*, IX(2): 209–24.

Goodnow, Frank. 1926. *China: An Analysis*. Baltimore: Johns Hopkins Press.

Gordon, Amy Glassner. 1986. "Autres Mondes, Autres Meurs: French Attitudes towards the Cultures Revealed by the Discoveries." In Pullapilly, Cyriac K. et al., ed. *Asia and the West: Encounters and Exchanges from the Age of Explorations*. Notre Dame, Indiana: Cross Cultural Books. 45–84.

Gottschalk, Louis and Lach, Donald. 1973. *Toward the French Revolution: Europe and America in the Eighteenth-Century World*. New York: Charles Scribner's Sons.

Gough, Kathleen. 1986. "Roots of the Pol Pot Regime in Kampuchea" *Contemporary Marxism* Spring 1986, No. 12/13, SOUTHEAST ASIA (Spring 1986), pp. 14–48.

Groslier, Bernard Philippe. 1956. *Angkor: Hommes et pierres*. Paris: Arthaud.

Groslier, Bernard Philippe. 1958. *Angkor et le Cambodge au XVIe siècle d'après les sources portugaises et espagnoles*. Paris: Presses Universitaire de France.

Groslier, Bernard Philippe. 2007 [1979]. trans. by Lustig Terry, Pottier Christophe. "The Angkorian Hydraulic City: Exploitation or Over-Exploitation of the Soil?" *Aséanie*, 20: 141–85.

Grosrichard, Alain. 1998. *The Sultan's Court: European Fantasies of the East*. London and New York: Verso.

Guardian 2020. "China the 'greatest threat to democracy and freedom,' US spy chief warns" *The Guardian*. December 3, 2020. www.theguardian.com/us-news/2020/dec/03/china-beijing-america-democracy-freedom

Guy, Basil. 1956. "Rousseau and China," *Revue de Litterature Comparee*, XXX: 531–6.

Guy, Basil. 1963a. *The French Image of China before and after Voltaire*. Genève: Institut Et Musee Voltaire.

Guy, Basil. 1963b. "The Chinese Examination System and France, 1569–1847." In Theodore Besterman, ed. *Studies on Voltaire and the Eighteenth Century*. Vol. 25. Genève: Institut Et Musee Voltaire. 741–71.

Haggard, Stephe. 1990. *Pathways from the Periphery: The Politics of Growth in the Newly Industrializing Countries*. Ithaca: Cornell University Press.

Hall, Kenneth R. 1975. "Khmer Commercial Development and Foreign Contacts under Sūryavarman I" *Journal of the Economic and Social History of the Orient*, 18(3): 318–36.

Halliday, Jon and Jung Chang 2005. *Mao: The Unknown Story*. New York: Alfred Knopf.

Hamashita, Takeshi. 2008. *China, East Asia and the Global Economy*. London: Routledge.

Hamilton, Gary H. 1990. "Patriarchy, Patrimonialism, and Filial Piety: A Comparison of China and Western Europe." *The British Journal of Sociology*, 41(1): 77–104.

Handler-Spitz, Rivi, Pauline C. Lee, and Haun Saussy, eds. 2021. *The Objectionable Li Zhi: Fiction, Criticism, and Dissent in Late Ming China*. Seattle: University of Washington Press.

Harvest 豐年社. 1955. "有病著要醫" (you got to see a doctor when you're sick) 豐年5(23): 20–1.

Hase, Patrick. 2013. *Custom, Land, and Livelihood in Rural South China: The Traditional Land Law of Hong Kong's New Territories, 1750–1950*. Hong Kong: Hong Kong University Press.

Hawkins, Mike. 1997. *Social Darwinism in European and American Thought, 1860–1945: Nature as Model and Nature as Threat*. New York and Cambridge: Cambridge University Press.

Hayes, James. 1977. *The Hong Kong Region, 1850–1911: Institutions and Leadership in Town and Countryside*. New York: Archon Books.

Hayford, Charles W. 1998. "What's So Bad about THE GOOD EARTH?" *Education about Asia*, 3(3): 4–7. www.asianstudies.org/publications/eaa/archives/whats-so-bad-about-the-good-earth/

Hazard, Paul. 1935. *La crise de la conscience européene (1680–1715)*. Paris: Boivin et LGF.

He, Fengquan 何芳川 1996. 澳門與葡萄牙大商帆: 葡萄牙與近代早期太平洋貿網的形成 (Macao and the Portuguese Gallean: Portugal and the Formation of the Early Modern Pacific Trade Network). Beijing: 北京大學出版社

Hegel, Georg Wilhelm Friedrich. 1955 [1805]. *Hegel's Lectures on the History of Philosophy* Vol. 1 (translated by Elizabeth Sanderson Haldane) London: Routledge and Kegan www.gutenberg.org/cache/epub/51635/pg51635-images.html

Hegel, Georg Wilhelm Friedrich. 1983 [1837]. "Introduction to the History of Philosophy." In Quentin Lauer, ed. *Hegel's Idea of Philosophy: With a New Translation of Hegel's Introduction to the History of Philosophy* New York: Fordham University Press. www.marxists.org/reference/archive/hegel/works/hp/hpintroduction.htm

Hegel, Georg Wilhelm Friedrich. 2001 [1822]. *The Philosophy of History*. (translated by J. Sibree) Kitchener, Ontario: Batoche Book.

Himel, Jeffrey. 2007. "Khmer Rouge Irrigation Development in Cambodia." www.genocide-watch.com/images/Cambodia_11_Apr_07_Khmer_Rouge_Irrigation_Development_in_Cambodia.pdf

Ho, Ping-ti. 1962. *The Ladder of Success in Imperial China, Aspects of Social Mobility, 1368–1911*. New York: Columbia University Press.

Hobsbawn, Eric. 1989. *The Age of Empire: 1875–1914*. New York: Vintage Book.

Hohnholz, Linda. 2008. "Donald Trump dismayed with the US and the economy" Eturbonews. June 6, 2008. https://eturbonews.com/donald-trump-dismayed-us-and-economy/

Holmes, Todd. 2020. *James C. Scott: Agrarian Studies and over 50 Years of Pioneering Work in the Social Sciences: The Yale Agrarian Studies Oral History Project*. UC-Berkeley: Oral History Center: The Bancroft Library.

Hon, Tze-ki. 2015. *The Cultural and Historical Debates in Late Qing and Republican China*. Leiden: Brill.

Hosne, Ana Carolina. 2014. "Friendship among Literati. Matteo Ricci SJ (1552–1610) in Late Ming China." *The Journal of Transcultural Studies*, 5(1): 190–214. https://doi.org/10.11588/ts.2014.1.11362

Hou, Yuon. 1982 [1955]. "The Peasantry of Kampuchea: Colonialism and Modernization." In Ben Kiernan and Chanthou Boua, eds. *Peasants and Politics in Kampuchea, 1942–1981*. London: Zed Books. 34–68.

Hou, Yuon. 1982 [1964]. "Solving Rural Problems: A Socialist Programme to Safeguard the Nation." In Ben Kiernan and Chanthou Boua, eds. *Peasants and Politics in Kampuchea, 1942–1981*. London: Zed Books, 134–65.

Huang, Philip C. C. 1985. *The Peasant Economy and Social Change in North China*. Palo Alto: Stanford University Press.

Huang, Philip C. C. 1991. "The Paradigmatic Crisis in Chinese Studies: Paradoxes in Social and Economic History." *Modern China* 17(3): 299–341.

Huang, Philip C. C. 2000. "Biculturality in Modern China and in Chinese Studies." *Modern China*, 26(1): 3–31.

Hui, P. K. 1995. *Overseas Chinese Business Networks: East Asian Economic Development in Historical Perspective*. unpublished Ph.D dissertation. SUNY-Binghamton.

Hung, Ho-fung. 2000. "Maritime Capitalism in Seventeenth-Century China: The Rise and Fall of Koxinga Revisited" IROWS working paper. https://irows.ucr.edu/papers/irows72/irows72.htm

Hung, Ho-fung. 2001. "Imperial China and Capitalist Europe in the Eighteenth-Century Global Economy." *Review: A Journal of the Fernand Braudel Center*, 24(4): 473–513.

Hung, Ho-fung. 2003. "Orientalist Knowledge and Social Theories: China and the European Conceptions of East-West Differences from 1600 to 1900." *Sociological Theory*, 21(3): 254–79.

Hung, Ho-fung. 2011. *Protest with Chinese Characteristics: Protests, Petitions, and Riots in Mid-Qing Dynasty*. New York: Columbia University Press.

Hung, Ho-fung. 2015. *The China Boom: Why China Will Not Rule the World*. New York: Columbia University Press.

Hung, Ho-fung. 2017. "The Global, the Historical, and the Social in the Making of Capitalism." Julian Go and George Lawson eds. *Global Historical Sociology*. New York and Cambridge: Cambridge University Press. 163–81.

Hung, Ho-fung. 2020. "China and the Global South." Thomas Fingar and Jean Oi. eds. *Fateful Decisions: Choices That Will Shape China's Future*. Palo Alto: Stanford University Press.

Hung, Ho-fung. 2022a. *Clash of Empires: From "Chimerica" to the "New Cold War."* New York and Cambridge: Cambridge University Press.

Hung, Ho-fung. 2022b. *City on the Edge: Hong Kong under Chinese Rule*. Cambridge and New York: Cambridge University Press.

Hung, Ho-fung. 2024. "China's 'State Capitalism' in Comparative and Historical Perspectives." *Economy and Society*, 53(3): 376–99.

Huntington, Samuel. 1996. *Clash of Civilizations and the Remaking of World Order*. New York: Simon & Schuster.

Huppert, G. 1971. "The Idea of Civilization in the Sixteenth Century." A. Molho and J. A. Tedeschi eds. *Renaissance Studies in Honour of Hans Baron*. Florence: G. C. Sansoni, 759–69.

Idema, Wilt L. 1991. "Preface." In JiaFong Wang and Laura Li, eds. *When West Meets East: International Sinology and Sinologists*. Taipei: Sinorama. 8–9.

Idema, Wilt L. 2023. "Studies on the History of Dutch Sinology: A Bibliographical Essay." *Journal of Chinese History*, 7(2): 327–47 www.cambridge.org/core/journals/journal-of-chinese-history/article/abs/studies-on-the-history-of-dutch-sinology-a-bibliographical-essay/58EB91CE57B6AD4F59EB10592F5DD5FA

Iiyama, Tomoyasu. 2023. "Contemporary Japanese Sinology." *Journal of Chinese History*, 7(2): 311–25.

Ikegami, Eiko. 1995. *The Taming of the Samurai: Honorific Individualism and the Making of Modern Japan*. Cambridge, MA: Harvard University Press.

Ince, Onur Ulas. 2024. From "Chinese Colonist" to "Yellow Peril": Capitalist Racialization in the British Empire. *American Political Science Review*, 118(4): 1748–62.

Isaacs, Harold. 1958. *Scratches on Our Minds: American Images of China And India*. New York: John Day.

Jacques, Martin. 2009. *When China Rule the World: The End of the Western World and the Birth of a New Global Order*. New York: Penguin Book.

Jacques, Martin. 2023. "To Understand China's Success, First Understand Chinese Civilization." Lujun Chen and Karl-Heinz Pohl eds. *East-West Dialogue*. London: Palgrave Macmillam.

Jackson, Peter. 2018. *The Mongols and the West: 1221–1410*. New York and London: Routledge.

Jenne, Jeremiah. 2015. "The Perils of Advising the Emperor: Yuan Shikai and Frank Goodnow." ChinaFile. December 30, 2015.

www.chinafile.com/reporting-opinion/viewpoint/perils-advising-empire

Jensen, Kurt Villads. 1998. "Riccoldo da Monte di Croce's Libellus ad nationes orientales" University of South Denmark. www2.historia.su.se/personal/villads-jensen/Riccoldo/0.introduction.pdf

Jensen, Lionel M. 1997. *Manufacturing Confucianism: Chinese Traditions and Universal Civilization*. Durham: Duke University Press.

Jiang, Shigong. 2019. (translated by David Ownby) "The Internal Logic of Super-Sized Political Entities: 'Empire' and World Order" Reading the China Dream. www.readingthechinadream.com/jiang-shigong-empire-and-world-order.html

Jin, Guantao and Liu Qingfeng 金觀濤與劉青峰. 1984. 興盛與危機：論中國社會的超穩定結構 (prosperity and crisis: on the ultrastable structure of the Chinese society). Beijing: 法律出版社.

Johns, Christopher M. S. 2016. *China and the Church: Chinoiserie in Global Context*. Berkeley: University of California Press.

Kalab, Milada. 1968. "Study of a Cambodian Village." *The Geographical Journal*, 134(4): 521–37.

Kant, Immanuel. 1996 [1794]. "What Is Enlightenment?" In Lawrence E. Cohoon, ed. *From Modernism to Postmodernism: An Anthrology*. Cambridge, MA: Blackwell.

Kay, Tamara and R. L. Evans. 2018. *Trade Battles: Activism and the Politicization of International Trade Policy*. Oxford University Press.

Keevak, Michael. 2011. *Becoming Yellow: A Short History of Racial Thinking*. Princeton, NJ: Princeton University Press.

Kennan, George. 1951. *American Diplomacy, 1900–1950*. Chicago: University of Chicago Press.

Kerkvliet, Benedict J. Tria and Mark Selden. 1998. "Agrarian Transformations in China and Vietnam." *The China Journal*, 40, 37–58.

Khieu, Samphan. 1976 [1959]. *Underdevelopment in Cambodia*. (doctoral dissertation partially translated by Laura Summers) printed in *IndoChina Chronicle*. September–November 1976.

Kiernan, Ben. 2001. "Myth, Nationalism and Genocide," *Journal of Genocide Research*, 3(2): 187–206.

Kiernan, Ben. 2006. "External and Indigenous Sources of Khmer Rouge Ideology." In Odd Arne Westad and Sophie Quinn-Judge, eds. *The Third Indochina War: Conflict between China, Vietnam and Cambodia*. Routledge.

Kim, Daegyeong. 2022. "Anti-Asian Racism and the Racial Politics of U.S.-ChinaGreat Power Rivalry." Doctoral dissertation, department of political science, UC-San Diego.

Kim, Young Kun. 1978. "Hegel's Criticism of Chinese Philosophy," *Philosophy East and West*, XXVIII(2): 173–80.

Kim Sungmoon. 2014. *Confucian Democracy in East Asia: Theory and Practice*. New York and Cambridge: Cambridge University Press.

Klump, Sarah Dixon. n.d. "Russian Eurasianism: An Ideology of Empire" Wilson Center. www.wilsoncenter.org/publication/russian-eurasianism-ideology-empire

Krader, Lawrence. 1975. *The Asiatic Mode of Production: Sources, Development and Critique in the Writings of Karl Marx*. ASSEN, the Netherlands: Van Gorcum & Comp. B. V.

Kroncke, Jedidiah. 2012. "An Early Tragedy of Comparative Constitutionalism: Frank Goodnow and the Chinese Republic." *Pacific Rim Law and Policy Journal*, 21(3): 535–90.

Kroncke, Jedidiah. 2016. *The Futility of Law and Development: China and the Dangers of Exporting American Law*. New York: Oxford University Press.

Kuhn, Thomas. 1962. *The Structure of Scientific Revolutions*. Chicago: University of Chicago Press.

Kuhn, Philip A. 1970. *Rebellion and Its Enemies in Late Imperial China: Militarization and Social Structure, 1796–1864*. Cambridge, MA: Harvard University Press.

Kuhn, Philip. 2002. *The Origins of the Modern Chinese State*. Stanford, CA: Stanford University Press.

Kuo John Wei Tchen and Dylan Yeats. 2014. *Yellow Peril! An Archive of Anti-Asian Fear* New York and London: Verso.

Kuzuoğlu, Uluğ. 2023. *Codes of Modernity: Chinese Scripts in the Global Information Age*. New York: Columbia University Press.

Lach, Donald F. 1965. *Asia in the Making of Europe Vol. I: The Century of Discovery*. Chicago: The University of Chicago Press.

Lach, Donald F. 1977. *Asia in the Making of Europe Vol. II: A Century of Wonder*. Chicago: The University of Chicago Press.

Lach, Donald F. and Van Kley, Edwin J. 1993. *Asia in the Making of Europe Vol. III: A Century of Advance*. Chicago: The University of Chicago Press.

Lamont, Michèle. 2001. "Three Questions for a Big Book: Collins's The Sociology of Philosophies." *Sociological Theory*. 19:1. 86–91.

Lantham, Michael E. 2000. *Modernization as Ideology: American Social Science and "Nation Building" in the Kennedy Era*. Chapel Hill: University of North Carolina Press.

Lanza, Fabio. 2017. *The End of Concern: Maoist China, Activism, and Asian Studies*. New Durham, NC: Duke University Press.

Lattimore, Owen. 1940. *Inner Asian Frontiers of China by Owen Lattimore*. New York: American Geographical Society.

Lattimore, Owen. 1950. *Pivot of Asia: Sinkiang and the Inner Asian Frontiers of China and Russia*. Boston: Little Brown.

Le Comte, Louis. 1696. *Nouveaux memoires sur l'etat present de la Chine*. II. Paris: Chez Jean Anisson directeur de l'Imprimerie Royale.

Leaf, Murray J. 1979. *Man, Mind, and Science: A History of Anthropology*. New York: Columbia University Press.

Lee, Ann. 2012. *What the U.S. Can Learn from China: An Open-Minded Guide to Treating Our Greatest Competitor as Our Greatest Teacher*. Oakland, California: Berrett-Koehler Publishers.

Lee, Paulin. 2012. *Li Zhi, Confucianism, and the Virtue of Desire*. Albany: SUNY Press.

Lee, Richard E. and Immanuel Wallerstein, eds. 2004. *Overcoming the Two Cultures: Science vs. the Humanities in the Modern World-System*. New York: Routledge.

Legge, Helen Edith. 1905. *James Legge: Missionary and scholar*. London: The Religious Tract Society.

Legge, James. 1893. *The Chinese Classics*. Oxford: Clarendon Press.

Legge, James. 1959 [1891]. *The Texts of Taoism*. New York: The Julian Press.

Legge, James. 1976 [1880]. *The Religions of China: Confucianism and Taoism Described and Compared with Christianity*. Folcroft, PA: Folcroft Library Editions.

Leites, Edmund. 1978. "Confucianism in Eighteenth-Century England: Natural Morality and Social Reform," *Philosophy East and West*, XXVIII (2): 143–60.

Lele, Jayant. 1993. "Orientalism and the Social Sciences." Carol A. Breckenridge and Peter van der Veer, eds. *Orientalism and the Postcolonial Predicament: Perspective on South Asia.* 45–75. Philadelphia: University of Pennsylvania Press.

Lenin, V. I. 1972 [1897]. "A Characterisation of Economic Romanticism" *Lenin Collected Works,* Progress Publishers, Moscow, Volume 2, pages 129–266. www.marxists.org/archive/lenin/works/1897/econroman/ii8ii.htm

Lenin, V. I. 1964 [1900]. "The War in China" *Lenin Collected Works,* Progress Publishers, 1964, Moscow, Volume 4, pages 372–7. www.marxists.org/archive/lenin/works/1900/dec/china.htm

Levenson, Joseph R. 1968. *Confucian China and Its Modern Fate: A Trilogy.* Berkeley and LA: University of California Press.

Levine, Nathan. 2024. "China and the Global Culture War: Western Civilizational Turmoil and Beijing's Strategic Calculus." Heritage Foundation. June 17, 2024. www.heritage.org/asia/report/china-and-the-global-culture-war-western-civilizational-turmoil-and-beijings-strategic

Li, Huaiyin. 2006. "The First Encounter: Peasant Resistance to State Control of Grain in East China in the Mid-1950s." *The China Quarterly,* no. 185, pp. 145–62.

Li, Laura. 1991. "Scholar of the Tao: French Sinologist Kristofer Schipper." In JiaFong Wang and Laura Li, eds. *When West Meets East: International Sinology and Sinologists.* Taipei: Sinorama. 112–21.

Li, Tana. 1998. *Nguyen Cochinchina: Southern Vietnam in the Seventeenth and Eighteenth Century.* Ithaca, NY: Cornell University Press.

Li, Tana and Nola Cooke. 2004. *Water Frontier: Commerce and the Chinese in the Lower Mekong Region, 1750–1880.* Lanham, MD: Rowman and Littlefield.

Li, Tana. 2024. *A Maritime Vietnam: From Earliest Times to the Nineteenth Century.* Cambridge: Cambridge University Press.

Liu, James T. C. 1973. "How Did a Neo-Confucian School Become the State Orthodoxy?" *Philosophy East and West,* 23(4): 483–505.

Liu, Lydia. 2000. *Tokens of Exchange: The Problem of Translation in Global Circulations* Durham, NC: Duke University Press.

Liu, Lydia. 2009. *The Clash of Empires: The Invention of China in Modern World Making*. Harvard University Press.

Lizzi, Francesco Giovanni. 2024. "Competitor, Rival but Partner No More? EU-China Economic Relations and the European Elections." CSDS Policy Brief. 16/2024. https://csds.vub.be/publication/competitor-rival-but-partner-no-more-eu-china-economic-relations-and-the-european-elections/

Locard, Henri. 2015. "The Myth of Angkor as an Essential Component of the Khmer Rouge Utopia." Michael Falser eds. *Cultural Heritage as Civilizing Mission: From Decay to Recovery*. New York: Springer. 201–22.

Ludden, David. 1993. "Orientalist Empiricism and Transformations of Colonial Knowledge." C. A. Breckenridge and Peter Van der Veer eds. *Orientalism and The Post-Colonial Predicament*. Philadelphia: University of Pennsylvania Press. 250–78.

Lux, Jonathan. 2015. "'Characters Reall': Francis Bacon, China and the entanglements of curiosity." *Renaissance Studies*, 29(2): 184–203.

MacMurray, J. V. A. 1915. "Chargé MacMurray to the Secretary of State." Papers Relating to the Foreign Relations of the United States, with the Address of the President to Congress December 7, 1915, Document 47. US State Department Office of the Historian. https://history.state.gov/historicaldocuments/frus1915/d47

Mahajani, Usha. 1964. "Is Australia a Part of Asia?" *The Australian Quarterly*, 36(2): 25–34. https://doi.org/10.2307/20633957

Mana, Ferran Perez. 2023. "Farewell to Revolution: The 'Chinese School of IR' and the Depoliticisation of IR theory in Post-Mao China." *International Politics*. 2023. https://link.springer.com/article/10.1057/s41311-023-00468-2

Mannheim, Karl. 2014 [1936]. *Ideology and Utopia: An Introduction to the Sociology of Knowledge*. London: Routledge.

Mair, Victor H. 1985. "Language and Ideology in the Written Popularization of the *Sacred Edict*." David Johnson, Andrew J. Nathan, and Evelyn S. Rawski eds. *Popular Culture in Late Imperial China*. Berkeley: University of California Press. 325–59.

Marchand, Suzanne L. 2009. *German Orientalism in the Age of Empire: Religion, Race, and Scholarship*. Cambridge and New York: Cambridge University Press.

Marks, Robert B. 1984. *Rural Revolution in South China: Peasants and the Making of History in Haifeng County, 1570–1930*. Madison: University of Wisconsin Press.

Marks, Robert. 1998. *Tigers, Rice, Silk and Silt: Environment and Economy in Late Imperial South China*. New York and Cambridge: Cambridge University Press.

Marx, Karl. 1853a. "The British Rule in India" *New-York Daily Tribune*, June 25, 1853 www.marxists.org/archive/marx/works/1853/06/25.htm

Marx, Karl. 1853b. "Revolution in China and In Europe" *New York Daily Tribune* June 14, 1853.

Marx, Karl. 1859. "Trade with China." *New York Daily Tribune* December 3, 1859. www.marxists.org/archive/marx/works/1859/12/03.htm

Marx, Karl. 1973 [c 1857]. *Grundrisse: Foundations of the Critique of Political Economy (Rough Draft)* (translated by Martin Nicolaus) New York: Vintage Book. www.marxists.org/archive/marx/works/1857/grundrisse/ch09.htm

Masatoshi Tanaka. 1984. "Popular Uprisings, Rent Resistance, and Bondservant Rebellions in the Late Ming." Linda Grove and Christian Daniels eds. *State and Society in China: Japanese Perspectives on Ming-Qing Social and Economic History*. Tokyo: University of Tokyo Press.

Mawdsley, Emma. 2008. "Fu Manchu versus Dr Livingstone in the Dark Continent? Representing China, Africa and the West in British broadsheet newspapers." *Political Geography*, 27(5): 509–29,

McClelland, Charles E. 1980. *State, Society, and University in Germany, 1700–1914*. New York and Cambridge: Cambridge University Press.

McCord, Edward. 1993. *The Power of the Gun: The Emergence of Modern Chinese Warlordism*. Berkeley: University of California Press.

McIntyre, Kevin. 1996. "Geography as Destiny: Cities, Villages and Khmer Rouge Orientalism." *Comparative Studies in Society and History*, 38(4): 730–58.

McManus, Stuart M. 2023. *Bringing Together China and the West: Books of Early Modern Western Sinology in The Chinese University of Hong Kong Library*. Hong Kong: Chinese University of Hong Kong Press.

Menache, Sophia. 1996. "Tartars, Jews, Saracens and the Jewish–Mongol 'Plot' of 1241." *History*, 81(263): 319–42.

Mertha, Andrew. 2025. *Bad Lieutenants: The Khmer Rouge, United Front, and Class Struggle to the Eve of the New Millennium, 1970–1997*. Ithaca, NY: Cornell University Press.

Migdal, Joel. 1974. *Peasants, Politics, and Revolution. Pressures toward Political and Social Change in the Third World*. Princeton, NJ: Princeton University Press.

Miles, Steven B. 2020. *Chinese Diasporas: A Social History of Global Migration*. New York and Cambridge: Cambridge University Press.

Mitter, Rana. 2005. *A Bitter Revolution: China's Struggle with the Modern World*. Oxford: Oxford University Press.

Montesquieu, Charles de Secondât. 1990 [1734]. "Considerations on the Causes of the Greatness of the Romans and their Decline." In Melvin Richter, ed. *Montesquieu: Selected Political Writings*. Indianapolis, IN: Hackett Publishing.

Moore, Ronald. 1973. "Report on the Panel Discussion: Wang Yang-ming and Japanese Culture" Philosophy East and West, January–April 1973, Vol. 23, No. 1/2, Proceedings of East-West Philosophers' Conference on Wang Yang-ming (January–April 1973), pp. 217–24.

Müller, Friedrich Max. 1882. *Introduction to the Science of Religion: Four Lectures Delivered at the Royal Institution in February and May, 1870*. London: Longmans Green & Co.

Müller, Friedrich Max. 1891. "On the 'Enormous' Antiquity of the East (Inaugural Address at the Royal Asiatic Society, March 4, 1891)," *Nineteenth Century*, 29: 796–810.

Müller, Friedrich Max. 1893. "Inaugural Address." In E. Delmar Morgan, ed. *Transactions of the Nineth International Congress of Orientalists, London, 1892*. 1–37. London: Committee of the Congress.

Mungello, David E. 1985. *Curious Land: Jesuit Accomodation and the Origins of Sinology*. Stuttgart: Franz Steiner Verlag Wiesbaden GMBH.

Mungello. 1999. *The Great Encounter of China and the West, 1500–1800*. Lanham, MD: Rowman and Littlefield.

Needham, Joseph. 1954. *Science and Civilisation in China. Vol. 1*. New York and Cambridge: Cambridge University Press.

Neill, Stephen. 1964. *A History of Christian Missions*. Middlesex, England: Harmondsworth.

Navarro, Peter and Greg Autry. 2011. *Death by China: Confronting the Dragon – A Global Call to Action* Pearson Education.

Nieuhof, Johannes. 1693 [1665]. *Het gezandtschap der Neérlandtsche Oost-Indische Compagnie, aan den grooten Tartarischen Cham*. Tot Amsterdam, By Wolfgang, Waasberge, Boom, van Someren, en Goethals www.biodiversitylibrary.org/item/135127#page/9/mode/1up

Nisbet, Robert. 1980. *History of the Idea of Progress*. New York: Basic Books.

New York Times 1964. "Soviet Charges China Glorifies Genghis Khan." *New York Times*. May 7, 1964.

Newman, Frank N. 2011. *Six Myths that Hold Back America: And What America Can Learn from the Growth of China's Economy*. New York: Diversion Books.

Newman, Robert. 1992. *Owen Lattimore and the "Loss" of China*. University of California Press.

Nguyen Me & Benoît Malbranque. 2014. "Les Chinois de Turgot." Institut Coppet. March 25, 2014. www.institutcoppet.org/les-chinois-de-turgot/

O'Leary, Brendan. 1989. *The Asiatic Mode of Production: Oriental Despotism, Historical Materialism and Indian History*. Oxford: Blackwell.

O'Neill, Robert K. 1986. "The Role of Private Libraries in the Dissemination of Knowledge about Asia in Sixteenth Century Europe." In Cyriac K. Pullapilly et al. eds. *Asia and the West: Encounters and Exchanges from the Age of Explorations*. Notre Dame, Indiana: Cross Cultural Books. 277–308.

Ocko, Jonathan K. 1990. "Hierarchy and Harmony: Family Conflict as Seen in Ch'ing Legal Cases." In Kwang-ching Liu, ed. *Orthodoxy in Late Imperial China*. Berkeley and LA: University of California Press. 212–30.

Osterhammel, Jürgen. 2018. *Unfabling the East: The Enlightenment's Encounter with Asia*. Princeton, NJ: Princeton University Press.

Ownby, David. 1999. "Chinese Millenarian Traditions: The Formative Age." *American Historical Review*, 104(5): 1513–30.

Page, Jeffrey M. 1975. *Agrarian Revolution: Social Movements and Export Agriculture in the Underdeveloped World*. Free Press.

Palat, Ravi. 1996. "Fragmented Visions: Excavating the Future of Area Studies in a Post-American World." *Review*, 19(3): 269–18.
Paris, Matthew. 1259. *Chronica Majora Manuscript*. Cambridge: Corpus Christi College.
Parker, Geoffrey and Lesley Smith, eds. 1997. *The General Crisis of the Seventeenth Century*. Routledge.
Parsons, Talcott. 1991 [1951]. *The Social System*. London: Routledge.
Parsons, Talcott. 1971. *The System of Modern Societies*. Englewoods Cliffs, NJ: Prentice-Hall.
Patton, George S. Jr. 1944. "Main concepts. Strategy. Tactics. Leadership." Speech to the Third Army. https://people.uncw.edu/kozloffm/pattonnew.doc
Patton, George S. Jr. 2002. (ed. by Charles M. Province) "Military Essays and Articles." The George S. Patton, Jr. Historical Society. www.pattonhq.com/pdffiles/vintagetext.pdf
Pennington, Brian. 2005. *Was Hinduism Invented? Britons, Indians, and the Colonial Construction of Religion*. Oxford: Oxford University Press.
Perdue, Peter. 2000. "Russia, Central Eurasia, China, Japan, 1500–1700: Centralization and Commercialization" http://web.mit.edu/course/21/21h.504/www/perdue_16.htm
Perdue, Peter. 2010. *China Marches West: The Qing Conquest of Central Eurasia*. Cambridge, MA: Belknap Press.
Perkins, Franklin. 2004. *Leibniz and China: A Commerce of Light*. New York and Cambridge: Cambridge University Press.
Perman, Tony. 2020. "Coronavirus in China kept me under quarantine. I felt safer there than back in the U.S." NBC News, March 14, 2020. www.nbcnews.com/think/opinion/coronavirus-china-kept-me-under-quarantine-i-felt-safer-there-ncna1158756
Perry, Elizabeth J. 1980. *Rebels and Revolutionaries in North China, 1845–1945*. Stanford: Stanford University Press.
Peycam, Philippe M. F. 2010. "Sketching an Institutional History of Academic Knowledge Production in Cambodia (1863–2009) – Part 1." *Sojourn: Journal of Social Issues in Southeast Asia*, 25(2): 153–77.
Piaia, Gregorio. 1996. "European Identity and National Characteristics in the Historia Philosophica of the Seventeenth and Eighteenth Centuries." *Journal of the History of Philosophy* XXXIV(4): 593–605.

Pilling, David. 2009. "When China Rules the World: The Rise of the Middle Kingdom and the End of the Western World" *Financial Times*. June 12, 2009.

Pillsbury, Michael. 2016. *The Hundred-Year Marathon: China's Secret Strategy to Replace America as the Global Superpower*. New York: St Martin's Griffin.

Polachek, James. 1983. "The Moral Economy of the Kiangsi Soviet (1928–1934)" *Journal of Asian Studies* 42(4): 805–29.

Polachek, James. 1992. *The Inner Opium War*. Cambridge, MA: Harvard Asia Center.

Polo, Marco. 1958 [c. 1300]. *The Travel of Marco Polo*. London: Penguin.

Pomeranz, Kennth. 2000. *The Great Divergence: Europe, China, and the Making of the Modern World Economy*. Princeton, NJ: Princeton University Press.

Popkins, Samuel. 1979. *The Rational PeasantThe Political Economy of Rural Society in Vietnam*. Berkeley: University of California Press.

Popov, Vladimir. 2021. "The Main Contradiction of the Modern Era" Inter Press Service. September 6, 2021. www.globalissues.org/news/2021/09/06/28673

Poznanski, Kazimierz. 2017. "Confucian Economics: How Is Chinese Thinking Different?" *China Economic Journal*, 10(3): 362–84.

Price, David H. 2016. *Cold War Anthropology: The CIA, the Pentagon, and the Growth of Dual Use Anthropology*. Durham, NC: Duke University Press.

Price, David H. 2024. *Cold War Deceptions: The Asia Foundation and the CIA*. Seattle: University of Washington Press.

Pugach, Noel. 1973. "Embarrassed Monarchist: Frank J. Goodnow and Constitutional Development in China, 1913–1915." *Pacific Historical Review*, 42(4): 499–517.

Pulleyblank, Edwin G. 1995. "European Studies on Chinese Phonology: The First Phrase." In Wilson Ming and John Cayley, eds. *Europe Studies China: Papers from the International Conference on the History of European Sinology*. London: Han-Shan Tang Books. 339–67.

Qi Zheng. 2012. "Carl Schmitt in China" *Telos* 160 (Fall 2012): 29–52.

Quan, Hansheng 全漢昇 1969. "明清間白銀的輸入中國" (Import of American silver into China in Ming and Qing times). 中國文化研究學報 2(1): 59–79.

Quan, Hansheng 全漢昇 1971. "自明季至清中葉西屬美洲的中國絲貨貿易" (The Chinese Silk Trade in Spanish America from Late Ming to Mid Qing) 中國文化研究所學報 4(2): 345–69.

Quesnay, François. 2011 [1767]. *Despotisme de la Chine*. Pierre Palpant www.chineancienne.fr

Rahman Taimur. 2008. "Lenin on the Asiatic Mode of Production" *Revolutionary Democracy*, XIV(2): 2008 https://revolutionarydemocracy.org/rdv14n2/asiatic.htm

Ramo, Joshua. 2004. *The Beijing Consensus*. Foreign Policy Centre.

Rawski, Evelyn S. 1998. *The Last Emperors: A Social History of Qing Imperial Institutions*. University of California Press.

Rawski, Evelyn S. 2015. *Early Modern China and Northeast Asia: Cross-Border Perspectives*. New York and Cambridge: Cambridge University Press.

Raymond, Chad, Mark Selden, and Kate Zhou 2000. "The Power of the Strong? Rural Resistance and Reform in China and Vietnam." *China Information*, 14(2), 1–30.

Readings, Bill. 1996. *The University in Ruins*. Cambridge, MA: Harvard University Press.

Redding, S. Gordon. 1993. *The Spirit of Chinese Capitalism*. New York: Walter de Gruyter.

Reed, Christopher A. 2021. "Nearly Lost in Translation (s): Chiang Kai-shek's China's Destiny and Its Extraordinary English Language Publishing History, 1943–1947." *Publishing History*, 84: 65–97.

Reichwein, Adolf. 1925. *China and Europe: Intellectual and Artistic Contacts in the Eighteenth Century*. New York: Barnes and Noble.

Reid, Anthony. 1988. *Southeast Asia in the Age of Commerce, 1450–1680: Volume One: The Lands below the Winds*. Yale University Press.

Reid, T. R. 2013. *Confucius Lives Next Door: What Living in the East Teaches Us about Living in the West*. Knopf Doubleday Publishing Group.

Ricci, Matteo. 1953. *China in the 16th Century: The Journals of Matthew Ricci, 1583–1610*. New York: Random House.

Riccoldo da Monte di Croce. 2009 [1300]. *Libellus ad nationes orientales* (redaz. Firenze 1300) www.e-theca.net/emiliopanella/riccoldo2/adno.htm

Ride, Lindsay. 1960. "Biographic Note." In James Legge, ed. *The Chinese Classics*. Hong Kong: Hong Kong University Press. 1–25.

Rieber, Alfred J. 2005. "Stalin as Georgian: the formative years." Sarah Davies and James Harris eds. *Stalin: A New History*. Cambridge and New York: Cambridge University Press. 18–44.

Roberts, Alasdair. 2020. "Bearing the White Man's Burden: American Empire and the Origin of Public Administration." *Perspectives on Public Management and Governance*, 3(3): 185–96.

Rocher, Rosane. 1993. "British Orientalism in the Eighteenth Century: The Dialectics of Knowledge and Government." In Carol A. Breckenridge and Peter van der Veer, eds. *Orientalism and the Postcolonial Predicament: Perspective on South Asia*. Philadelphia: University of Pennsylvania Press. 215–49.

Rohmer Sax. 1913. *The Insidious Dr. Fu-Manchu: Being a SomeWhat Detailed Account of the Amazing Adventures of Nayland Smith in His Trailing of the Sinister Chinaman*. New York: A. L. Burt.

Romein, Jan M. 1978. *The Watershed of Two Eras: Europe in 1900*. Middletown, Connecticut: Wesleyan University Press.

Rossabi, Morris. 1994. "The Reign of Khubilai Khan." In Herbert Franke and Denis C. Twitchett, eds. *Cambridge History of China. Vol 6*. New York and Cambridge: Cambridge University Press. 414–89.

Rowbotham, Arnold H. 1942. *Missionary and Mandarin: The Jesuits at the Court of China*. New York: Russell and Russell.

Rowe, William T. 2001. *Saving the World: Chen Hongmou and Elite Consciousness in Eighteenth-Century China*. Palo Alto: Stanford University Press.

Rowe, William T. 2002. "Social Stability and Social Change." In Willard J. Peterson, ed. *The Cambridge History of China*. Vol. 9. New York and Cambridge: Cambridge University Press. 473–562.

Rowe, William T. 2007. "Owen Lattimore, Asia, and Comparative History" *The Journal of Asian Studies*, 66(3): 759–86.

Rowe, William T. 2010. *China's Last Empire: The Great Qing*. Harvard University Press.
Rozman, Gilbert. 2003. "Center-Local Relations: Can Confucianism Boost Decentralization and Regionalism?" Daniel A. Bell and Hahm Chaibong eds. *Confucianism for the Modern World*. New York and Cambridge: Cambridge University Press. 181–200.
Rule, Paul A. 1986. *K'ung-tzu or Confucius? The Jesuit Interpretation of Confucianism*. London: Aleen & Unwin.
Said, Edward W. 1978. *Orientalism: Western Conception of the Orient*. London: Penguin Bks.
Said, Edward W. 1985. "Orientalism Reconsidered" *Cultural Critique*, 1: 89–107.
San Francisco Call 1901. "Chinatown is a Menace to Health: Memorial of the Exclusion Convention Addressed to the President and Congress." *The San Francisco Call*. November 23, 1901 http://chroniclingamerica.loc.gov/lccn/sn85066387/1901-11-23/ed-1/seq-3/
Saussy, Haun. 2022. *The Making of Barbarians: Chinese Literature and Multilingual Asia*. Princeton, NJ: Princeton University Press.
Sautman, Barry. 1992. "Sirens of the Strongman: Neo-Authoritarianism in Recent Chinese Political Theory" *The China Quarterly*, 129: 72–102.
Schipper, Kristofer. 1995. "The History of Taoist Studies in Europe." In Wilson Ming and John Cayley, eds. *Europe Studies China: Papers from the International Conference on the History of European Sinology*. London: Han-Shan Tang Books. 467–91.
Schmidt, Stephan. 2011. "Mou Zongsan, Hegel, and Kant: The Quest for Confucian Modernity." *Philosophy East and West* 61(2): 260–302.
Schwab, Raymond. 1984. *The Oriental Renaissance: Europe's Rediscovery of India and the East 1680–1880*. New York: Columbia University Press.
Schwartz, Benjamin I. 1951. *Chinese Communism and the Rise of Mao*. Cambridge, MA: Harvard University Press.
Schwartz, Benjamin I. 1964. *In Search of Wealth and Power: Yen Fu and the West*. Cambridge, MA: Harvard University Press.
Scott, James C. 1976. *The Moral Economy of the Peasant: Rebellion and Subsistence in Southeast Asia*. New Haven: Yale University Press.

Scott, James C. 1998. *Seeing Like a State: How Certain Schemes to Improve the Human Condition Have Failed*. New Haven, CT: Yale University Press.

Sebes, Joseph S. J. 1988. "The Precursors of Ricci." In Charles E. Ronan and Bonnie B. C. Oh, eds. *East Meets West: The Jesuits in China, 1582–1773*. Chicago: Loyola University Press.

Selden, Mark. 1994. "Pathways from Collectivization: Socialist and Post-Socialist Agrarian Alternatives in Russia and China." *Review* (Fernand Braudel Center), 17(4): 423–49.

Sewell, William H. Jr. 1985. "Ideologies and Social Revolutions: Reflections on the French Case." *The Journal of Modern History*, 57(1): 86–96.

Sewell, William H. Jr. 2005. *Logics of History: Social Theory and Social Transformation*. Chicago: Chicago University Press.

Shambaugh, David. 2023. "The Evolution of American Contemporary China Studies: Coming Full Circle?" *Journal of Contemporary China*. DOI: 10.1080/10670564.2023.2237918

Shen Daming 沈大明. 2007. 《大清律例》與清代的社會控制 *(Qing legal code and social control in the Qing)*. Shanghai: 上海人民出版社.

Shih Shu-mei, Chien-hsin Tsai, and Brian Bernards, ed. 2013. *Sinophone Studies: A Critical Reader*. New York: Columbia University Press.

Shin, Doh Chull. 2012. *Confucianism and Democratization in East Asia*. New York and Cambridge: Cambridge University Press.

Shlapentokh, Dmitry. 2007. "Dugin, Eurasianism, and Central Asia" *Communist and Post-Communist Studies*, 40(2): 143–56. https://online.ucpress.edu/cpcs/article-abstract/40/2/143/70/Dugin-Eurasianism-and-Central-Asia?redirectedFrom=fulltext

Simon of Saint-Quentin 2019 [c. 1253]. Pow, Stephen, Tamás Kiss, Anna Romsics, Flora Ghazaryan. trans and ed. *Historia Tartarorum*. www.simonofstquentin.org

Skinner, William. 1964. "What the Study of China Can Do for Social Science." *Journal of Asian Studies* 23(4): 517–22.

Skinner, William G. 1977. *The City in Late Imperial China*. Palo Alto: Stanford University Press.

Skocpol, Theda. 1982. "What Makes Peasants Revolutionary?" *Comparative Politics*, 14(3): 351–75.

Société Asiatique de Paris ed. 1949. *Actes du XXI Congrès International des Orientalistes*. Paris: Imprimerie Nationale.
Sommer, Mathew H. 2000. *Sex, Law, and Society in Late Imperial China*. Stanford University Press.
Spence, Jonathan D. 1984. *The Memory Palace of Matteo Ricci*. New York: Viking Penguin.
Spence, Jonathan D. 1992a. "Matteo Ricci and the Ascent to Peking." In Jonathan D. Spence, ed. *Chinese Roundabout*. New York: W.W. Norton. 37–49.
Spence, Jonathan D. 1992b. "Looking East: The Long View." *Chinese Roundabout*. 78–92. New York: W.W. Norton.
Spence, Jonathan D. 1998. *The Chan's Great Continent: China in Western Minds*. New York: W. W. Norton.
Spieckermann, Marie-Luise. 1983. "The Idea of Teleology and the Theory of Scientific Progress at the Beginning of the Eighteenth Century." In Haydn Mason, ed. *Transactions of the Sixth International Congress on the Enlightenment*. Oxford: The Voltaire Foundation.
Standen, Edith A. 1976. "The Story of the Emperor of China: A Beauvais Tapestry Series." *The Metropolitan Museum of Art Journal*, 11: 103–17.
Stein, Burton. 1989. "Eighteenth Century India: Another view" *Studies in History*, 5(1): 1–26.
Steinmetz, George. 2007. *The Devil's Handwriting: Precoloniality and the German Colonial State in Qingdao, Samoa, and Southwest Africa*. Chicago: Chicago University Press.
Steinmetz, George. 2023. *The Colonial Origins of Modern Social Thought: French Sociology and the Overseas Empire*. Princeton, NJ: Princeton University Press.
Stone, Lawrence. 1981. *The Past and the Present Revisited*. London: Routledge and Kegan Paul.
Suckling, Norman. 1967. "The Enlightenment and the Idea of Progress." In Theodore Besterman, ed. *Studies on Voltaire and the Eighteenth Century*. Vol. LVIII. Geneve: Institut Et Musee Voltaire. 1461–81.
Swen, Litian. 2021. *Jesuit Mission and Submission: Qing Rulership and the Fate of Christianity in China, 1644–1735*. Leiden: Brill.
Swidler Ann and Jorge Aditi. 1994. "The New Sociology of Knowledge." *Annual Review of Sociology* 20: 305–29.

Tan, Hongkai. 2024. "Marco Polo spirit of mutual learning still valuable." *China Daily*. November 11, 2024. www.chinadaily.com.cn/a/202411/11/WS673147daa310f1265a1cc8d9.html

Taylor, Jay. 2011. *The Generalissimo: Chiang Kai-shek and the Struggle for Modern China*. Cambridge, MA: Belknap Press.

Teng, Michael. 2014. *Ancient Chinese Wisdom to Transform Your Business: Lessons from Zheng He, Confucius and Sun Zi*. Singapore: Corporate Turnaround Centre Pte Ltd.

Ter Haar, Barend J. 2017. *Guan Yu: The Religious Afterlife of a Failed Hero*. Oxford: Oxford University Press.

The Economist. 2009. "Enter the dragon" *The Economist*. July 9, 2009.

Thomas, Nicholas. 1994. *Colonialism's Culture: Anthropology, Travel and Government*. London: Polity Press.

Thompson, D. G. 1986. "General Ricci and the Suppression of the Jesuit Order in France: 1760–4." *Journal of Ecclesiastical History*, 37(3): 426–41.

Thompson, Martyn P. 1994. "Ideas of Europe during the French Revolution and Napoleonic Wars." *Journal of History of Ideas*, 55(1): 37–58.

Thompson, Mark R. 2001. "Whatever Happened to 'Asian Values'?" *Journal of Democracy*, 12(4): 154–65. https://web.archive.org/web/20160208020234id_/www.risingpowersinitiative.org:80/wp-content/uploads/Thompson1.pdf

Time 1956. "RUSSIA: Go East, Young Man!" *Time* June 4, 1956. https://content.time.com/time/subscriber/article/0,33009,866946,00.html

Times Higher Education. 2021. www.timeshighereducation.com/news/hong-kong-university-close-mecca-china-studies

Trevor-Roper, Hugh. 1967. *Religion, the Reformation and Social Change* London: Secker & Warburg.

Trompf, G. W. 1978. *Friedrich Max Mueller: As a Theorist of Comparative Religion*. Bombay: Shakuntala Publishing House.

Trotsky, Leon. 1941. *Stalin: An Appraisal of the Man and His Influence*. New York: Harper & Brothers. www.marxists.org/archive/trotsky/1940/xx/stalin/ch01.htm

Tsou, Tang. 1963. *America's failure in China*. 2 vols. Chicago: University of Chicago Press.

Tsu, Jing. 2022. *Kingdom of Characters: The Language Revolution That Made China Modern*. Riverhead Books.

Tu, Weiming. 1976. *Neo-Confucian Thought in Action: Wang Yang-Ming's Youth*. Berkeley: University of California Press.

Tu, Weiming. 2017. "Chinese Philosophy: A Synoptic View" Eliot Deutsch and Ron Bontekoe eds. *A Companion to World Philosophies*. Oxford: Blackwell. 1–23.

Tuan, Rocky. 2023. "Preface." McManus, Stuart M. 2023. Bringing Together China and the West: Books of Early Modern Western Sinology in The Chinese University of Hong Kong Library. Hong Kong: Chinese University of Hong Kong Press xii.

Turner, Bryan S. 1978. *Marx and the End of Orientalism*. London: George Allen & Unwin.

Turner, Bryan S. 1994. *Orientalism, Postmodernism, and Globalism*. London and NY: Routledge.

Turvey, Calum G. 2019. "John Lossing Buck and Land Utilization in China." H. Hu, F. Zhong, and C. Turvey eds. *Chinese Agriculture in the 1930s: Investigations into John Lossing Buck's Rediscovered 'Land Utilization in China' Microdata*. Cham: Palgrave Macmillan. 33–54.

Tyner, James A. et al. 2018. "Khmer Rouge Irrigation Schemes during the Cambodian Genocide." *Genocide Studies International*, 12(1): 103–19.

Van Kley, Edwin J. 1973. "News from China; Seventeenth-Century European Notices of the Manchu Conquest." *Journal of Modern History*, XLV(4): 561–82.

Van Kley, Dale. 1975. *The Jansenists and the Expulsion of the Jesuits from France, 1757–1765*. New Haven, CT: Yale University Press.

Veg, Sebastian. 2020. "The 'Restructuring' of Hong Kong and the Rise of Neostatism." *Tocqueville 21*. June 27, 2020. https://tocqueville21.com/le-club/the-restructuring-of-hong-kong-and-the-rise-of-neostatism/

Vico, Giambattista. 1948 [1744]. *The New Science* (translated by Thomas Goddard Bergin and Max Harold Fisch). Ithaca, NY: Cornell University Press.

Vogel, Ezra. 2016. "Milestones in the History of the Universities Service Centre for China Studies." *The China Journal*, 75, 1–8.

Voltaire. 1759a [1756]. *An Essay on Universal History, the Manners, and Spirit of Nations: From the Reign of Charlemaign to the Age* of Lewis XIV. Volume 1 [English translation of Essai sur les moeurs et l'esprit des nations by Nugent]. London: J. Nourse.

Voltaire. 1759b [1756]. An Essay on Universal History, the Manners, and Spirit of Nations: From the Reign of Charlemaign to the Age of Lewis XIV. Volume V [English translation of Essai sur les moeurs et l'esprit des nations by Nugent]. London: J. Nourse.

von Glahn, Richard. 1991. "Municipal Reform and Urban Social Conflict in Late Ming Jiangnan." *Journal of Asian Studies*, 50(2): 280–307.

von Glahn, Richard. 2016. *The Economic History of China: From Antiquity to the Nineteenth Century*. New York and Cambridge: Cambridge University Press.

Vukovich, Daniel. 2012. *China and Orientalism: Western Knowledge Production and the PRC*. London: Routledge.

Wade, Robert. 1990. *Governing the Market: Economic Theory and the Role of Government in East Asian Industrialization*. Princeton, NJ: Princeton University Press.

Wakeman, Frederic 1972. "The Price of Autonomy: Intellectuals in Ming and Ch'ing Politics." *Daedalus*, 101: 42–3.

Wakeman, Frederic Jr. 1986. "China and the Seventeenth-Century Crisis." *Late Imperial China*, 7(1): 1–26.

Wakeman, Frederic Jr. "A Revisionist View of the Nanjing Decade: Confucian Fascism." *The China Quarterly*, 150: 395–432.

Wakeman, Frederic Jr. 1998. "Boundaries of the Public Sphere in Ming and Qing China." *Daedalus*, 127(3): Early Modernities 167–89.

Walder, Andrew 1986. *Communist Neo-Traditionalism: Work and Authority in Chinese Industry*. Berkeley and LA: University of California Press.

Wallace, William A. 1991. *Galileo, the Jesuits, and the Medieval Aristotle*. London: Variorum.

Wallerstein, Immanuel. 1974. *The Modern World-System I: Capitalist Agriculture and the Origins of the European World-Economy in the Sixteenth Century*. San Diego: Academic Press.

Wallerstein, Immanuel. 1980. *The Modern World-System II: Mercantilism and the Consolidation of the European World-Economy, 1600–1750*. New York: Academic Press.

Wallerstein, Immanuel. 1989. *The Modern World-System III: The Second Era of Great Expansion of the Capitalist World-Economy, 1730s–1840s* New York: Academic Press.

Wallerstein, Immanuel. 1991. *Geopolitics and Geoculture: Essays on the Changing World-System*. New York and Cambridge: Cambridge University Press.

Wallerstein, Immanuel. 1992. "The West, Capitalism, and the Modern World-System." *Review* XV(4): 561–619.

Wallerstein, Immanuel et al. 1996. *Open the Social Sciences: Report of the Gulbenkian Commission on the Restructuring of the Social Sciences*. Stanford: Stanford University Press.

Wallerstein, Immanuel. 1997. "The Unintended Consequences of Cold War Area Studies." Noam Chomsky et al. eds. *The Cold War & The University: Toward an Intellectual History of the Postwar Years*. New York: The New Press. 195–232.

Wallerstein, Immanuel. 2011. *The Modern World-System IV: Centrist Liberalism Triumphant, 1789–1914* University of California Press.

Wang, Gang-wu. 2002. *The Chinese Overseas: From Earthbound China to the Quest for Autonomy*. Cambridge, MA: Harvard University Press.

Wang Wenwen. 2020. "Now is the time for Western media to learn about collectivism" *Global Times*. February 1, 2020. www.globaltimes.cn/content/1179823.shtml

Wasserstrom, Jeffrey. 1991. *Student Protests in Twentieth-Century China: The View from Shanghai*. Stanford: Stanford University Press.

Wasserstrom, Jeffrey. 2006. "Misreading China: It's time to move beyond old stereotypes." *Christian Science Monitor*. April 7, 2006. www.csmonitor.com/2006/0407/p09s03-coop.html

Waterson, James. 2013. *Defending Heaven: China's Mongol Wars, 1209–1370*. Frontline Books.

Watson, James. 1975. *Emigration and the Chinese Lineage: The Mans in Hong Kong and London*. University of California Press.

Watson, James. 1983. "Rural Society: Hong Kong's New Territories." *The China Quarterly*, 95: 480–90.

Webb, John. 1669. *An Historical Essay Endeavouring a Probability that the Language of the Empire of China Is the Primitive Language*. London: Printed for Nath. Brook.

Weber, Max. 1951 [1915]. *The Religion of China: Confucianism and Taoism*. Glencoe: The Free Press.

Weber, Max. 1958 [1916]. *The Religion of India: The Sociology of Hinduism and Buddhism*. Glencoe: The Free Press.

Weber, Max. 1973 [1908]. "The Power of the State and the Dignity of the Academic Calling in Imperial Germany: The Writing of Max Weber on University Problem." *Minerva*. Vol 11, No. 4. 571–632.

Weber, Max. 1992 [1905]. *The Protestant Ethic and the Spirit of Capitalism*. London: Routledge.

Weil, Robert. 1996. *Red Cat, White Cat: China and the Contradictions of "Market Socialism."* Monthly Review Press.

Well, Samuel. 1894. *New Physiognomy, or, Signs of Character, as Manifested through Temperament and External Forms, and Especially in "the Human Face Divine"* New York: Fowler & Wells Co.

Weinberger, Eliot. 2016. "What Is the I Ching?" *The New York Review of Books*. February 25, 2016. www.nybooks.com/articles/2016/02/25/what-is-the-i-ching/?utm_source=chinafile&utm_medium=link&utm_campaign=none

Weitzman, Arthur J. 1967. "The Oriental Tale in the Eighteenth Century: A Reconsideration." In Theodore Besterman, ed. *Studies on Voltaire and the Eighteenth Century*. Vol. LVIII. Geneve: Institut Et Musee Voltaire, 1839–55.

White, Ben. 2014. "Professional Blindness and Missing The Mark: The Anthropologist's Blind Spots: Clifford Geertz on Class, Killings and Communists In Indonesia" *Rozenberg Quarterly*. http://rozenbergquarterly.com/professional-blindness-and-missing-the-mark-the-anthropologists-blind-spots-clifford-geertz-on-class-killings-and-communists-in-indonesia

Will, Pierre-Etienne. 2023. "French Sinology." *Journal of Chinese History*, 7: 525–74.

Will, Pierre-Etienne and Bin R. Wong. 1991. *Nourish the People: The State Civilian Granary System in China, 1650–1850*. Ann Arbor: University of Michigan Press.

Wittfogel, Karl. 1957. *Oriental Despotism: A Comparative Study of Total Power*. New Haven: Yale University Press.

Wolf, Eric. 1969 *Peasant Wars of the Twentieth Century*. Harper and Row.

Wong, R. Bin. 1997. *China Transformed: Historical Change and the Limits of European Experience*. Ithaca, NY: Cornell University Press.

Wood, Frances. 1997. *Did Marco Polo Go to China?* New York: Perseus.

Woodside, Alexander. 1990. "State, Scholars, and Orthodoxy: The Ch'ing Academies, 1736–1839." In Kwang-ching Liu, ed. *Orthodoxy in Late Imperial China*. Berkeley and LA: University of California Press. 158–86.

Wu Jen-shu 巫仁恕 2011. 激變良民：傳統中國城市群眾集體行動之分析 (Rebellious Good Subjects: An Analysis of Urban Collective Action in Traditional China). Beijing: 北京大學出版社

Xi Jinping. 2013. "Address to the First Session of the 12th National People's Congress." March 17, 2013. http://en.qstheory.cn/2020-09/21/c_607581.htm

Xi Jinping. 2023. "Xi calls for efforts to build modern Chinese civilization" Xinhua News, June 3, 2023. https://english.news.cn/20230603/197012efecbf4a34992b6df61a05310c/c.html

Xu Xiaohong, Ivan Png, Junhong Chu & Yehning Chen. 2024. "The Misruling Elites: The State, Local Elites, and the Social Geography of the Chinese Revolution" *Theory and Society*. Vol 53, No. 2. p. 465–508.

Yang Nianqun 楊念群 1997. 儒學地域化的近代化形態：三大知識群體互動的比較研究 (Modern form of regionalization of Confucianism: a comparative study of the interaction among three intellectual groups). Beijing: 三聯書店

Ye Gaoshu. 葉高樹 2002. 清前期的文化政策 (cultural policy of early Qing period) Taipei: 稻香出版社.

Yongzheng Emperor 雍正皇帝 1724. 御製朋黨論 (Imperial discourse on friendship and cliques) https://ctext.org/wiki.pl?if=en&chapter=99087&remap=gb

Yü Ying-shih. 1967. *Trade and Expansion in Han China, A Study in the Structure of Sino-Barbarian Economic Relations*. Berkeley: University of California Press.

Yü Ying-shih. 余英時 2004. 宋明理學與政治文化 (Philosophy of principle and political culture in Ming and Qing) Taipei: 允晨文化

Yü Ying-shih. 2021 [1986]. *The Religious Ethic and Mercantile Spirit in Early Modern China*. Translated by Yim-tze Kwong. Edited by Hoyt Cleveland Tillman. New York: Columbia University Press.

Yü Ying-shih. 余英時 2022a. 余英時評政治現實 (Yü Ying-shi on political realities). Taipei: 印刻

Yü Ying-shih. 余英時 2022b. 余英時政論集 (collection of Yü Yingshi political commentaries). Taipei: 聯經出版公司

Zarakol, Ayşe. 2022. *Before the West: The Rise and Fall of Eastern World Orders*. Cambridge: Cambridge University Press.

Zarrow, Peter. 2005. *China in War and Revolution, 1895–1949*. London: Routledge.

Zhang, Longxi. 1988. "The Myth of the Other: China in the Eyes of the West." *Critical Inquiry*, 15(1): 108–31.

Zhang, Longxi. 1999. *Mighty Opposites: From Dichotomies to Differences in the Comparative Study of China*. Palo Alto: Stanford University Press.

Zhao Qinghe 趙慶河 1995. 讀書雜誌與中國社會史論戰 (The Reading magazine and the debate on Chinese social history) Taipei: 稻禾出版社

Zhao Tingyang. 2021 [2011]. *All under Heaven: The Tianxia System for a Possible World Order*. Berkeley and LA: University of California Press. Trans. by Joseph E. Harroff.

Zhou Daguan 周達觀 n.d. [c. 1297]. 真臘風土記 (The Customs of Cambodia). https://ctext.org/wiki.pl?if=gb&res=311919

Zhou, Zhenhe. 周振鶴 2006. "聖諭, 聖諭廣訓與相關的文化現象" (Sacred Edits, Amplified Instructions of the Sacred Edicts, and Related Cultural Phenomenon)" Zhou Zhenke 周振鶴ed. 聖諭光訓: 集解與研究. 351–632. Shanghai: 上海書店出版社

Zhu Guanglei 朱光磊 2021. "現代新儒家的陽明學研究" (Research on Yangming School of Modern Neo Confucianism) 文化中國. No. 109: 24–32.

Zürcher, Erik. 1994. "Conception, Birth and Early Childhood of the Documentation Center." In Woei Lien Chong and Ingrid d'Hooghe, eds. *China Information: Anniversary Supplement to Vol. IX, No.1*.

Zürcher, Erik. 1995. "From 'Jesuit Studies' to 'Western Learning.'" In Wilson Ming and John Cayley, eds. *Europe Studies China: Papers from an International Conference on the History of European Sinology*. London: Han-Shan Tang Books. 264–79.

INDEX

Abdel-Malek, Anouar, 6
Abel-Rémusat, Jean-Pierre, 113
absolute monarch, 104
absolutism, 104
academia
  Cold War Western, 18
  Europe's, 17
  hegemony of US, 164
  mainstream Western, 188
  Western, 8, 150, 175, 186, 196, 256
academic knowledge, 4
academic production, 5
accommodation policy, 40, 50
  Jesuits', 43, 63
Age of Empire, 129
alliance
  Christian–Mongol, 30
  Muslim–Confucianist, 255
  Soviet–China, 24
  US-led Western, 238, 261
Amin, Samir, 189, 191
Amoy, 125
ancestor worship, 210
Anderson, Perry, 184
antiquity, 79, 81, 93, 95
  Chinese, 48
  Greco–Roman, 47
  Greek and Roman, 46
  Indian, 118
  Occidental, 47
anti-war movement, 173, 246
Arab Studies, 6
Area Studies, 159, 164, 171, 245

the formation of US, 160
the institutionalization of, 165
aristocracy, 104
  feudal, 104
aristocrats, 104
Aryan, the, 135
Asian stagnation, 179
Asian Tigers, 235
Asian values, 235–42
atheism, 41
atheists, 95
Austria, 26
autarky, 189, 192
authoritarianism, 252
authority, intellectual and moral, 46
autocracy, 211, 220

balance of power, between the East and West, 103
barbarianism, 96
benevolence, 222
Bergesen, Albert, 10
Biden, Joe, 2
Black Death, the, 34
Bolsheviks, 184–7
Bose, Sudhindra, 229
Bourdieu, Pierre, 12
bourgeois class, 103
bourgeoisie. *See also* bourgeois class
  rising financial power of the, 106
Bouvet, Joachim, 85–6
Brucker, Johann Jacob, 91
Buck, John Lossing, 166

304 / Index

Buck, Pearl, 248–50
Buddhism, 40, 112, 123, 126, 141, 157
C. de Bridia, 27
Calvinism, 149, 151–2, 235
Calvinists, Protestant, 56
canonization
  colonial, 109
  of Marx, 173
  of Taoism and Confucianism, 111
Canton. *See* Guangzhou
capital accumulation, 1
capitalism, 2, 149
  authoritarian, 237
  model of, 2
  the rise of, 149
capitalist development. *See* capitalism
capitalist modernization. *See* capitalism
capitalist spirit, 150, 152
Cathay, 4, 33–4
Catholic Church, 4, 26, 49, 54, 73
  discontent against the, 64
Catholicism, 36, 40–1
CCP. *See* Chinese Communist Party
Cheng-Zhu School, of neo-
  Confucianism, 223
Chiang, Kai-shek, 214–19
China
  debt trap, 254
  idealized and rationalized image of, 61
  invasion of Vietnam, 199
  a military crusade against, 39
  model, 2
  Mongol, 31
  Mongol-ruled, 31
  the social scientific approach to the study of, 164
  South, 34
  the study of, 45
China Studies, 4–6, 18, 162–5, 245–7
  de-Orientalization of, 173
  in other Asian societies, 172
  Western, 172
China/Area Studies, 8
Chinese Communist Party, 188
  the formation of the, 212

Chinese Exclusion Act, 23
Chinese phonology, 128
chinoiserie, 64, 102
Chomsky, Noam, 197
Christendom, 42
Christianity, 4, 15, 32, 38, 40, 42–3, 74, 122–3, 137, 149, 151, 219, 236, 252
  converting the Khan to, 30
chronology
  Biblical, 59
  Chinese, 54, 59
  orthodox Biblical, 54
Chuang Tzu. *See* Zhuangzi
civil war, 204, 215
civilizations, 42
  Asian, 6, 43, 109
  Chinese, 7, 47, 50, 65, 112
  Confucianist, 254
  Eastern, 5
  European, 6
  high, 42
  homogenous, timeless Asian, 186
  Indian, 110
  non-Western, 5, 7, 118
  ocean and Western, 214
  Western, 2, 4
class conflicts, 177
class interest, 104
Classicism, 64
Classics
  Chinese, 120, 171
  Confucian, 84, 120
  Confucianism's state-sanctioned, 112
  Confucianist, 41, 113
  Jesuits-translated, 112
  of Taoism, 115
  Taoist, 113, 120
clergy, 126
Cold War, 24, 150, 160, 169–70, 175, 186, 245
collectivism, 160, 214–15, 217, 220, 237–9, 241, 252, 255
  Confucianist, 240
  Eastern, 242
collectivization, 192

Collins, Randall, 11–12
colonialism, 103, 129
  French, 190
colonization, 88
communal property, 179–80
communal villages, 182
communalism, 216, 231, 233, 235
communism, 187–8
Communist Party of Kampuchea. *See* Khmer Rouge
Communist totalitarianism, 186
Confucianism, 2, 9, 18, 40, 112, 123, 126, 137, 141, 150, 153–7, 208, 220, 235
  atheist interpretation of, 40
  essentialization of, 236
  Jesuit interpretation of, 58
  radical, 224
Confucius, 41, 59, 77, 91, 93, 100, 138
  the Classics of, 79
consciousness, 98
conservatives, cultural, 214
Constantinople, the fall of, 34
court
  French, 44, 104
  Mongol, 27
  Prussian, 104
  Qing, 16
  Spanish, 35
COVID-19 pandemic, 3, 239
cultural revolution, 211–12
Cultural Revolution, 198
  of 1966–1968, 213
cultures
  Chinese, 140, 232
  Confucianist, 214, 251
  Eastern, 117
  Greco-Roman, 93
  non-European, 43
  non-Western, 160
  Oriental, 110
  stereotypical image of traditional Chinese, 215
  total rejection of Chinese traditional, 213
  traditional, 212

traditional Chinese, 211, 214
wholesale importation of Western, 211

Daode Jing, 113, 122
Darwin, Charles, 130
Darwinian evolutionism, 130, 144
Darwinism, 17
de Groot, J. J. M., 125–8, 139–43, 156
delinking, 191
democracy, 2
  Confucian, 235
  liberal, 213
de-Orientalization, 175, 203
  of China Studies, 246–7
dependency theory, 188
Dermigny, Louis, 103
despotism, 82, 93, 98
  Asiatic, 94
  enlightened, 80–1
  Oriental, 94, 99, 213, 216, 241, 244
Diderot, Denis, 95
disenchantment, 153
Du Halde, Jean-Baptiste, 61–2
Dugin, Aleksandr, 240
dynasty
  Qin, 41
  Tang, 81

East, the, 25, 30
East Indian Company, 45, 180
Edkins, Joseph, 128
education, lack of, 208–9
Emperor Taizong, 81
Empires
  Chinese, 37, 50
  European, 109
  Iberian, 34
  Khmer, 193–4
  Ming, 34, 48
  Mongol, 4
  Ottoman, 6, 34
  Portuguese maritime, 35
  Qing, 48, 73, 203
  vast Chinese, 82
Encyclopédie, 95

306 / Index

Enlightenment, 4, 47–8, 72–3
   Oriental, 74
   radical, 95, 99
   Sinophilic, 90
environmental determinism, 133
epistemology
   essentializing and homogenizing, 255
   Orientalist, 236, 244
essentialism, 65, 175
ethics, Confucian, 80
ethnography, 169
ethnonationalism, 17, 133
EU–China relations, 3
eugenics, 130
Eurasia, 25, 30
Eurocentrism, of Western Sinology, 232
Europe
   Christian, 64
   Enlightenment, 64
European colonization, 47
European concert, 91
European supremacy, 92

factionalism, 228
Fairbank, John King, 162, 218
familial relationship, 155
Fénelon, François, 92
feudalism, 213
   the crisis of, 45–8, 71
filial loyalty, 222
filial piety, 223, 226
fiscal crisis, of the Bourbon
   dynasty, 106
France, 45
free trade, 31
freedom, 98
French Revolution, 89, 95, 106
Fu, Manchu, 250
Fu Xi, 79, 86
Fujian, 35

Genghis Khan, 26, 28
genocide, Cambodian, 197
geography, 96
Germany, 117
global financial crisis, 2–3, 252

Gobineau, Arthur de, 129
God, 40, 120, 138
   Biblical, 65
   existence of, 123
   monotheistic, 40, 58, 122
Golden Age, the, 79
González de Mendoza, Juan, 38
Goodnow, Frank, 204–11, 229
Gregory XIII, Pope, 39
Groslier, Bernard Philippe, 192
Gu, Yanwu. *See* Ku, Yen-wu
Guangzhou, 34–5
Guyuk Khan, 27

Han Chinese, 53
Harvard School, 162
Hegel, Georg Wilhelm Friedrich, 97–9
hegemony
   Mongol Empire's, 25
   world, 11
High Imperialism, 135, 146
Hinduism, 110, 157
historiography
   China-centered, 8
   European, 42
Hong Kong, 169, 256
human nature, 127
humanities, 110
Hungary, 26
Huntington, Samuel, 237, 255

idealization, 4–5, 74, 117, 138, 245
   of China, 7, 15, 252, 255, 261
   naïve, 243
   of a non-Western civilization, 8
   romantic, 8, 135
   Romanticist, 195
   utopian, 182
identity
   Christian–Latin, 46
   crisis, European, 90
   new European, 92
ideologies
   imperialist and ethnonationalist, 133
   racist, 130
   state, 40

idolatry, 55
   of the Chinese, 37
imperialism, 129, 144, 198
   Western, 7
India, 6
   agrarian society, 180
   British administration of, 180
   individualism, 160, 215, 217, 231, 239, 241, 255
   Western, 240, 242
Industrial Revolution, 88
Innocent IV, Pope, 27
intellectuals
   China's liberal, 213
   Chinese, 18, 212
   early modern, 46
   fields, 11–13
   Indian, 110
   leftist, 187
   liberal, 214
   May Fourth, 212
   networks, 11–13
   radical non-establishment, 188
   rival networks of, 244
   Western, 188
intelligence, 207
inter-Asian studies, 8
inter-imperial rivalry, 17, 133, 144
irrationality, 154, 160, 220, 244
   of the Chinese culture, 212
Islam, 6, 110

Jacques, Martin, 240
Jansenism, 100
Jansenists, French, 55
Japan, 172
Jesuits, 4, 15, 39–42, 49, 73, 85, 99–101, 112, 244, 257
   Portuguese and Spanish, 37
   Spanish, 38
Jews, 29
Jiaqing Emperor, 228
Julien, Stanislas, 114

Kang, Youwei, 229
Kangxi Emperor, 62–3, 81, 226

Kant, Immanuel, 72, 97
Kennan, George, 24
Khmer Rouge, 189–95, 198
KMT, 214, 219
knowledge
   academic production of, 243
   Catholic, 67
   co-reproduction of Orientalist, 211
   monastic, 33
   Orientalist, 5, 171, 182, 203
   scientific and mathematical, 86
   Sinological, 9
knowledge production, 4, 71, 109
   academic, 3, 9
Ku, Yen-wu, 229
Kublai Khan, 4, 31, 62

laissez-faire, 81
languages
   Chinese, 41, 128
   European, 128
   Indo–European, 128
Lanza, Fabio, 198
Lao-tzu. *See* Laozi
Laozi, 113, 139
Lattimore, Owen, 163, 167
Le Comte, Louis, 59
leadership
   US global, 3
   Western, 2
Legge, James, 115, 120–4, 137–9, 156
Leibniz, Gottfried Wilhelm, 85–6
Leiden University, 125
Lenin, V. I., 182, 184
Levenson, Joseph, 168
Li, Zhi, 224
liberalism, 236
   Western, 215
literati, 112
lixue. *See* Cheng-Zhu School, of neo-Confucianism
logic, 209
longue durée, 5
Louis XIV, 55

Macao, 34–5
macro-sociology of knowledge, 5
macro-world-historical perspective, 10
magic, 154–5
Manchu Conquest, 45, 48–53, 80
Manchu state. *See* states, Qing
Manchus, the, 48
Manila, 35–6
Mao, Zedong, 253
Maoism, 173, 189
Maoists. *See* Maoism
Martini, Martino, 49
Marx, Karl, 176–84
Marxian approach. *See* Marxian paradigm
Marxian paradigm, 173
Marxism, 212
mathematics, 85
May Fourth New Culture movement, 211
merchants, 30
meritocracy, 251
meritocratic examination system. *See* meritocratic examinations
meritocratic examinations, 80
missionaries, 15, 36, 49, 58, 61, 63
  Jesuit, 85
  Portuguese and Spanish, 39
  Protestant, 120
mode of production, Asiatic, 176–84, 186, 193, 213, 216
modernity, 195
  Chinese, 212
  Japan's, 234
  the rise of, 17
  Western, 231, 244
modernization, 159
  theory, 150, 160, 162, 245
monarchy, 211
Mongol Conquest. *See* Mongols, the
Mongolia. *See* Mongols, the
Mongols, the, 4, 23–34, 67, 244
monotheism, 41, 122–3
Montesquieu, 93
moral economy, of the peasants, 195
moral laws, 77
morality
  Biblical, 59
  Chinese, 77, 79
  Confucian, 41
  natural, 79
Mou, Tsung-san, 231
Mou Zongsan. *See* Mou, Tsung-san
Müller, Friedrich Max, 111, 118, 121, 124, 135–6
Mungello, David, 9

Nanking University, 166
nation building, 203
nationalism, 218
  the rise of, 117
nation-states, 47, 134
natural laws, 80–1
  of evolution, 89
natural order, 154
natural sciences, 85
naturalists, 95
Near East, the, 27, 30
neo-Confucianism, 222–9
Netherlands, the, 51–3
network analysis, 11
network/field perspective, 10
New Asia College, 234
New Confucianism, 221, 229–35
Nieuhof, Johan, 52, 55

Opium War, 178, 229
Orient, the, 91, 94
Oriental despot. *See* Oriental despotism
Oriental despotism, 177, 179–80, 184
  Tsarist, 185
Oriental Renaissance, 102, 109
Orientalism, 5–10, 102, 109
  academic, 144
  the demise of European, 159
  nineteenth-century, 111
  Romantic, 17, 117
  scientific-racist, 17, 245
  self-, 221, 256
  Western, 215
orthodoxy
  Catholic, 44
  religious, 46

Osterhammel, Jürgen, 7
Oxford University, 120

Paris, 45, 189
Paris, Matthew, 15, 28–30, 244
Parsons, Talcott, 159
particularism, 11, 160, 243
Paul IV, Pope, 44
philology, 74–6, 128
philosophers
  Enlightenment, 4, 92
  kings, 80
  millenarian, 88
  political, 80
  Sinophilic, 4, 244
  Sinophilic Enlightenment, 88
  Sinophobic, 92, 106, 244
philosophy
  Chinese, 84, 97, 127
  Chinese moral, 41
  Confucian, 58–9, 83
  Confucianist, 79
  Eastern origin of, 91
  Enlightenment, 64
  European, 91
  the idealist tradition of German, 151
  modern, 91
  natural, 91
  non-European, 92
Physiocratic school, 82
Poivre, Pierre, 81
Poland, 26
polarization, 67
political economy, 81
  domestic, 3
  global, 3
  of the world-system, 11
political sociology, of the rise and fall of Sinophilia, 102–6
Polo, Marco, 4, 15, 31–3, 243
polytheism, 122
Popov, Vladimir, 241
populists, Russian, 181–2
Portugal, 34–5
Pot, Pol, 189
predestination, 56, 65
Prester John, 26, 28

Primitive Language, 74–5
printing press, 71
private property, 177
progress, 72
  discourse of, 95
  The Eurocentric idea of, 89–92
  the idea of, 48, 88
  the ideology of, 106
Protestantism, 36, 47

Quesnay, François, 81–4

races
  Aryan and Semitic, 136
  dark, 130
  dark-skinned, 205
  inferior, 133
  white, 130
  "yellow," 4, 130
racism, 7, 129
  scientific, 17, 135, 205
rapprochement, to China, 24
rationalism, 119, 133, 150
rationality, 116, 133, 154–5, 160
reason, 73
reductionism, 65, 175
Reformation, 36, 46, 71
regime
  Chinese Communist, 186
  "Confucian fascist," 217
  Khmer Rouge, 190, 192
  KMT, 234
  Qing, 50
  Russia's tsarist, 181
  Stalin, 186
reification
  of any non-Western civilization, 245
  Orientalist, 166
religions, 40, 111
  Asiatic, 150
  in China, 56
  Chinese, 37, 65, 122, 139, 150
  Chinese official and folk, 125
  folk, 114
  natural, 76
  non-Christian, 42

religions (cont.)
    Occidental, 149
    Oriental, 111, 118
religious tolerance, 127
Renaissance, 46–7
Republic of China, 204
republicanism, 205
revelation, 40, 123
revolution
    Chinese Communist, 187
    Communist, 196
    peasant, 188
    Vietnamese communist, 198
Ricci, Matteo, 39–41, 44
Riccoldo, da Monte di Croce, 30
Rites Controversy, the, 54–8
River Elegy, 214
Romantic movement. *See* Romanticism
Romanticism, 17, 116–19
    the decline of, 144
romanticization, 182
    of Asian peasants and Asiatic communal villages, 187
    of the pre-colonial Asian countryside, 195
Rome, 36, 45
Rousseau, Jean-Jacques, 96, 216

Said, Edward, 5–10
salvation, 55, 65, 152
Samphan, Khieu, 189, 191
Schlegel, Gustaaf, 127
Schmitt, Carl, 238
scholars
    biblical and non-biblical, 76
    China, 5
    China Studies, 9
    Chinese, 172
    Chinese official, 238
    diasporic Chinese, 221
    Western China Studies, 257
Schwartz, Benjamin I., 168
science, 85, 109, 116
    pseudo-, 129
    racist pseudo-, 133
Science, 139

scientific methods, 110
scientific racism, the rise of, 144
Scientific Revolution, 72–3, 85, 89
secular liberalism, 127
segregation, 130
Semite, the, 135
Seven Years' War, 106
Shangdi. See God
Sihanouk, King, 197
silver, 48
Simon of Saint Quentin, 27
Sinologists
    Japanese, 172
    Romantic, 244
    scientific-racist, 244
Sinology, 146
    European, 158, 164
    nineteenth-century, 113
    racist, 4
    Romantic, 4, 119, 245
    scientific-racist, 129, 156, 245
    Western, 41
Sinophiles, 55, 92, 95, 103, 106
Sinophilia, 15, 49, 91, 94–5
    the demise of, 99
    early Enlightenment, 71
    a final blow to, 100
    the rise of, 51
    a surge of, 54
Sinophobes, 55, 104, 106
Sinophobia, 53, 94, 97, 99
    late Enlightenment, 88
Sino-Portuguese war, in 1522–1523, 34
Sino-Soviet relations, 25
Sixtus V, Pope, 54
Skinner, G. William, 167, 170
social engineering, 212
social history, 173
social sciences, 150, 164, 172, 246
    Parsonian, 165
    universalist, 165
social scientific methods, 168
social scientific theory, 166
social theories, 149
Society of Jesus, the, 36, 39, 45, 54, 61, 99
sociology

of intellectual change, 10–13
of knowledge, 8
Socrates, 93
Soviet Union, 24–5, 184–7
Spain, 35–6
spirituality, Eastern, 119
Stalin, 185–6
states
   absolutist, 103, 106
   Chinese, 19, 39, 82, 94, 142, 239
   despotic, 211, 213
   European, 51
   French, 45
   imperial, 222
   Manchu, 49
   Ming, 35
   one-party authoritarian, 213
   Prussian-German, 134
   Qing, 226–8
statism, 217, 237
Steinmetz, George, 7
stereotypes, 3, 248
   of China, 33
   of Fu Manchu, 253
   Orientalist, 165
   romantic, 197
   Western, 203
structural functionalism, 159
Sun, Yat-sen, 204
superiority
   China's moral, 127
   Chinese, 79
   of the Chinese civilization, 100
   Europe's, 92
   European, 43, 91
supernatural, the, 123
superstition, 116
symbolic interaction theory, 11

Taiwan, 53
Tao, 154
Taoism, 112, 123, 126, 138, 141, 150, 153–7, 209
   canonization of, 113–16
Tartars, 28–30
term question, 120
Thevet, André, 42

thinkers
   early Enlightenment, 86
   Enlightenment, 16, 58, 65
   Sinophilic, 106
Tian, 40, 121
Tokugawa government, 74
trade
   the Asian, 44
   China, 35
   China–Nagasaki, 35
   France–Asia, 45
   traditionalism, 142
Trump, Donald, 1–3
Tu, Weiming, 233
Turgot, Robert Jacques, 84

underdevelopment, 188, 191
Universal History, 42–3, 88
Universal Language, 75–6
universalism, 11, 160, 243
   ethnocentric, 173
universality. *See* universalism
Universism, 141
universities, 109, 134
   de-theologizing, 71
   German, 134
   nineteenth-century, 4
   Western, 4
Universities Service Center, 169, 256
US–China rivalry, 2, 255

Valignano, 39
Vatican, the, 35–6
Voltaire, 50, 77–80

Wallerstein, Immanuel, 10
Wang Yangming. *See* Wang Yangming School, of neo-Confucianism
Wang Yangming School,
   of neo-Confucianism, 223, 225, 228
Weber, Max, 146, 149–58
Westernization, 212–13
Westphalian system, 47
white supremacy. *See* racism

Wittfogel, Karl, 186
World War II, 24
world-system, capitalist, 10
worldview
    Catholic, 47
    Christian, 47
    Christian–Latin, 47
    Eurocentric and theological, 43
    medieval, 90
    theological, 46

Xiamen, 126. *See also* Amoy
Xiao jing, 226

xinxue. *See* Wang Yangming School, of neo-Confucianism

yellow peril, 23, 130, 250
Yi Jing, 85–6
Yongzheng Emperor, 64, 227
Yuan, Shikai, 204
Yuon, Hou, 189–90

Zhao, Zhiyang, 213
Zheng, Chenggong, 53
Zhu, Xi, 40
Zhuangzi, 115